Jesus said, "You shall know the truth, and it will set you free." Much of America is having a hard time listening to truth and finding true freedom. Check out ole Starnes's rendition of why our culture is turning away from timeless truths and turning on the messengers that espouse them.

—PHIL ROBERTSON
"THE DUCK COMMANDER"

This book strikes a healthy balance of painting an accurate picture of challenges to American culture and liberty while also providing timely, down-to-earth instruction on what everyday citizens can do to truly make America great again. Well done!

—BRAD DACUS
PRESIDENT, PACIFIC JUSTICE INSTITUTE

While many on the Left have predicted the demise of the conservative Christian voice in politics, Todd provides an encouraging and prophetic primer on the reengagement of Christians in culture. This work provides a playbook for a new generation of believers to stand for truth.

—EMIR CANER
PRESIDENT, TRUETT MCCONNELL UNIVERSITY

Todd Starnes is a combination of Andy Griffith, Mark Twain, and William Wallace. His fun-filled wit and Southern-flavored worldview make this book a must-read for anyone ready to push back against the rising tide of evil set against our American values. This nation is desperate for unique warriors, like Todd, who recognize if God's people don't get it right, our nation never will. So if you're tired of getting pushed around and told what you can and can't believe or say, then *The Deplorables' Guide to Making America Great Again* is for you!

—DAVID AND JASON BENHAM
AUTHORS, WHATEVER THE COST AND LIVING AMONG LIONS

Todd whimsically and effectively summarizes the incredible year that was 2016, and he lays out a path forward that includes a comprehensive overview of some of our biggest cultural challenges and how we can save America from the enemies within before it is too late. A must-read for all ages!

—CHARLIE KIRK
FOUNDER AND EXECUTIVE DIRECTOR, TURNING POINT USA

My dear friend Todd Starnes is one of America's greatest patriots. He uses his wit and passion to promote the fact that our nation was founded on Judeo-Christian principles and can remain free only as we honor God, who is the author of our liberty. God bless you, Todd, for another great book!

—CH (COL) Ron Crews, USAR, Retired
Executive director, Chaplain Alliance for Religious Liberty

It's time to make America great again, and my friend Todd Starnes points out the way in his excellent new book. Using his trademark Southern humor, Todd shows us how to push back against secularism and resist the mind-set that would relegate Christianity to the margins of society. We can make a difference in our nation, and Todd shows us how. This book is a must-read.

—Robert Jeffress
Pastor, First Baptist Dallas

Todd Starnes once again proves that he is among the most gifted and timely writers of our time. This book reminds the reader of just how close America came to sliding into the moral abyss in 2016 while providing dozens of inspirational examples of ordinary Americans who stood up to the Goliath of liberalism, whether in government, the media, the courts, or academia, and like David of old said, "Not on my watch."

I consider myself well-informed when it comes to the culture war in our nation, but Todd, in his role as a Christian reporter, lives on the frontlines, and *The Deplorables' Guide to Making America Great Again* will quicken the silent warrior within you as you get acquainted with many who have courageously stood on behalf of us all. I wholeheartedly endorse this book and look forward to giving it to pastors across the nation in hopes of inspiring them to join us in the battle for the soul of America.

—Rick Scarborough
Vision America

If you want to know why the Left thinks you are a "Deplorable" and what to do about it, read *The Deplorables' Guide to Making America Great Again*. Todd Starnes is a Southern-fried conservative and more importantly, a Christian, who has a gift for speaking the truth and saying it in a way that makes it memorable!

—Jerry Johnson
President, National Religious Broadcasters

★ ★ ★ THE ★ ★ ★ DEPLORABLES' GUIDE

TO MAKING AMERICA GREAT AGAIN

TODD STARNES

FRONT LINE

Most CHARISMA HOUSE BOOK GROUP products are available at special quantity discounts for bulk purchase for sales promotions, premiums, fundraising, and educational needs. For details, write Charisma House Book Group, 600 Rinehart Road, Lake Mary, Florida 32746, or telephone (407) 333-0600.

THE DEPLORABLES' GUIDE TO MAKING AMERICA GREAT AGAIN
by Todd Starnes
Published by FrontLine
Charisma Media/Charisma House Book Group
600 Rinehart Road
Lake Mary, Florida 32746
www.charismahouse.com

Scripture quotations marked ESV are from the Holy Bible, English Standard Version. Copyright © 2001 by Crossway Bibles, a division of Good News Publishers. Used by permission.

Scripture quotations marked HCSB are taken from the Holman Christian Standard Bible®, Copyright © 1999, 2000, 2002, 2003, 2009 by Holman Bible Publishers. Used by permission. Holman Christian Standard Bible®, Holman CSB®, and HCSB® are federally registered trademarks of Holman Bible Publishers.

Scripture quotations marked KJV are from the King James Version of the Bible.

Scripture quotations marked MEV are from the Modern English Version. Copyright © 2014 by Military Bible Association. Used by permission. All rights reserved.

Scripture quotations marked NKJV are taken from the New King James Version®. Copyright © 1982 by Thomas Nelson. Used by permission. All rights reserved.

Cover design by Justin Evans

Visit the author's website at toddstarnes.com

Library of Congress Control Number: 2017930722
International Standard Book Number: 978-1-62999-170-2
E-book ISBN: 978-1-62999-171-9

17 18 19 20 21 — 987654321

Printed in the United States of America

To my Friend from Findlay

*The people who know their God
shall stand firm and take action.*
—DANIEL 11:32, ESV

CONTENTS

ACKNOWLEDGMENTS

I T TAKES A lot of "deplorable" people to write a book like this—a basketful at the very least! And I'm proud to say that I associate with a number of people the Left holds in contempt—folks who go to church, drive pickup trucks, shoot guns, and pledge allegiance to the flag, folks who take a knee to pray, not protest.

In truth these good people are not deplorable; they are red-blooded American patriots. And without their support and guidance and prayers this book would not have been birthed.

I'm blessed with a wonderful Southern family. It's hard to fit most of us on the front porch, but we still manage to squeeze in everyone. Of course Aunt Lynn and Uncle Jerry and Aunt Norma and Uncle Bob have been there from day one with great words of encouragement and at times consternation.

Caleb, you are a great blessing to me. I'm proud to call you a friend and a colleague here at Fox News. But most importantly I'm honored to call you a brother in the Lord. Book signings are just not the same unless someone asks, "Is Caleb here too?"

Shannon, your prayers and notes have been a source of great encouragement to me.

Dalton, thank you for being my eyes and ears in the Heartland.

Joseph, I can't think of a finer graphics designer in the nation. Your work has just been tremendous. Thank you for the long hours and the last-minute changes. You've created a beautiful website and beautiful program materials for our retreats and conferences.

Paul and Michelle Cox, you folks are like family. Thank you for your friendship and our family vacations—even the ones that I don't attend because of a pressing engagement with Governor Huckabee.

William, Morris and Sandy, Mylon and Wendy, John and Joni, Gerald and

Donna, Carl and DonnaLynn, Mark and Mardi—I could fill these pages with heartfelt thanks. Of all the Deplorables, you are the most deplorable.

I'm also blessed with great spiritual counsel from Mike Huckabee, Dr. Steve Gaines, Mark Blair, Dr. Robert Jeffress, Dr. Emir Caner, Dr. John Yarbrough, Tony Perkins, Jason and David Benham, Jerry Falwell Jr., and Jerry Johnson.

Franklin and Will Graham, thank you for letting us share your stories with the nation, and thank you for opening up The Cove at the Billy Graham Training Center for my annual retreat.

A huge thank-you to the team at Fox News Channel, FoxNews.com, and Fox News Radio.

What can I say about Charisma Media? It has been such a joy to work with these fine folks. Thank you, Steve Strang, Tessie DeVore, Adrienne Gaines, and Debbie Marrie.

And a special thank-you to the best literary agent in America, Frank Breeden, along with the entire team at Premiere Authors and Premiere Speakers.

Thank you also to the producers, anchors, and reporters who share my stories with the nation. And that includes the wonderful broadcasters at American Family Radio, Bott Radio Network, and the hundreds of Fox Radio stations that carry my daily commentary.

Most importantly "to God be the glory; great things He hath done."

—Todd
New York City, 2016

INTRODUCTION

I'VE LIVED IN New York City for more than a decade now among the indigenous liberal population in the borough of Brooklyn. Many people ask me, "Todd, why would you subject yourself to such harsh living conditions?" And I tell them that to truly understand the American liberal, I felt as if I needed to study them in their natural habitat.

Peace prevailed with my Far-Left neighbors until I showed up at the summer block party with a case of Rush Limbaugh's original Two If by Tea.[1] It's delicious and refreshing. I figured they could drink their liberal Kool-Aid while I sipped Rush's freedom-touting sweet tea. My neighbors were not amused.

Then my cover as a conservative was literally blown when my vegan neighbors caught me smoking a pork butt. For you readers who live in the Upper East Side, *pork butt* is not a euphemism for some untoward behavior. It's just good eatin'. Well, the smell of smoking meat nearly set off a small panic on Brooklyn's Fifth Avenue. Just imagine nearly getting trampled by a thundering herd of vegetarian hipsters stampeding to their safe spaces. You'd be surprised how fast they can move in those skinny jeans.

So it's appropriate and neighborly to issue a warning to you, dear reader, especially if you suffer from microaggressions or other liberal social diseases. It's about to get politically incorrect up in this book.

I'm one of those people Hillary Clinton was talking about in 2016—an "irredeemable Deplorable." Mrs. Clinton matter-of-factly dubbed half of Donald Trump's supporters a bunch of xenophobic, homophobic, Islamophobic bigots.[2] I'm surprised she didn't say we hated puppies too.

For the record, I'm an irredeemable Deplorable who has been redeemed by the blood of the Lamb (more on that later). And I also happen to love puppies.

But if you take offense at cultural appropriation or season 2 of *The Dukes of Hazzard*, you might want to carefully put down this book and immediately proceed to your closest essential oils shop to recover your peace. It ain't gonna get better for you.

You see, in 2008 President Barack Obama promised to fundamentally transform the United States of America. And ladies and gentlemen, he fulfilled that campaign promise. In less than eight years our former president turned the most exceptional nation on earth into a vast wasteland of perpetually offended snowflakes. We've gone from the greatest generation to the entitlement generation.

Instead of creating and innovating and fighting and winning and dreaming and doing, many of our fellow countrymen are hunkered down in their government-subsidized dwellings, waxing poetic about gender fluidity, taking selfies, and debating which lives matter and which lives do not.

The country's gone plumb nuts.

It remains to be seen whether President Donald Trump will defend religious liberty or capitulate to the social justice warriors. My prayer is he stands firm against the coming onslaught, but only time will tell. And that's the problem—we don't have much time.

Franklin Graham called it when he said we are close to a moral tipping point.[3] There is a deep-seated antagonism and hostility toward Christianity in every seat of power in the nation.

Consider the evidence. What used to be wrong by any historical standard, including the Bible, is now trumpeted as right and laudable. What used to be right is now defined as beyond impolite—and actually evil. The Supreme Court took the throne to redefine what God already defined for time and eternity, replacing the testimony of the Almighty and of human history with the opinion of five frail individuals.[4] At the same time the nation has become a killing field for Islamic radicals.[5] Unborn babies are slaughtered, and some worry their parts may be auctioned off to the highest bidder.[6]

It certainly feels like we're stumbling in greater darkness than ever before.

Under the Obama regime Christian Americans were hauled into court and thrown into jail, bullied and slandered by those who preach tolerance and diversity. (See chapter 4.) As you will see in the pages of this book, it's been open season on gun-toting Bible-clingers in America. Solomon wisely advised not to impose a fine on a righteous man or strike the noble for their uprightness (Prov. 17:26). In biblical terms former president Obama is no King Solomon.

Last year I wrote a column about the football team at the US Military Academy. The team was investigated because players and coaches were caught praying in the locker room.[7] They were investigated because they petitioned the Almighty. If George Washington had been a general in President Obama's military, he would've been court-martialed and hauled off to jail.

Our public schools have been turned into radical indoctrination centers for the social justice crowd, leading the charge in a massive assault on the family. Sexual revolutionaries have been given carte blanche to sow seeds of confusion in our children, poisoning their minds with their desire for a genderless society.[8] (See chapter 5, "Indoctrination 101.")

You would think at some point in this story the church would stand up and shout, "Enough!" We led the way in other times of great crisis—the American Revolution and the Civil War come to mind. But a sort of spiritual malaise has blanketed many churches today. Pastors refuse to discuss cultural issues from the pulpit, fearing reprisal from the Left. One well-known evangelical leader even cautioned Christians about bringing God into their workplace.[9] That, my friends, sounds like an order to retreat.

These days some churches resemble the Cowardly Lion more than the Lion of Judah.

I can't tell you how many times ministers have told me they refuse to discuss controversial issues inside the church house because it might offend people. I'm not sure where they find that commandment in the Bible, "Thou shalt not offend thy congregation." If I remember correctly, Jesus offended a good many people. How it grieves my heart to know that sinners might be spending an eternity apart from God simply because the body of Christ wanted to be "nice."

On March 30, 1863, President Abraham Lincoln called on the nation to fast and pray and repent—to ask God for a "pardon" for our national sins.

> We have been the recipients of the choicest bounties of Heaven; we have been preserved these many years in peace and prosperity; we have grown in numbers, wealth, and power as no other nation has ever grown. But we have forgotten God. We have forgotten the gracious hand which preserved us in peace and multiplied and enriched and strengthened us, and we have vainly imagined, in the deceitfulness of our hearts, that all these blessings were produced by some superior wisdom and virtue of our own. Intoxicated with unbroken success, we have become too self-sufficient to feel the necessity of redeeming and preserving grace, too proud to pray to the God that made us.[10]

Can you imagine a modern president calling the nation to fast and pray like this? Can you imagine former president Obama opining that we have become "too proud to pray to the God that made us"? (My apologies to those of you who just choked on your iced tea.) Well, the man whose face is on billions of pennies and five-dollar bills told a nation to return to God with repentance and humility. We could do a lot worse than take that advice again.

I say President Lincoln's proclamation is as relevant today as it was in 1863. If we don't turn this thing around—to put it in intellectual terms—we're toast.

So what are those of us who cherish traditional American values going to do about all this left-wing wackadoodle nonsense? That is the point of this book. That is the point of your life—at least part of it—in the coming years because if you and I don't do something, there's nothing the White House can do by itself. If we don't get on board and row—hard—we could find ourselves drifting back to where we were. These opportunities don't come along often. It's time to call this what it is: a historic moment in the life of our country.

If each of us responds rightly, we get our country back.

But if we sit back in our rocking chairs...

Remember the five Houston pastors who nearly got thrown in jail because they refused to comply with the mayor's subpoena? Remember that story?[11]

I never could figure out how a conservative town such as Houston would elect a mayor who was so liberal. I mean just about everybody's a Baptist in that part of the country. Even the Methodists are Baptists. But it turns out that most of the city's churchgoing crowd never bothered to show up on Election Day. They stayed home like the vast majority of the city's registered voters.[12] That decision nearly got those pastors thrown in jail.

President Ronald Reagan famously said freedom is just one generation away from extinction.[13] As we learned last November, freedom's flame was nearly extinguished by the possible election of one woman in a pantsuit who pledged to continue the "transformation" of America.

But I've sensed a great stirring across the fruited plain: Students are defending their faith and their country in classrooms. Farmers and schoolteachers, construction workers and police officers are standing up for what they believe. The silence is over. Voices are being raised in every sector of society, and they're saying, "Enough! This 'transformation' is not making us great; it's killing us. Let's get back to what works and make our great nation the envy of the world again."

I was especially moved by a story from Brandon, Mississippi, which you will read about later in this book. The marching band had been pulled off the field. School leaders feared that one of the songs might have violated a federal court order. The song was "How Great Thou Art."

That Friday night at the end of the second quarter fans sat quietly in the stands as the football teams trotted off the field. Suddenly a lone voice began humming a familiar tune. Others joined in—hairdressers and electricians, moms and dads, and cheerleaders. The melody rose from below the press box until it became a mighty choir of hundreds who rose up in defiance, belting out the forbidden song: "Then sings my soul, my Savior God, to Thee"!

They took a stand for religious liberty that humid night in the great state of Mississippi, and that kind of sentiment is spreading like wildfire across this land.

To quote a statement often attributed to the Christian theologian and martyr Dietrich Bonhoeffer, though its origin is unknown, "Silence in the face of evil is itself evil: God will not hold us guiltless. Not to speak is to speak. Not to act is to act."

This is a moment for every Bible-believing Christian in America to speak and to act. God's little lambs can no longer go silently where the Left leads us. Our duty is to be civil—not silent. We must roar like lions!

God is not finished with America. I know—and you know deep down in your gut—that we can still be a force for good in this world. We can once again be that shining city on a hill President Ronald Reagan spoke of.[14]

But let's be clear: making America great again does not start at the White House. It starts at your house, and mine. This book is a guide—a how-to, an inspirational guide—to help us get started on that task. We're going to take a look at the cultural landscape—the good, the bad, and the snarky. And at the end of each chapter I'll provide marching orders, practical ways you can make America great again right where you live and work.

Fellow Deplorables, put on your work boots, grab a baloney sandwich, and let's get to work! We've got a country to save.

Chapter 1

THE HAPPY WARRIOR

I'M A FAN of war movies—*Saving Private Ryan, Patton, The Great Escape*, and just about every film starring John Wayne. But I'm especially fond of *The Patriot*, a film set in South Carolina in the days leading up to the Revolutionary War. It's the fictional story of Benjamin Martin and his family and the sacrifices they made to secure our freedom.

In one poignant scene Benjamin's son Gabriel was tasked with recruiting an army to fight the British. He interrupted a worship service in a small country church and made his plea. But his petitions fell on deaf ears until finally a young lady in the congregation rose to her feet to rebuke their hesitancy.

This is what she said:

> Half the men in this church, including you, father, and you, reverend, are as ardent patriots as I. Will you now, when you are needed most, stop at only words? Is that the sort of men you are? I ask only that you act upon the beliefs of which you have so strongly spoken and in which you so strongly believe.[1]

After a long pause, Gabriel Martin asked a question that I pose to you in these pages: "Who's with us?"

One by one the farmers and shopkeepers rose to their feet—with their sons by their sides. American citizens were rising up to fight for religious liberty, to fight for freedom. As they gathered in the front yard of the church, the men were startled to discover there was one more recruit—the parson, armed with a musket.

"A shepherd must tend his flock and at times fight off the wolves," he declared.[2]

While *The Patriot* is a fictionalized story, there were some parallels to reality. In truth the fight for our freedom was birthed in church houses from Boston, Massachusetts, to Charleston, South Carolina.

The Reverend Oliver Hart, the pastor of what is now known as the First Baptist Church of Charleston, was dispatched by the Provincial Congress of South Carolina to help recruit volunteers to fight the British. He traveled across the upstate and delivered messages about the need to "enforce the necessity of a general union in order to preserve themselves and their children from slavery."[3] He preached politics from the pulpit way back in 1775.

When the Founding Fathers needed to round up an army to fight for our freedom, they called on the Baptists. In "From Dissenters to Patriots: Baptists and the American Revolution," Baylor University history professor Thomas Kidd explains why those good Baptists grabbed their guns. "They were convinced that the American Revolution heralded liberty from Britain, but more importantly, liberty for their religion, the true faith of the gospel. And as they accepted the war as a godly cause, they began to see the new American nation as a place uniquely favored by God."[4]

President Obama once said America is no longer just a Christian nation. But there is no dispute that many of our Founding Fathers were devout Christian men who flavored our founding documents with truths gleaned from almighty God and His Word.

Yet many Christians and Christian leaders have disengaged. They've avoided discussing or debating the culture war—fearing they might offend people.

So, many evangelical Christian voices have been silenced—by their own hand. Many have bought into a wrong-headed notion that we should practice our faith only inside the walls of the church house. And there is now a prevailing belief—among Democrats and some Republicans—that Christianity should be erased from the public marketplace.

John Stonestreet addressed that issue in a brilliant *BreakPoint* commentary titled "You Really Want Us to Keep Our Faith to Ourselves?" He imagined what a world would look like without Christianity's influence.

For starters, he noted, we wouldn't have volunteers working in prisons to rehabilitate the incarcerated, and there would be fewer free clinics and hospitals because it has been Baptist, Methodist, Catholic, and other Christian organizations that have been leaders in building medical facilities, not Buddhists or atheists. The same goes for soup kitchens, rescue missions, adoption agencies, and disaster relief organizations. "And good luck sustaining free, public education to the millions of students once religious schools shut their doors," he said. "When Christians 'keep it to ourselves,' *everybody* loses."[5]

John Inazu, an associate professor of law and political science at Washington University School of Law in St. Louis, Missouri, warned that Christians who have avoided the culture wars may no longer have that choice. He referenced the

2015 Supreme Court ruling that redefined marriage, pointing to an amicus brief filed by religious freedom expert Douglas Laycock.[6]

Although Laycock argued in favor of same-sex marriage, in his brief he also expressed grave concerns about the future of religious liberty:

> Must pastors, priests, and rabbis provide religious marriage counseling to same-sex couples? Must religious colleges provide married student housing to same-sex couples? Must churches and synagogues employ spouses in same-sex marriages, even though such employees would be persistently and publicly flouting the religious teachings they would be hired to promote? Must religious organizations provide spousal fringe benefits to the same-sex spouses of any such employees they do hire? Must religious social-service agencies place children for adoption with same-sex couples? Already, Catholic Charities in Illinois, Massachusetts, and the District of Columbia has closed its adoption units because of this issue.
>
> Religious colleges, summer camps, day care centers, retreat houses, counseling centers, meeting halls, and adoption agencies may be sued under public accommodations laws for refusing to offer their facilities or services to same-sex couples. Or they may be penalized by loss of licensing, accreditation, government contracts, access to public facilities, or tax exemption.[7]

And those are the observations of a pro-gay marriage religious liberty advocate!

Just last year the chairman of the US Commission on Civil Rights warned that religious exemptions of issues involving sexual orientation and gender identity "significantly infringe upon these civil rights."[8]

Following are some of Martin Castro's remarks:

> The phrases "religious liberty" and "religious freedom" will stand for nothing except hypocrisy so long as they remain code words for discrimination, intolerance, racism, sexism, homophobia, Islamophobia, Christian supremacy or any form of intolerance.
>
> Religious liberty was never intended to give one religion dominion over other religions, or a veto power over the civil rights and civil liberties of others. However, today, as in the past, religion is being used as both a weapon and a shield by those seeking to deny others equality. In our nation's past religion has been used to justify slavery and later, Jim Crow laws. We now see "religious liberty" arguments sneaking their way back into our political and constitutional discourse (just like the concept of "state rights") in an effort to undermine the rights of some

Americans. This generation of Americans must stand up and speak out to ensure that religion never again be twisted to deny others the full promise of America.[9]

Friends, now you understand why it is imperative that Christians take a stand to defend religious liberty. Otherwise we're going to be worshipping in underground churches.

CRACKS IN THE FOUNDATION

Religious liberty is our first freedom, and I've often said if we allow the secularists to undermine that specific freedom, everything else will crumble. And we are already beginning to see cracks in the foundation.

The US Department of Defense (DoD) in 2015 published a "sexism course" that attacked the Bible, the US Constitution, and the Declaration of Independence. The DoD said all three contributed to modern sexism.[10]

Previously, in 2013, the DoD published a training document that depicted the Founding Fathers as extremists, and conservative organizations as hate groups. The Defense Equal Opportunity Management Institute training guide was obtained by Judicial Watch under a Freedom of Information Act request. It was acquired from the Air Force but originated with the Pentagon.

"This document deserves a careful examination by military leadership," Judicial Watch President Tom Fitton told me. "Congress needs to conduct better oversight and figure out what the heck is going on in our military."[11]

Included in the 133 pages of lesson plans is a student guide titled "Extremism." Under a section titled "Extremist Ideologies" the document states, "In U.S. history, there are many examples of extremist ideologies and movements. The colonists who sought to free themselves from British rule and the Confederate states who sought to secede from the Northern states are just two examples."[12]

It was "disturbing insight into what [was] happening inside Obama's Pentagon," Fitton said. "The Obama administration [had] a nasty habit of equating basic conservative values with terrorism."[13]

The training guide warned that active participation in groups that are regarded as extremist organizations is "incompatible with military service and is, therefore, prohibited."[14]

"It's craziness," Fitton said. "It's political correctness run amok."[15]

The training documents also focus on those who cherish individual liberty. The DoD warns students to be aware that "nowadays, instead of dressing in sheets or publicly espousing hate messages, many extremists will talk of individual liberties, states' rights, and how to make the world a better place."[16]

The document relied heavily on information obtained from the Southern Poverty Law Center, a left-wing organization that has a history of labeling conservative Christian organizations such as the Family Research Council (FRC) as "hate groups."

In April 2013 I obtained an e-mail sent by a lieutenant colonel at Fort Campbell to three dozen subordinates warning them to be on the lookout for any soldiers who might be members of "domestic hate groups" such as the FRC and the American Family Association. "When we see behaviors that are inconsistent with Army Values—don't just walk by—do the right thing and address the concern before it becomes a problem," the e-mail advised.[17]

At the time the Army denied there was any attack on Christians or those who hold religious beliefs. But it does make one wonder what President Obama and his minions at the Pentagon were up to. "The notion that the Army is taking an antireligion or anti-Christian stance is contrary to any of our policies, doctrines, and regulations," an Army spokesman told me at the time.[18]

However, in a separate incident an Army training instructor listed evangelical Christianity and Catholicism as examples of religious extremism—along with al Qaeda and Hamas. The same Army spokesman said the training session was an "isolated incident not condoned by the Department of the Army."[19]

You could say that it's at least a good thing the DoD hadn't resorted to slandering our Founding Fathers or the Declaration of Independence because in 2016 Rep. Barbara Norton managed to do both during a bizarre rant on the floor of the *Chambre des Représentants de Louisiane*, as they say in Cajun country. "All men are not created equal," the gentle lady from Shreveport ranted. "We're teaching them a lie."[20]

Rep. Norton was fired up hotter than a bottle of Tabasco from Avery Island.

State lawmakers had been asked to consider a bill authored by Republican Rep. Valarie Hodges that would have required children in grades four, five, and six to recite portions of the Declaration of Independence. "I want students to understand that the Declaration of Independence is the cornerstone of our republic—and what gives us liberty," Rep. Hodges told me. "I want them to not just memorize it, but understand what that document did—it changed the course of history."[21]

A noble cause indeed—to teach young Americans that they live in a most exceptional nation. "It's important that we fight for these values," she told me. "The future of our republic depends on the next generation, whether or not they are prepared for citizenship."[22]

And as my Fox News colleague Jesse Watters demonstrates on a weekly basis in his "Watters' World" segment on *The O'Reilly Factor*, our public school system is doing a subpar job of teaching kids what it means to be an American.

"Instead of believing that America is an exceptional nation, there are some radicals who want to rewrite history and teach our children the opposite of what is truth," Rep. Hodges said.[23]

And that brings me back to Rep. Norton's railing about the Declaration of Independence. "When I think back in 1776, July Fourth, African Americans were slaves, and for you to bring a bill to request that our children will recite the Declaration, I think it's a little bit unfair to us to ask those children to recite something that's not the truth," she said.[24]

Louisiana state house Speaker *pro tempore* Walt Leger III (another Democrat) took issue with the "all men are created equal" portion of the Declaration of Independence and said it needed to be taught with historical context. "Men and women were not seen as equals at that time, nor were blacks considered to be men that were equal to others," he said during a committee hearing.[25]

Rep. Hodges was dumbfounded by the hostility. "I feel sadness that that level of hatred was displayed against the Founding Fathers and the documents that give us the ability as women and black people and Caucasians to run for office," she said. "The lack of understanding to me is saddening and frightening."[26]

Hodges ended up pulling her bill under pressure from lawmakers and a mountain of amendments.

There you have it: Democrats don't believe we should teach young Americans "that they are endowed by their Creator with certain unalienable rights." And they sure don't want them to pursue happiness. That, boys and girls, is what we call a self-evident truth.

While many of his contemporaries are hunkered down, Franklin Graham is one of those lone voices crying in the wilderness. "I believe we are perilously close to the moral tipping point for the survival of the United States of America," Graham wrote in *Decision* magazine. "I refuse to be silent and watch the future of our children and grandchildren be offered up on pagan altars of personal pleasure and immorality."[27]

Instead of ignoring the rotting of America's culture, the president and CEO of the Billy Graham Evangelistic Association decided to do something about it. Last year Graham launched the "Decision America Tour," a series of prayer rallies at the capitol buildings of all fifty states. "The only hope for America is not the Democratic Party, and it's not the Republican Party," Graham told me. "The only hope for America is God."[28]

I caught up with Graham just after his inaugural prayer gathering in Des Moines, Iowa, in January 2016. More than two thousand people turned out in frigid weather—to petition the Almighty.

It was one of the rare moments in Iowa when politicians were not recognized nor allowed to speak. "If a candidate showed up, [we were] not going to recognize them," Graham said at the time. "We're not going to give them a microphone."[29]

That's because the "Decision America Tour" was not about politics. "It's trying to lead this nation in prayer, confessing the sins of our country, asking for God's forgiveness, and encouraging Christians to get engaged in the political process," he told me.[30]

Graham did what many young ministers refuse to do—address issues that some might consider to be politically incorrect. He told me that while a number of older pastors understand the gravity of the situation, many younger pastors do not. "The younger pastors, so many are caught up in the pop culture, and the pastor in a church is more about being cool," he said. "We're beginning to put theology in the backseat, and I'm concerned about the church."[31]

And that's when he dropped this evangelical bombshell: "To be honest with you, the problems we have in America today are the failure of the church."[32]

I reckon that comment will make a lot of folks start wiggling in the pews. But Graham has a valid point. The government has taken on many responsibilities that were once in the hands of the local church. "The churches have allowed the government to take away their responsibility, and so the government is feeding people, the government is clothing people, the government is now in charge of health care," Graham said.[33]

Graham's message is crystal clear: it's time for Christians to reengage the culture. "We as a nation are in trouble, and only God can fix it," he said.

OUR MANDATE AS CHRISTIAN CITIZENS

So what do we do? Where do we begin?

At the beginning of this chapter I told you about some Christ-following patriots who took a stand to defend their freedom. They fought for what they believed and helped shape the government of this great nation. Yet in the years since then Christians have tended to swing back and forth between engagement and passivity when it comes to government participation.

One moment they are founding a nation and infusing the Declaration of Independence and Constitution with Bible references and principles. The next they're retreating into church activities and leaving the public square to the secular and power-hungry.

In the 1980s Jerry Falwell rolled up his sleeves, climbed into the political ring, and led the nation to a come-to-Jesus moment (as we say in the South). Falwell, one of my great heroes of the faith, raised up an army of Christian legislators, congressmen, school board members, and county supervisors. Prayer meetings sprung up on Capitol Hill. Liberal policies rolled ever-so-slowly back.

The Supreme Court's decisions came to more closely reflect the views of the supreme being by Christian reckoning.

Then somehow complacency set in. Reagan brought morning to America, but instead of seizing the day, conservatives went into hibernation. My friend the evangelist Alex McFarland told me Falwell was often quoted as saying, "Christians quit when they lose, and they quit when they win."[34] The post-Reagan era lends credence to that belief.

Maybe the Reagan Revolution lost steam under Bush 41. Maybe the dispiriting election of Bill Clinton sent us into retreat.

Or maybe Christians just thought they'd done enough for a while and returned to their plows rather than the polls. So goes participation among the faithful. One year we vote in droves. The next we seem to disappear from the political map. Elections hinge on us—yet sometimes we roar, and sometimes we yawn. Christians, Falwell was known to have said, oftentimes think too small, aim too low, and quit too soon.[35] Verily, verily.

Many Christians now are just confused. "Is it right to participate in politics?" they wonder. "Can Christians seek higher office? Or do we consent to live under whatever kind of government our fellow citizens foist on us?"

The Left would like us to believe we shouldn't get involved in politics. They want us to think that because of the separation of church and state we should just sit down and shut up. But if we followed that line of thinking, our grits would really be cooked. As Christians we have a mandate to engage in politics and the culture. Our marching orders don't come from the White House or the courthouse. They come from a much higher authority—the Word of God.

Several years ago I was given a copy of a sermon delivered by Dr. Adrian Rogers, the late pastor of Bellevue Baptist Church in Memphis, Tennessee, and one of the greatest American preachers of all time. The message was titled "Christian Citizenship." The sermon was delivered in 1998, but its central message is timeless. I'm going to lean heavily on that sermon for the thoughts ahead because they are so profound. (Thanks to Love Worth Finding for graciously agreeing to allow me to include Dr. Rogers's powerful words in this book.)[36]

The questions Dr. Rogers poses are these: What is Christian citizenship? What are our responsibilities, our duties, our rights? Is the Bible oblivious to human government? Or did God ordain human government—and tell His people to stay out of it? What are Christians to do, and how should we think and behave in relationship to government?

Many Christians have dropped out of the political process because they fear turning their faith into a social gospel. The social gospel is a dilution, dare I say even a bastardization, of the actual gospel. It shifts emphasis off the Son of God and onto man's social responsibility toward others. Being kind and generous and self-sacrificing is nice, but it's not the heart of the Christian gospel. It is certainly a result, but too often these zealous reformers of society turn Jesus into a common community organizer who just happened to tell better stories and inspire more people than, say, Socrates or Mother Teresa.

No, friends. Jesus didn't leave heaven to come to Earth and die just so you and I would put a few extra bucks in the offering plate. There's a lot more at stake than that—like where we are going to spend the "Sweet By and By" once you give up the ghost. And unless Jesus Christ is your Lord and Savior, it doesn't matter how many water wells you dig in a third world country or how many silver dollars you put in the Salvation Army bucket.

So some people are rightly wary of wandering from the blazing fire of faith into some lackluster social expression. They refuse to give government and civic participation much attention, thus leaving the election of some politicians in the hands of the too-earthly-minded.

Other believers have simply given up hope. They say, as Dr. Rogers put it, that America has crossed the point of no return, that there is no going back to our foundations. Recalling the catacombs, these Christians hunker down to wait for Jesus to rescue them.

Others skip politics because they see politics as dirty—and who can blame them? Nobody whose thoughts are on heaven wants to soil himself with dishonest doings.

Still others are intimidated. The ACLU and other left-wing tribes have pranced and lied and misinformed so many people about a so-called separation of church and state that even believers think we have no rights, privileges, or prerogatives in civil society—that we have been disenfranchised completely in the political arena. As Dr. Rogers put it, they tell us, "Why don't you shut up and go back inside your little stained-glass prisons and leave it to us to take care of it?"[37]

But the Bible says not to drop out, not to give up hope, and not to feel disenfranchised. So many American Christians have bought the secular lie that the church and state must be separate, meaning having no influence on each other. Rightly understood, separation of church and state keeps the state from meddling in church business, but it was never intended to keep the church from speaking out and influencing the government. The meaning of this phrase, coined by Thomas Jefferson in a letter written after his presidency, has been twisted to mean the opposite of his original intent.

Our Founding Fathers clearly intended our government to be influenced by Christians. That's why they wrote in the Declaration of Independence, "We hold these truths to be self-evident, that all men are created equal, that they are endowed by their Creator with certain unalienable Rights."[38] The rights did not come from the government but from God. Why would they say our rights derive from God and then ask churches to have no influence at all on the government? It makes no sense.

When the founders wrote in the Bill of Rights, "Congress shall make no law respecting an establishment of religion,"[39] it was to keep America from having a state-mandated, state-supported church as they had in England. Yet left-wingers, bent on their own secular religious agenda, have used this as a cudgel to keep Christians out of the public square.

So what must we do as Christian citizens? Yes, we all know that heaven is our ultimate home, but for now we've got to mow the grass and weed whack the front porch on this planet. Leaving the government to God-dishonoring people would be a travesty of our calling as humans. Here are the five duties of a Christian toward the government, as enumerated by Dr. Rogers.

1. Pay for your government.

Paul wrote, "For this cause pay ye tribute also: for they are God's ministers, attending continually upon this very thing. Render therefore to all their dues: tribute to whom tribute is due; custom to whom custom; fear to whom fear; honour to whom honour" (Rom. 13:6–7, KJV). Whether it's income tax, sales tax, fees, or whatever, we are required to pay them. Even Jesus paid His taxes. That is not to say that the taxes are always fair—remember, our government is just as fallen as we are because of sin and the influence of evil. But if taxes aren't fair, that's our signal to get involved and make sure the evil of over-taxing is restrained and people are rewarded with lower taxes so they can make their own financial decisions.

I'll say it again: If you don't like how much government costs, get involved and help make changes. It won't get done by complaining.

2. Pray for our government.

Paul wrote elsewhere, "Therefore I exhort first of all that you make supplications, prayers, intercessions, and thanksgivings for everyone, for kings and for all who are in authority, that we may lead a quiet and peaceful life in all godliness and honesty, for this is good and acceptable in the sight of God our Savior" (1 Tim. 2:1–3, MEV). You might have to pray for your senator or congressman or the president through gritted teeth—but you should still do it. Prayer works, even on those in power. Proverbs 21:1 informs us, "The king's heart is in the hand of the LORD, as the rivers of water; He turns it to any place He will" (MEV).

3. Praise our republic.

The Bible says in Romans 13:7 to give honor to whom honor is due. And 1 Peter 2:17 says, "Honor the king" (MEV). Some Christians feel conflicted waving an American flag because the Bible says our (ultimate) citizenship is in heaven. But that's like not being proud of the earthly family in which God placed you. For the time being we are Americans. There's nothing wrong with patriotism. At the very least it's a way of honoring a country to which honor is due.

4. Preach to our country.

I'm with Dr. Rogers, who declared: "God's people dare not be silent. As long as they're killing babies and practicing infanticide, I will not be silent. As long as we have a government that's trying to normalize sexual perversion, I will not be silent. As long as they're handing out condoms to high school and junior high school students in so-called 'God-blessed America,' I will not be silent. And as long as a free-born American is told he cannot pray out loud anywhere, I will not be silent. We must preach to our government. And we must say to our government, 'Whatever is morally wrong is not politically right!'" [40]

5. Participate in our government.

Jesus said, "Render to Caesar the things that are Caesar's, and to God the things that are God's" (Mark 12:17, MEV). Our highest allegiance is to God; our lesser allegiance is to our country. We have no Caesar. But by great fortune and the will of God we are a government of the people, by the people, and for the people. If we do not participate in this government to the extent we are able, we have not rendered to our "Caesar" the things that belong to him.

So what do we do? Here is your first batch of marching orders:

MARCHING ORDERS

1. **Engage.** Sign up to receive e-mails from patriotic, constitutional, pro-family, conservative organizations. You don't have to make it your life's work, but be a regular consumer or checker of conservative websites and radio shows. These are the life-stream of the conservative movement, which is rising to reclaim this country, and you will know when to raise your voice about a certain issue, you will know what to pray for, and you will be equipped and informed for sharing your perspective with others.

2. **Join something local.** Maybe you've never done this before. There are school boards, parent groups, and neighborhood associations that form the lowest rung of civic participation, but these are

great places to learn to deal with people of all stripes. You will hone your message and your ability to persuade and prevail. It's like progressing through the farm leagues in baseball. Be a living, breathing part of the American experiment. And maybe you'll find that you like it, and someday people will call you Mayor, Council Member, or Senator.

3. **Get to know your representatives.** Read up on these people. They make laws for you! Drop them an e-mail, or give them a call now and then, maybe annually, and tell them what you appreciate and do not appreciate about their voting record. This is even more effective if you can say you represent such-and-such group, which advocates locally for such-and-such issue. Even if that group includes five other people, give yourselves a name. Citizens for Accuracy in Textbooks. Patriots for Improved Public Morality. Dub yourself the president, and enter the conversation. You will be noticed.

None of this takes very long—it just takes diligence. If we don't mow the front yard, weeds will take over. If we don't tend to our civic lawn, the same thing happens. It's time to mow some grass, Deplorables!

Chapter 2

THE GREAT UNRAVELING

I SORT OF FIGURED the country was on a slippery slope to you know where when my good buddy Phil Robertson got in trouble for delivering a prayer—at a NASCAR race.

Brother Phil drew the ire of a bunch of Jesus-bashing, liberal lug nuts after he petitioned the Lord during a NASCAR invocation to put a "Jesus man in the White House."[1] Aren't you glad the Lord answered that prayer?

Phil also mentioned the Bible and guns, and he thanked the good Lord for the US Armed Forces—just like any good, churchgoing Christian man would do.[2] But the duck commander's heartfelt invocation caused the mainstream media to blow a collective head gasket. Sports commentators and journalists suggested pre-race prayers were too "Southern" and too "redneck," as if there's something wrong with being a Southern-fried redneck.[3]

The *Deadspin* sports blog called Brother Phil an "unapologetic bigot" and a "duck call industrialist."[4] The Associated Press auto-racing writer accused Brother Phil of pushing an agenda—and accused NASCAR of "clouding its image with politics."

"There are Democrats who enjoy NASCAR," AP writer Jenna Fryer sneered. "Jews and atheists and women, too."[5]

The *Orlando Sentinel* published a column titled "NASCAR Doesn't Need Phil Robertson's Prayers." Writer David Whitley opined, "What if at next Sunday's race, someone got up and prayed for gun control, the Koran and that a Muhammad-woman be put in the White House? Most of the people defending Robertson would be throwing tire irons at their TVs."[6]

Well, I sincerely doubt a devout Muslim would be asking Allah to put a "Muhammad-woman" anywhere near the White House. And let's be honest, you don't see too many burkas at Bristol.

After Brother Phil's prayer sports writer Christopher Olmstead contemplated whether or not religion still belongs in NASCAR. "For a sport that is trying to become a global success is it appropriate to attach a certain religion or religious tone to yourself?" he wrote. "For a sport that might have several drivers who might not believe in God or religion is it appropriate to hold the pre-race invocation? For a sport that is trying to reach out to different cultures around the world who may believe in a higher power other than God, is it appropriate to have the invocation?"[7]

It's tempting to tell Brother Phil's critics to blow it out their tailpipes, but that's not the Christian thing to do. And besides, Brother Phil has more supporters than detractors, including the president of Texas Motor Speedway. "He said what he felt and believed and there are a lot of people that agree with him and a lot that disagree with him," Eddie Gossage told the Fort Worth Star-Telegram. "Nowadays, you cannot say what you think because of political correctness. So I guess everyone has a right to free speech or nobody does."[8]

Prayer is an important part of Southern culture. It's what we do. It's who we are—whether we're asking the good Lord to bless the butter beans or offering an unspoken prayer request before Bible study. And that's why the mainstream media may be in for a rude awakening if they think they can "prayer-shame" the good, churchgoing racing fans of America. It's not going to happen. Why, NASCAR without Jesus would be like biscuits without gravy.

You might be wondering right now, "Where is Todd going with this?" Well, the incident at that NASCAR race demonstrates the unraveling of our cherished American traditions and institutions. It's one of many signs all around us that act as warning lights on the dashboard, telling us, "You better get to Jiffy Lube, or else your engine's going to give up the ghost."

Are we paying attention to the signs?

Consider what happened when lawmakers in Tennessee tried to make the Holy Bible the official state book. State senator Kerry Roberts told The Tennessean that the legislation was meant to commemorate the historical nature of the Good Book, referencing George Washington's inauguration. "He used the Bible for his swearing in," Roberts told the newspaper. "The attitude of these people was not to keep religion out of government. It was to keep government out of religion."[9]

Try telling that to the editorial board of the Tennessean. The newspaper issued a blistering rebuke of lawmakers who supported the so-called Bible bill, calling them theocrats and comparing them to Muslim ayatollahs. "This is Tennessee, not Tehran," they sneered. "We are governed by the people, not the religious authorities."[10]

OK, folks. Let's take a deep breath here. I would suggest the newspaper's editorial board might have had a valid point—if, in fact, the lawmakers were beheading people, throwing citizens off buildings, and torturing ministers. But they are not.

The move to make the Bible the official state book is akin to a state having an official vegetable or an official snack. In other words, the Bible bill would have no discernable impact on people's daily lives. There will be no forced conversions or baptisms in the Volunteer State.

The newspaper went on to suggest that the bill was "clearly an attack on religious minorities, and secular, agnostic or atheistic people, who are also protected by the state and federal constitutions."[11] The editorial said it was "also an attack on religious people who have a strong interest in ensuring that government does not endorse one way to worship God over another."[12]

Those Tennessee lawmakers should be commended for their efforts to honor the Holy Bible. We are, after all, one nation under God. So why not recognize His Book? But imagine what kind of a nation we would be if folks went one step further and decided to live by the teachings of the Good Book.

By the way, Tennessee's official state beverage is milk. I wonder if the *Tennessean* is going to accuse lawmakers of attacking those who are lactose intolerant.

It has been said that America will never be destroyed from the outside, but if we falter and lose our freedoms, we will destroy ourselves. Those words were never truer than during a *CBS News Sunday Morning* segment featuring esteemed anchor Charles Osgood. Since you may have been in Sunday school at that hour, let me recap what happened.

Osgood opened the episode with a question meant to shock viewers: "Is the US Constitution truly worthy of the reverence in which most Americans hold it?"[13]

Mission accomplished.

From there Mr. Osgood introduced a gentleman by the name of Louis Michael Seidman, a professor of constitutional law at Georgetown University, who began his commentary with this statement: "I've got a simple idea: Let's give up on the Constitution. I know, it sounds radical, but it's really not. Constitutional disobedience is as American as apple pie."[14]

From that point the anti-Constitution constitutional law professor held forth on his quest to "take back our own country." He demanded that we "stop deferring to an ancient and outdated document."[15]

"We have a right to the kind of country we want," he declared. "We would not allow the French or the United Nations to rule us, and neither should we allow people who died over two centuries ago and knew nothing of our country as it exists today."[16]

I'm from the South, so I know when somebody is cooking my grits. But I don't believe that's what Professor Seidman was doing. I think he genuinely believes that nonsense. And that concerns me. There is an effort afoot to undermine not only the US Constitution but also our Founding Fathers.

Call it the "Great Unraveling."

The evidence is all around us, in a thousand headlines in various newspapers and localities. That's how unraveling happens—one small thread at a time. Consider the following examples.

HANDOUT PAINTS FOUNDING FATHERS AS RACISTS

In the fall of 2014 Sommer Bauer, the mother of an eight-year-old, told me her son was given a Nation of Islam handout at Harold McCormick Elementary School in Elizabethton, Tennessee. The handout asked, "What does it take to be on Mount Rushmore?" The handout then explained that George Washington hailed from Virginia, a "prime breeder of black people." It alleged Theodore Roosevelt called Africans "ape-like." There were also disparaging remarks made of Thomas Jefferson, whom the handout claimed enslaved two hundred Africans, as well as of Abraham Lincoln.[17]

Sommer said her jaw dropped when she followed the link to a website that was listed on the handout. Imagine her surprise when up popped the Nation of Islam home page. The Nation of Islam believes there is no God but Allah. They also aren't all that keen on white or Jewish folks. "It raised a number of red flags," Sommer said. "They are basically saying our Founding Fathers are racists."[18]

Sommer told me she reached out to the teacher for an explanation, hoping it was an honest mistake. "At first she did not recall which paper it was," she said. "Later in the day she found the paper and told me she didn't like what it said and said she must have printed it by mistake."[19]

The teacher also told Sommer that her son was not supposed to take the Nation of Islam handout home. It was supposed to stay in the classroom. That bit of news caused her great alarm. "I was caught off guard," she told me. "I reassured my son that he needed to feel safe enough to bring anything that the school gave him home to me. Ultimately while his teachers do care for him, his mother and his father have his absolute number one best interests at heart. He knows he needs to bring everything home to me," she said.[20]

Sommer then reached out to the principal to find out how Nation of Islam material ended up in her son's third-grade classroom. She said the principal was cordial and promised to investigate. She's still waiting for answers.

Ed Alexander, superintendent of the Elizabethton City school system, sounded genuinely horrified when I read him the contents of the handout. "My goodness, that we would promote bigoted or racist points of view—merciful heavens," he said. "I can assure you that is not the case."[21]

Alexander told me the handout was never meant for public distribution. He said the child took the handout from the teacher's workstation without her permission. He said the teacher had been preparing for a presentation on Mount Rushmore and had discarded the controversial handout. "It was not an authorized handout," Alexander said.[22]

Julie West is the president of Parents for Truth in Education, a Tennessee-based group that is opposed to the national Common Core educational initiative. Although there is no indication the Nation of Islam assignment was connected to Common Core, West said she is alarmed by whatever happened at Harold McCormick Elementary School. "The fact that students were cautioned against allowing their parents to see anything is deeply troubling," West told me. "The only reasonable explanation is they don't want parents to know what it is their children are learning."[23]

I certainly don't mean to be an apologist for the school, but what if it was just an honest-to-goodness mistake?

"Whatever the reason it came into the classroom, it's not OK," West said. "These are not advanced high school students. This is third grade. They should be learning the basics of our country."[24]

So what's the bottom line?

"We had a teacher who apparently never looked at something, never read something, before it was distributed to a class of third-graders," West said. "In addition she warned the students not to take it home."[25]

That does seem a bit odd.

I've interviewed Sommer Bauer at least a half dozen times. Her story has remained consistent. The teacher gave her two explanations for what happened in the classroom. The superintendent gave me a third.

I find it hard to believe an eight-year-old boy would steal a handout from a teacher's desk, bring it home, and then concoct an elaborate tale to cover up the crime. But let's suspend reality for just a moment and say the little boy did take that handout. Regardless there's no disputing the fact that it was on the teacher's desk.

And I do believe the good people of Elizabethton deserve to know how and why a handout from the Nation of Islam ended up on school property because it might be one more thread coming loose in the fabric of our nation.

THE US FLAG, A SYMBOL OF RACISM?

I wish the case in Elizabethton were isolated, but something similar happened on the Left Coast. In this instance a group of university professors signed a letter showing solidarity with six students who passed a resolution that, had it taken effect, would have banned the American flag at the University of California, Irvine. Why did the students want Old Glory removed? Because, according to the students, the American flag contributes to racism.

The letter supporting the failed resolution claimed that "nationalism, including U.S. nationalism, often contributes to racism and xenophobia, and that the paraphernalia of nationalism is in fact often used to intimidate."[26] Hundreds across the nation signed the offensive letter, including some UC Irvine professors. "We admire the courage of the resolution's supporters amid this environment of political immaturity and threat, and support them unequivocally," the letter read.[27]

How those professors can sleep at night knowing their salaries are paid for by a bunch of xenophobic racists is beyond me.

The UC Irvine student government association had voted 6–4 (with two abstentions) to remove Old Glory from a campus lobby for the sake of cultural inclusivity. The un-American knuckleheads blathered on about how "the American flag has been flown in instances of colonialism and imperialism."[28]

Breitbart quoted an unnamed student who said the student government association feared the flag might hurt the feelings of illegal aliens. "There were people who were like, 'The flag triggers me'—that was their exact wording, too," the student said.[29]

The flag triggers me too, but in a whole different sense of the word. Count me as one who would gladly take up arms to defend her if the freedoms she represented were ever endangered.

Over a weekend the executive leadership of the student government met and vetoed the legislation, and by the following Monday the flag was once again posted in the campus lobby.[30] "Our campus is patriotic and proud," student government President Reza Zomorrodian told me at the time. "We did something right for our campus."[31]

A legislative meeting to discuss the controversy was canceled after the university received a "viable threat of violence." While the threat was not specific, university officials said they were taking it seriously and urged students to be diligent. "Regardless of your opinion on the display of the American flag, we must be united in protecting the people who make this university a premier institution of higher learning," Chancellor Howard Gillman wrote in a statement posted on the university's website.[32]

Meanwhile, a group of California lawmakers is working on a bill that would prohibit publicly funded universities from banning the American flag.[33] Let me tell you how I think it should work: you ban the flag; we ban your student loans. As that great American Merle Haggard once said so eloquently, "If you don't love it, leave it."[34]

If we can't unite around the flag, are we really united at all?

SCHOOL TELLS KIDS TO REMOVE AMERICAN FLAGS ON 9/11

Sometimes good intentions have unintended consequences. Principal Aaron Fulmer of Woodruff High School in Woodruff, South Carolina, made national headlines after he directed students to remove American flags from their pickup trucks on September 11.[35]

The patriotic teenagers had mounted large American flags in their truck beds in violation of a long-standing school policy. The policy, which has been in place for more than twenty years, bans anything that creates a disturbance on campus or draws an unusual amount of attention to itself.[36] "A bumper sticker is not going to do that from a distance, but a pole flag is," school superintendent Rallie Liston told me in a telephone interview. "The American flag was never an issue for us. It was never anti-American flag. It was just no pole flags—period."[37]

Liston said the original rule was created to prevent students from showing up at school with Confederate flags. "It was inflammatory," the superintendent told me. "Finally, we reached a point where we said no more pole flags."[38]

American flag bumper stickers are fine. So are American flag T-shirts. But students simply cannot fly American flags in their pickup trucks. Such behavior is impermissible. As the superintendent explained, the policy prevents students from showing up with something offensive. "If it's an American flag, everybody is excited about it," he said. "But what if it's the Nazi flag or another flag you might not be congruent with?"[39]

As you might imagine, the school's decision led to lots of protests and name-calling. A group of parents even stood outside the school, waving American flags.[40]

Superintendent Liston said accusations that the school is anti-American are as far from the truth as can be. "These are the most God-fearing, flag-waving, patriotic people you will ever find," he said. "They are God and country."[41]

But he said with the growing fears over the Islamic State and the school's plans to commemorate 9/11, he realized he might have made a mistake. "We dropped the ball with 9/11," he told me matter-of-factly. "In hindsight we apologize to any veteran or service person for this happening. That was not our intent. It was just a rule that has been consistently enforced." [42]

I think it's safe to say the school learned its lesson. "I don't want to ever get in the position where we take the American flag down again," Liston told me. [43]

Superintendent Liston seems like a true Southern gentleman, and I believe his apology is sincere. As we say in the South, you know when somebody's cooking your grits. And Superintendent Liston was not cooking my grits.

Nevertheless it's deeply troubling when any public school suppresses the patriotism of American teenagers. It's another small step toward the total breakdown we all saw coming before us as voters jumped in to try to prevent it.

ACADEMY REPLACES MOTHER TERESA WITH OPRAH

You can tell a country is unraveling when it replaces real heroes with celebrities.

For years boys and girls at South Arbor Charter Academy in Ypsilanti, Michigan, had been inspired by Heroes Hall, a corridor featuring murals that honored the space shuttle Columbia astronauts, Mother Teresa, Betsy Ross, and Albert Einstein. But many parents were furious after the principal had the murals replaced with paintings honoring former president Obama, Oprah, *Harry Potter* author J. K. Rowling, Apple cofounder Steve Jobs, poet Maya Angelou, and Walt Disney. [44] "This is no longer a hall of heroes," parent Craig Bergman told me. "Now we have a hall of celebrities." [45]

The original mural had been a part of the Michigan charter school for years. It included a diverse group of national and global "heroes"—from Gandhi to the astronauts who were killed when the space shuttle Columbia exploded over Texas. [46]

Parent Todd Holliday told me the new mural sends the wrong message to children in the school for kindergartners through eighth-graders. "My biggest concern is my kid seeing these murals for the next four years, thinking they represent what a hero is," Holliday told me. "They might be successful business-people, but they aren't really heroes." [47]

Bergman said the school's new mural really transforms the concept of what makes a person a hero. "The mere fact that you have talent doesn't mean you are a hero," he said. "I want someone who made a life investment—perhaps they even sacrificed their life so that our society and so our world could be a better place." [48]

So what was going on here? Why did the South Arbor Charter Academy remove a mural memorializing the fallen Columbia astronauts and replace it with one honoring President Obama? School spokesperson Jennifer Hoff said it was part of an intentional shift from "historical heroes" to "modern-day heroes."

"Heroes Hall has been a part of the school's fabric for years," she said. "In fact, the old mural had been on the wall for at least eleven years. As with all things over time, it was showing its age from the activities of being an active school and needed some repair."[49]

So why not just hire an artist and touch up Mother Teresa? Why paint over her entire face? And who made that decision?

Bergman told me the principal appointed a blue-ribbon panel of four staffers to select who the new heroes should be. "There was no parental involvement," he said. "The principal of the school handpicked and self-appointed [the group]. Once they gave her their final decisions, she solely approved the list."[50]

And judging from who they selected, it's pretty clear the new-and-improved Heroes Hall is not—*ahem*—fair and balanced. "Previously it was very well-balanced and respected a lot of different thoughts," Bergman said. "Instead it's become more of a political issue. There's definitely a certain genre of pictures here."[51]

Hoff said Heroes Hall is a "tangible way for students to see that despite circumstances in life, you can achieve great things through hard work, dedication, and the moral focus virtues."[52] What, pray tell, are "moral focus virtues"?

According to Hoff, the school culture is built on virtues that emphasize "wisdom, respect, gratitude, self-control, perseverance, courage, encouragement, compassion, and integrity."[53] And the new heroes, she said, embody those virtues.

She said Rowling shows the children wisdom, Steve Jobs shows the children integrity, Oprah represents compassion, Disney represents courage, and Maya Angelou shows the children perseverance. As for President Obama, well, he shows the children encouragement, Hoff said. "Our goal all along is to encourage our students to believe in themselves, work hard, and be brave enough to dream," she said.[54]

But that's just not sitting well with folks such as Bergman. "They may be some of the most influential people in American history, but they are not heroes," he said.[55]

For the record, the children are not required to sing praise songs or genuflect in the presence of the president's mural. Yet.

At the end of the day, the school is going to do what the school is going to do. But it's really a shame the principal didn't ask the public for their recommendations. How about the Navy SEALs who got Osama bin Laden? What about the firefighters and police officers who died on 9/11 or those who defended our consulate in Benghazi? Those are true American heroes.

ACLU CRACKS DOWN ON SCHOOL
YARD PATRIOTISM

Some heroes are small.

For more than a decade boys and girls at Glenview Elementary School in Haddon Heights, New Jersey, would start the day by gathering on the playground to recite the Pledge of Allegiance. Then they would conclude their patriotic service by saying, "God bless America."[56]

It was a tradition birthed by two kindergarten teachers in the aftermath of the terrorist attacks on September 11, 2001, a way to honor those who lost their lives on that terrible day. But that tradition ended on a winter day in 2016, thanks to the American Civil Liberties Union of New Jersey.[57]

The school's principal sent a letter to parents advising them that "the administration has decided to discontinue the official endorsement of reciting 'God bless America' at the end of the morning Pledge of Allegiance."[58]

ACLU-NJ legal director Ed Barocas said reciting the phrase "God bless America" is unconstitutional. "The Establishment Clause of the First Amendment to the United States Constitution prohibits the government from not only favoring one religion over another, but also from promoting religion over non-religion," he wrote in a letter to the school district's attorney. "The greatest care must be taken to avoid the appearance of governmental endorsement in schools, especially elementary schools, given the impressionable age of the children under the school's care and authority."[59]

Principal Sam Sassano told me the children saying "God bless America" had nothing to do with religion. "It wasn't taught with any intention of having any type of religious overtones," the principal said. "It was taught to show patriotism."[60]

Sassano said he took pride in watching the young patriots voluntarily say the phrase, "especially since there are so many people out there every day risking their lives to protect us and keep us safe."[61]

Nevertheless the final decision to stop the practice was determined by the school district, fearing a costly lawsuit. "Budgets across the state of New Jersey are very tight," the principal said. "We have to be very cautious how we spend taxpayer funds. The amount of legal fees to fight something like this in court could really break a budget."[62]

So thanks to the ACLU, students will no longer be allowed to invoke God's blessing upon America. "I'm very, very upset about this," said Debi Krezel, the parent of a sixth-grader. "Being a daughter, a sister, niece, and cousin of veterans and first responders, [as well as] an American and a taxpayer, why are my rights and my child's rights being taken away?"[63]

Krezel had nothing but praise for Sassano, and she said she understands why the district had to do what it did, but that still doesn't make it right. "I don't think it's fair to us or our children," she told me. "What are they going to take from us next? We are slowly chipping away the values and beliefs and traditions that [the nation] was created upon."[64]

Sassano stressed to me that no child has ever been forced to recite the Pledge of Allegiance or say, "God bless America." It's entirely voluntary. "We teach the children to be respectful," he said. "So if they choose not to recite the pledge, they stand quietly. Nothing is forced on the child."[65]

Hiram Sasser, the director of litigation for First Liberty Institute, told me the ACLU is off base. "Kids cannot be required to say it, but leading in the recitation of it is as constitutional as the national motto, 'In God We Trust,'" Sasser told me.[66]

The ACLU is one of those big organizations picking and pulling at the threads of what holds us together as Americans. When this well-funded, completely left-wing group picks on a bunch of children and bullies yet another small, patriotic community, it's nothing short of shameful.

In my estimation there's nothing civil about the American Civil Liberties Union—or American, for that matter. They are contributing to the "Great Unraveling" that is taking place before our eyes.

STUDENT PUNISHED FOR SAYING, "GOD BLESS AMERICA"

Again, the stories are all around us. A Florida high school student was disciplined after a national atheist organization took offense when he concluded the morning announcements by saying, "God bless America."[67]

A spokesperson for the Nassau County School District told me the student at Yulee High School deviated from the approved script on the morning of February 9 and uttered the words "God bless America," which apparently caused two atheist students to experience angst. "It wasn't part of the scripted morning announcements," district spokesperson Sharyl Wood said. "The principal took the appropriate steps in speaking with the student and disciplining the student."[68]

Disciplining the student? What's the penalty these days for asking God to bless America? Thirty lashes?

Instead of reporting their angst to the principal, the atheist students reached out to the American Humanist Association (AHA).[69] The group's legal arm—the

Appignani Humanist Legal Center—fired off a testy letter to the principal and school district on the students' behalf. "It is inappropriate and unlawful for a public school to start the school day with an official statement over the intercom stating, 'God Bless America,' for such a statement affirms God-belief, validates a theistic worldview, and is invidious toward atheists and other nonbelievers," the AHA wrote in a letter to the principal of Yulee High School.[70]

The AHA said the student violated the Constitution and broke the law by invoking God's name over the public address system. The organization demanded the school immediately cease and desist under the threat of a lawsuit. "The daily validation of the religious views of God-believers resigns atheists to second-class citizens," the AHA wrote in its letter. "Because attendance is mandatory, the students have no way of avoiding this daily message either."[71]

Later that day, the AHA received a mea culpa from the principal, assuring them such behavior would not happen again. Principal Natasha Drake told the AHA:

> Thank you for bringing this matter to my attention. I want to point out that the statement "God Bless America, keep us safe" that was made last week on the morning announcements was not approved by school Administration nor was it in the scripted announcements. The student on his own accord made the statement. I have called the student in this morning and directed him that at no time is he to add or take away from announcements that have been pre-approved and that if he did it again, he would no longer have the privilege of making the morning announcements. I am disappointed that the students who filed the complaint did not do so with me first, as I would have addressed it immediately. Once again, thank you for bringing this concern to my attention. It is our desire and intention to respect the beliefs and constitutional freedoms of all our students at Yulee High School.[72]

So why in the world does the school district have a problem with God blessing America?

"As an official representative of a governmental agency, schools aren't allowed to promote or inhibit religion," Wood told me. "Individual students are certainly permitted to express their religious beliefs but not on behalf of the governmental body."[73] She explained that once the student delivered the morning announcements, the student became a representative of the government, and invoking God to bless our fruited plain became a no-no.

Sweet Lord Almighty, good readers.

"We can't say, 'God bless America' or 'Hail to Muslims.' Nobody can get up there and say there is no God," Wood explained. "We have respect for all people's faiths and religions."[74]

The school district is also frustrated that the atheist students declined to speak directly to school leadership. The kids may have feared repercussions. But Wood said, "We have an anonymous tip line the students could have used to make a report."[75]

Of course the school district has an anonymous tip line for students. You never know when you might need to report a student for suddenly shouting, "Bless you!" after a teacher sneezes.

I asked Jeremy Dys, an attorney with the religious freedom advocacy group First Liberty Institute, to weigh in on this nonsense, and he said the atheists don't have a prayer. "Whether a student is being patriotic or engaging in religious speech, there is no law in this country forbidding a student from telling his or her classmates, 'God bless America,' and it is illegal for a school to censor a student for doing so," he said.[76]

Dys also wonders why atheists are so determined to censor the patriotic speech of a red-blooded American high school student. "Regardless of this attempt by secularists to whitewash over this demonstration of patriotism by a teenager, America's students do not give up their right to free speech and the expression of their religious beliefs when they go to school," he said.[77]

I'd still like to know how they disciplined the morning announcement reader for such an "egregious" act, but the district spokesperson refused to tell me. Lord love 'em, but I'm not sure what's worse, perpetually offended atheists or constitutionally ignorant educators.

THE SECOND AMERICAN REVOLUTION

Thank God there are good examples—people who are drawing us together, making us stronger, stopping the "Great Unraveling" from happening at the local level. One group of patriotic teenagers in the birthplace of the American Revolution held its ground and fought back against school administrators' attempts to cancel an "American Pride" dance and replace it with a more inclusive event.[78]

These students at Lexington High School in Lexington, Massachusetts, said the administration had canceled their plans for a red, white, and blue dance because it excluded other nationalities. Instead the administration suggested a more inclusive "National Pride" dance.[79] "It was suggested by the advisers that the students [have a] national pride theme so they could represent their individual nationalities," Assistant Superintendent Carol Pilarski told Boston NBC affiliate WHDH. "Maybe it should be more inclusive, and it should be national pride."[80]

Word of the administration's objections to an American-themed dance spread across town like the shot heard round the world. "[It's] a lot of hypersensitivity to being politically correct," one student told the television station.[81]

"People consider America to be a melting pot," said another student. "So the fact that it was even considered offensive is what people are a little surprised about."[82]

Principal Laura Lasa told me the dance had never been canceled. They merely wanted to "dialogue" with students about inclusivity.[83] Whatever.

First it was the redcoats, and now the good people of Lexington have to fight off an invading horde of un-American educators. But instead of Paul Revere there was a school full of courageous teenagers riding through the countryside shouting, "The liberals are coming! The liberals are coming!"

And they won. That's what happens when we simply stand for what is right and refuse to be cowed by cultural extremists, people to whom even the American flag and American-themed dances are now verboten.

I'm sure if I sat down and interviewed each of you reading this book, you would have an example from your town, school, or workplace that depicts this "Great Unraveling." It's all around us. But the good news is that people like you and me are now uniting to stop it. Every war is won by a thousand people staying at their posts and completing their assignments bravely.

I bet you can think of something right now that you can do at work, at school, or in your neighborhood to gain back ground that has been lost. Your local acts of courage are every bit as important as what gets reported on TV. It changes the climate of fear and uncertainty around you. It emboldens others to be brave as well. It's how America became great to begin with.

With each of us doing our part, the "Great Unraveling" can become the "Great Renewal" of America's principles and traditions. Following are some simple, easy ways to do your part.

MARCHING ORDERS

1. **Get proud and patriotic again.** Read up on accurate accounts of our nation's founding. Don't let people tell you that Thomas Jefferson, George Washington, and Benjamin Franklin were mere deists, or that the founders were bad men who had only their economic interests in mind to the detriment of everyone else. Arm yourself with facts, quotes, and historical references to refute that garbage. We've let liberals play stupid with our history for long enough.

2. **Let your patriotism show.** Post memes on social media with quotes from our founders. Do this especially around civic holidays. It may seem small, but that kind of thing seasons the conversation and gets into people's minds. If we express patriotism only in private, we will lose the public square.

3. **Research and talk about the great Americans who made this country what it is.** Enough of minor liberal heroes being elevated to places of high public esteem. Let's honor the people who really pulled their weight and built the foundations of freedom and prosperity we have long enjoyed.

4. **Involve your kids and grandkids in groups that affirm America and our Christian heritage.** Trail Life USA and American Heritage Girls are among the fastest-growing programs for young people in the country. Both were birthed in the wake of decisions by the Boy Scouts of America and the Girls Scouts to stray from their founding principles.

5. **Take a patriotic family vacation.** Pile the kids in the station wagon (an homage to *National Lampoon*) and hit the road. Visit the Freedom Trail in Boston or the Liberty Bell in Philadelphia. Explore the rich history of Charleston, South Carolina, and Williamsburg, Virginia. Take the family on a walking tour of the National Civil Rights Museum in Memphis, Tennessee, or visit one of our great national parks. Show your kids why we're proud to be Americans.

Chapter 3

PANTSUITS, YUGE HANDS, AND THE 2016 PRESIDENTIAL RACE

★ ★ ★ ★

S YOU CAN imagine, there was great weeping and gnashing of teeth in my liberal Brooklyn neighborhood on election night. Horrified millennials stumbled into the streets, searching for the nearest watering hole—looking to drown their sorrows in shots of wheatgrass. Meanwhile I was chugging an Abita Root Beer and doing the Boot Scootin' Boogie in the middle of Sixth Avenue. Well, that might be a slight exaggeration.

What a privilege to have a front-row seat to one of the most historic presidential elections in modern history—the night Donald J. Trump defeated Hillary Clinton. It was the twenty-first century's version of "Dewey Defeats Truman." That infamous 1948 headline was a mistake created by an overconfident newspaper that never expected Truman to win.[1] Much the same could be said of Trump.

Many networks were preparing to announce at 11:00 p.m. Eastern that Clinton had won the election. But those plans were popped in the nose after Trump pulled ahead in battleground states such as Florida and North Carolina...and then Ohio and Pennsylvania.

Who knew there were so many deplorable Americans of voting age so highly motivated to make America great again?

The Almighty spared the republic. We had been given a second chance. It was a glorious night.

After watching hundreds of people celebrating in the Fox News plaza, I rushed back to my office on the far right side of the building to see how the other cable networks were handling the shocking news. It appeared that several of the anchors needed emergency oxygen.

Trump's victory triggered microaggressions from coast to coast. The mainstream media suffered a psychotic breakdown. Millennials curled into fetal positions in their parents' basements. Hollywood self-medicated. Feminists burned their pantsuits. Establishment Republicans ordered martinis, extra dry. And our enemies soiled themselves.

Oh, the humanity.

We the people, the silent majority, decided it was time to take back our country. We had had enough of the name-calling, the threats, the bullying, and the violence. Enough was enough.

Liberals called us Nazis. Establishment Republicans called us foolish. Progressive evangelicals called us sinners. The mainstream media called us backwater bigots. And Hillary Clinton called us every name in her great big basket.

We the people decided it was time to drain the swamp. It was time to restore traditional American values and protect the Constitution and defend our sovereignty. We decided it was time to save those precious unborn babies and defend religious liberty. It was time to stand up for the American working man, bring jobs back from China and Mexico, and eradicate the scourge of Obamacare.

Granted, Trump is far from a gun-toting, Bible-clinging conservative. We understood that going into the booth on Election Day. But he promised to be our voice. He promised to be our defender. He promised to protect the unborn and appoint conservatives to the courts.

The alternative was simply unacceptable. Donald Trump may be a lot of things, but at least he's not Hillary Clinton. And that was a motivating factor for many voters. We were, in a word, desperate.

WRONG VALUES

A Fox News poll found that barely 50 percent of Americans said they were proud of their country, down 19 points from 2011.[2] And it's no wonder. For the past eight years we've had a president who waged war on our traditions and questioned our values. He told the world that we were not an exceptional nation. At a gathering in Asia he put it this way:

> Sometimes people say, "Ah, why are the Americans talking about these issues? This is none of their business; they shouldn't be meddling in other people's business. And also, America is not perfect. Look, it still has racial discrimination. It still has its own problems. It should worry about its own problems." And I agree with that in the sense that we definitely do still have problems we have to work on. We still have discrimination, we still have situations where women are not treated equally.[3]

He went on to suggest Americans are lazy. "If you're in the United States, sometimes you can feel lazy and think we're so big we don't have to really know anything about other people," he said.[4]

So the man who's played dozens and dozens of rounds of golf since putting his hand on the Bible had the nerve to call us lazy. Worse, he stood on foreign soil and declared we were no longer just a Christian nation.[5]

He later lectured attendees at the National Prayer Breakfast, telling the mostly Christian audience about terrible things done in the name of Jesus Christ. "From a school in Pakistan to the streets of Paris, we have seen violence and terror perpetrated by those who profess to stand up for faith, their faith, professed to stand up for Islam, but, in fact, are betraying it," he said, carefully avoiding the words *radical Islam* or *jihad* or *Islamic extremist*. "And lest we get on our high horse and think this is unique to some other place, remember that during the Crusades and the Inquisition, people committed terrible deeds in the name of Christ."[6]

The Community-Organizer-in-Chief could not leave the stage without reminding us what a terrible people we are. "Slavery and Jim Crow all too often was justified in the name of Christ," he said.[7]

It was a shocking, arrogant display of hostility toward the religion of America's founders. Bishop E. W. Jackson told a gathering of pastors in Washington, D.C., that he barely recognized his country anymore. "It bothers me to think my own country is a strange land," he said. "I never thought there would be a day when my nation would persecute the Bible-believing Christians for standing for what the [Word] of God says and reward those who come against it as if they are heroes, as if they are great Americans for standing up against God, but that's where we are."[8]

TIME magazine suggested we live in a divided nation. They named then President-elect Trump their person of the year and in a backhanded compliment called him the "President of the Divided States of America."[9] In other words, it's Los Angeles, San Francisco, and New York City versus the rest of us.

Texas senator Ted Cruz got in a bit of trouble during the Republican primary when he referenced what he called "New York values."[10] Now, all of us folks who are not New York City liberals know exactly what Cruz was talking about—the vast gap between the cultural and political values of the Big Apple and the American breadbasket.

But Cruz was slammed by Democrats and the mainstream media (and Donald Trump too) for what they considered an attack on the 9/11 victims.[11] Of course his remark had nothing to do with 9/11. And to suggest that he was referring to the brave firefighters and police officers who were massacred in the 2001 terrorist attacks is not only disgusting but an outright lie.

But liberal politicians have never let the truth get in the way of their ugly agendas. "I am disgusted at the insult that Ted Cruz threw at this city and its people," New York City Mayor Bill de Blasio said. "The bottom line is he does not understand in the least New York values." [12]

New York governor Andrew Cuomo called Cruz's comment "offensive" and said if "he had any class he would apologize" to the people of New York. [13] That's the same governor who once said "extreme conservatives" who are pro-life and pro-gun are not welcome in his state. "They have no place in the state of New York because that's not who New Yorkers are," the governor told a radio host in 2014. [14]

What was truly offensive is how liberal politicians and the mainstream media intentionally distorted what Cruz said. So let's talk about those "New York values" that Senator Cruz referenced.

He was referring to the permissive New York values celebrating public debauchery that would make the citizens of Sodom and Gomorrah blush. Just ask the families from the Heartland who've been accosted by topless women in Times Square. [15]

Remember Occupy Wall Street, which turned public parks into human cesspools? People defecating on police cars? [16] He was talking about those values too, along with the values that propelled citizens into the streets to justify violence against police officers. [17]

Senator Cruz was talking about the values that banned churches from public spaces and relegated Christians to second-class citizens. [18]

You see, in the land New Yorkers like to call flyover country, character counts. A man's word matters. Those are the values Senator Cruz found missing in New York.

HOW CHRISTIANS VOTED

And that brings me to the plight of evangelical Christians, the values voters. For some Trump was like a bucket of store-bought chicken at a Wednesday night church supper. It may have been a culinary heresy, but folks still ate it. For others Trump's religious values, or lack of them, disqualified him from holding public office. A popular quote by renowned pastor Charles Haddon Spurgeon was the rallying cry for that crowd: "Of two evils, choose neither." [19]

But was our best and only option to throw in the towel? Would Christians get to claim the moral high ground by electing Hillary Clinton president?

"The idea of not voting—you're sacrificing your Christian worldview on the altar of political expediency," Samuel Rodriguez, president of the National

Hispanic Christian Leadership Conference, told me at the time. "It is silly to talk about not voting for either candidate. Every single Christian should vote." [20]

I especially appreciated Franklin Graham's spiritual leadership during the 2016 presidential race. "You don't just stay home and not vote—you vote," the president of the Billy Graham Evangelistic Association told me. "Vote for the candidates that best support biblical truth and biblical values." [21]

But what if your candidate was not exactly an altar boy in good standing? "In some races it may not always be clear," Graham said. "You may have to hold your nose and choose of the two." [22]

So what were the Lutheran church ladies and Baptist deacons and Church of God Sunday school teachers supposed to do? Should Christians vote for Donald Trump? I reached out to my friend Arkansas governor Mike Huckabee for guidance on that question. "I'm not going to try and suggest that Donald Trump is in any way the reincarnation of the apostle Paul," Huckabee told me before the election. "But he's been very open to not only dialogue with but listen to and understand where many people in the faith community are coming from." [23]

Besides, Huckabee pointed out, the Republicans have nominated people who are far more contemptuous of the evangelical community. Anybody remember Sen. John McCain's infamous "agents of intolerance" rhetoric? In 2000 McCain said segments of the religious right were divisive and even un-American. [24]

So again, what was a good, churchgoing person supposed to do? Pray, Graham said. Instead of endorsing a candidate, Graham held prayer gatherings outside capitol buildings in all fifty states. Tens of thousands of Americans attended the "Decision America Tour" events in 2016. [25] "We aren't supporting political candidates," Graham said at the time. "I'm encouraging Christians to vote. The problem in our country today is that we have allowed the progressive to take God out of our government. We have allowed godless secularism to take control of Washington." [26]

But that was still not enough to convince some evangelical elites, many of whom browbeat their fellow believers with the idea that a vote for Trump was akin to renouncing Christ. [27] To be honest though, Donald Trump could've walked the aisle at a Billy Graham Crusade while waving a King James Bible and singing "Amazing Grace," and it still would not have been enough to sway the holier-than-thou club.

And for all you folks who quoted Spurgeon, I would offer this rebuttal: not to vote is to vote.

Sympathy for Trump went up as Americans were repulsed at the images of his supporters being bullied and battered from San Jose to San Diego to Chicago to Minneapolis. [28] In San Jose men were sucker punched and women pelted with bottles and eggs by a violent crowd waving Mexican flags. CBS in San Francisco reported that "another young man was chased down like prey. He ran until finding some police officers who stopped his attackers."[29]

ABC News reported that the rioters smashed the taillights of a car. The vicious mob even turned their wrath on police, attacking them with whatever they could find.[30] They also burned the American flag—on American soil.[31] But they did not burn the Mexican flag. If they love Mexico so much, they should pack their belongings and head to the border.

It was a classic example of how the Left tries to silence the opposition—through intimidation and violence. They were not protesters; they were criminals, enemies of free speech, common street thugs.

One of the most disturbing images from the campaign came from California. A small child held a sign that read "Make America Mexico Again."[32]

And that kind of attitude is what did it for many people. There was a time in this nation's history when having 13 million people breach your border would have been considered an invasion. We used to fight wars over such a hostile act. But these days instead of repelling the invaders, the Obama administration gave them food stamps, health care, and a voter registration card.[33]

We've been invaded, and our government has provided aid and comfort to the enemy. In both Indiana[34] and California[35] the protesters tried to bully and intimidate law-abiding Americans into silent submission. They tried, but they failed. Trump rallied America. He talked about the issues that mattered to those of us in the non-coastal states.

You see, "We the People" decided not to be silent anymore. We will not allow our sovereignty to be violated further. The American taxpayers have reached a boiling point. We are tired of illegals taking American jobs. We are tired of illegals living off our tax dollars. And more than anything we are tired of lawmakers who refuse to defend American sovereignty.

The truth is we don't know who or what has been coming across our southern border. We don't know what dangers lurk in our neighborhoods. And we wanted a president who would put American lives first. We wanted a president who would do whatever it takes to keep our families safe.

Many conservative pundits still do not understand why Americans flocked to Trump. They seem bewildered that so many voters ignored the warnings of establishment Republican overlords such as Mitt Romney and the uppity-ups at *National Review*. So for all you RINOs (Republicans in Name Only) who are confused, let me explain what's happened here.

The folks who pay the bills in this country are fed up. We're tired of being called racists, homophobes, and xenophobes. We're tired of having our principled values defined as ugly fears. The silent majority is mad as a wet hen—and we're not going to take it anymore. The epic election of 2016 was the starting line, not the finish line. We're far from done. Just wait to see what this country looks like when we're finished with her.

Here's your next batch of ideas for making America great again:

MARCHING ORDERS

1. **Call your representatives at the local, state, and federal levels.** When you do, they should answer, "Hi, Susan. How can we help you today?" I'm not saying to pester them, but how will they know what you think unless you tell them? I suggest you keep their phone numbers posted on the fridge or wall in your kitchen so every time an issue of significance comes up, you can jump on the line and weigh in. You may be surprised how your voice can sway their stance.

2. **When Election Day comes around, don't rely solely on the party's voter guide.** Increasingly parties have their own interests and lose touch with their base of supporters. Make sure you vote on the issues, not the party. That will send a signal to them on election night that we're not just sheep to be herded in whatever direction they wish.

3. **Get involved in a political party.** If you want more direct influence, consider joining the local arm of your political party. You may even find yourself on a ballot someday.

4. **Volunteer to be a poll watcher or to work the polls on Election Day.** It's a lot of fun. You'll meet your neighbors, and you'll enjoy the great feeling of participating in one of the world's greatest traditions—helping to ensure that an American election is free and fair.

Chapter 4

PAUL, SILAS, AND SWEET HOME ALABAMA

O NE SUMMER WHEN I was knee high to a butter bean, I attended vacation Bible school (VBS) at my grandmother's Methodist church in Whitehaven, Tennessee. It was a source of contention with my Southern Baptist mother, who was a dunker, not a sprinkler. But I must confess, I enjoyed spending my summers with the Methodists. My preference had less to do with theology than it did with vacation Bible school snacks. The Methodists served Oreo cookies and Kool-Aid. The Baptists served generic store-bought versions of both because it saved money for the missions offering. You were a kid once. You tell me which you would have preferred.

One year the VBS teacher gave us a stirring felt-board lesson on Paul and Silas. I can't recall the elderly lady's name, but she was about as Southern as sweet tea. For the sake of my story we'll just call her Miss Bertha. That's probably close anyway.

All of us third-graders were enraptured with her tale of how Paul and Silas were doing Monday night visitation when somebody called the law. She told us how a few deputies put a "whooping" on Paul and Silas.

"I heard tell them boys were smacked upside their heads with a cast iron skillet," she said in her high-pitched twang. "And then they got themselves throwed in the jail."

Lord Almighty, my little fingers were trembling so hard I nearly dropped my Oreo.

"But instead of hollering for their mama and them in the county lockup, Paul and Silas commenced to singing," Miss Bertha declared.

Well, we just had to know what those fellows were singing. So we peppered Miss Bertha with all sorts of queries. Was it "Sweet Home Alabama"? "Free Bird"? "Play That Funky Music"?

She gave us a stern lecture on listening to that "devil music" and then opined that many New Testament scholars believe Paul and Silas probably traveled with a copy of the Red-Back Hymnal.

Well, you know how the story goes. There was a violent earthquake that shook the foundations of the jail. The shaking was so fierce, the chains came off the prisoners. But instead of escaping, Paul and Silas and all the other prisoners stayed put. The jailer was so stunned, he fell down trembling and asked what he should do to be saved. (See Acts 16:16–40.)

"Sweet Jesus, revival broke out!" Miss Bertha shouted. "Folks started getting saved all over town. And the next day the sheriff ordered them deputies to release Paul and Silas."

I casually mentioned to Miss Bertha that my mama said Paul and Silas were actually Baptists and wondered why she had left out the part about everybody getting dunked in the pond. If there'd been a cast-iron skillet handy, I suspect Miss Bertha might would've used it.

There is a supersized spiritual truth bomb lurking in that familiar passage of Scripture from the Book of Acts. In the face of adversity and persecution, Paul and Silas were happy warriors. Now I don't mean they were giggling while being beaten. But they refused to allow their dire circumstances to quench the Spirit. They were being physically abused, yet Paul and Silas were mindful of their testimony. They sang, they prayed, and they ministered to their fellow prisoners.

In a *Guideposts* article, my friend Michelle Cox wondered at how precious that music must have sounded as it echoed through the darkened chambers of that hellish prison.[1] Indeed.

How many of us would consider doing the same? I'll be the first to confess that I don't do well with persecution. My first instinct is to lash out. But that's not what God calls us to do. We are to handle adversity and hardship knowing that He is in control.

But that does not mean we cannot call out injustice. In Acts 16:35–37 the chief magistrates ordered Paul and Silas released. "Go in peace" was the instruction they were given. But Paul was not having any of that.

> They beat us in public without a trial, although we are Roman citizens, and threw us in jail. And now are they going to smuggle us out secretly? Certainly not! On the contrary, let them come themselves and escort us out!
>
> —ACTS 16:37, HCSB

In Southern vernacular Paul was giving the law enforcement a version of, "Now wait just one cotton-picking minute."

Paul was righteously indignant. And sure enough, not only did the magistrates escort him and Silas out of the jail, but they also apologized. I love that. Revival came to Philippi. Justice was served, and Paul and Silas received an official police escort and a public apology. I'd take a beating for that.

Persecution didn't disappear with those brave men. In America during the past eight years Christians have gotten their own taste of it, from their own governments, no less. But in many cases the police escort and public apology never materialized. Consider these actual instances.

THE BAPTIST FLOWER SHOP LADY—PUBLIC ENEMY NO. 1

Barronelle Stutzman is a grandmother, a devout Baptist, and the owner of a small flower shop, and in early 2015 she was being treated as Washington state's Public Enemy No. 1. The seventy-two-year-old Christian is opposed to gay marriage, and her religious belief could cost Stutzman her business, her life savings, and even her home.[2]

A Washington judge ruled in 2015 that Stutzman, the owner of Arlene's Flowers, violated the law when she refused to provide flowers to a same-sex couple for their wedding.[3] "If you disagree with the state, then you're out of business," she told me at the time. "As a business owner, it's really frightening that they can rule that everything I have will be lost because of my disagreement with a stand."[4]

Superior Court Judge Alex Ekstrom found Stutzman had violated the state consumer protection and antidiscrimination law. He rejected arguments that her actions were protected by her freedom of speech and religion. The *Seattle Times* reported that Judge Ekstrom determined that "while religious beliefs are protected by the First Amendment, actions based on those beliefs aren't necessarily protected."[5]

So it's OK to believe in God so long as you don't follow the tenets of your faith? Wow. Welcome to the new America with the brand-new, redefined First Amendment.

"For over 135 years, the Supreme Court has held that laws may prohibit religiously motivated action, as opposed to belief," Ekstrom wrote in remarks reported by the *Seattle Times*. "The Courts have confirmed the power of the Legislative Branch to prohibit conduct it deems discriminatory, even where the motivation for that conduct is grounded in religious belief."[6]

Kristen Waggoner, an attorney with Alliance Defending Freedom who is representing Stutzman, called the ruling "terrifying."

"A government that can force you to say something and express a message that is so deeply contrary to your core beliefs is terrifying," Waggoner told me. "We are entering a whole new realm when we force people to express themselves and use their hearts, their heads, and their hands to create something that violates who they are."[7]

Waggoner accused Washington Attorney General Bob Ferguson of being on a personal crusade to destroy the elderly grandmother. "He's using the full power of his office to personally and professionally destroy her," she said. "He's trying to send a message—you better shut up if you disagree, or you are going to lose everything you own."[8]

Waggoner is referring to the attorney general's decision to seek legal fees and penalties against not only Arlene's Flowers but also Stutzman personally. The law allows for penalties of up to two thousand dollars per violation,[9] and Waggoner said the flower shop has been inundated with requests to provide flowers to gay weddings. Each one of those requests would be a violation. "Every time someone comes in you get tagged with a two-thousand-dollar fine," Waggoner said. "They're setting her up."[10]

And should they lose, there's a very real chance Stutzman could lose her home. "The killer part is the attorneys' fees and the court costs," Waggoner said. "She is liable to the state and the American Civil Liberties Union." She estimated the costs of an appeal reaching well into seven figures.[11]

A spokesman for the attorney general's office told the *Seattle Times* they anticipated going after both Stutzman and her business. "The law is clear: if you choose to provide a service to couples of the opposite sex, you must provide the same service to same-sex couples," the attorney general said in a prepared statement.[12]

Stutzman told me she has no plans to renounce her faith or her religious beliefs—no matter what the state may do. "There's the ACLU's side and the attorney general's side, and then there's God's side," she said. "Which side would you like to be on?"[13]

Stutzman's run-in with the government came about after what she thought was an innocent conversation with longtime customer Robert Ingersoll back in 2013. Ingersoll asked her to provide flowers for his upcoming wedding to Curt Freed. "He came in, and we were just chitchatting, and he said that he was going to get married," Stutzman recalled in court documents. "And I just put my hands on his and told him because of my relationship with Jesus Christ I couldn't do that, couldn't do his wedding."[14]

That led to a lawsuit, pitting the state of Washington and the gay couple against Stutzman. The legal battle has also served as a life lesson for her twenty-three grandchildren. She hopes they learn that it's important to stand up for their convictions. "Don't let someone bully you into doing what they want you to do if it's against your convictions," she said.[15]

Waggoner said her client has been graceful under a barrage of hateful attacks. "It's all about name calling and bullying and shaming people into shutting up," she said.[16]

Remember when our elected leaders told us that same-sex marriage would not impact anyone? Remember how we were told to live and let live? "We were sold a lie," Waggoner told me. "It's clear same-sex marriage does affect us. It's depriving people of their freedom—of their God-given freedoms."[17]

And as Stutzman learned, woe be to any Christian business owner who refuses to participate in a same-sex wedding. "It's me today," Stutzman said. "I'm just a little grain of sand, but it's you tomorrow."[18]

Her case is still being adjudicated, but if she loses, she could lose not only her business but also her home and her life savings. Not too long ago the state offered Stutzman a deal—confess to your sin and pay a two-thousand-dollar penalty plus one dollar and promise to never discriminate.[19]

She declined. "You are asking me to walk in the way of a well-known betrayer, one who sold something of infinite worth for thirty pieces of silver," Stutzman wrote in a letter to Ferguson. "That is something I will not do."[20] This is one granny whom you don't want to cross. I admire her more than I can say. She is a lamb who simply will not be silenced.

THE BENHAM BROTHERS: MUST-NOT-SEE TV

You might have heard the story about twins David and Jason Benham who were in production for *Flip It Forward*, a show that was expected to debut on HGTV, the nation's seventh-most-watched cable channel. According to *Entertainment Weekly*, the North Carolina brothers "would have followed families creating their dream homes from fixer-uppers."[21]

After the network announced the show was on the fall lineup, the militant lobbying group Right Wing Watch labeled David Benham, son of well-known evangelical pastor Flip Benham, an "anti-gay extremist" and reported on comments he made about homosexuality, abortion, and divorce.[22]

"If our faith costs us a television show, then so be it," the Benhams said. Sure enough, it did.[23]

The Benhams, who are graduates of Liberty University, said they were saddened to hear about HGTV's decision to cancel their show. "With all of the grotesque things that can be seen and heard on television today you would think there would be room for two twin brothers who are faithful to our families, committed to biblical principles, and dedicated professionals," they wrote.[24]

I'd be willing to bet that's what the Robertson family of A&E's *Duck Dynasty* fame thought too.

HGTV refuses to say why they decided not to go forward with the show. The channel's only statement, on Twitter, read: "HGTV has decided not to move forward with the Benham Brothers' series."[25] But its decision was announced after Right Wing Watch published the scathing attack on the brothers.

Among the Benhams' trespasses were David's leadership of a prayer rally outside the Democratic National Convention in Charlotte in 2012. They also took issue with comments he made to Christian radio host Janet Mefferd about the rally. "We don't realize that, OK, if 87 percent of Americans are Christians and yet we have abortion on demand; we have no-fault divorce; we have pornography and perversion; we have homosexuality and its agenda that is attacking the nation; we have adultery; we have all of the things; we even have allowed demonic ideologies to take our universities and our public school systems while the church sits silent and just builds big churches," Benham told the host. "We are so complacent, we are so apathetic, and we are very hypocritical in the church. That's why the Bible says judgment begins in the house of God. So when we prayed at 714, we asked God and our city to forgive us for allowing these things in the house of God."[26]

Right Wing Watch also took issue with his support for a North Carolina amendment that protected traditional marriage and his support of the pro-life movement.[27] I'm shocked that Right Wing Watch didn't document the number of times the brothers were caught eating a Chick-fil-A sandwich.

By the way, Billy Graham supported North Carolina's traditional marriage amendment.[28] Does Right Wing Watch think he's an antigay extremist?

The brothers reject any accusations that they are antigay or discriminate. They said anyone who says otherwise is not telling the truth. "As Christians we are called to love our fellow man," they wrote. "Anyone who suggests that we hate homosexuals or people of other faiths is either misinformed or lying."[29]

"Over the last decade, we've sold thousands of homes with the guiding principle of producing value and breathing life into each family that has crossed our path, and we do not, nor will we ever, discriminate against people who do not share our views," they wrote.[30]

It's too bad HGTV and those militant gay activists don't share similar guiding principles.

Mefferd told me this is a classic case of LGBT activists trying to marginalize and silence others. "This is an effort by the LGBT movement to silence the voices of people who do not agree with them on this issue and to send a message to the American public that anybody who does not get on board with their point of view does not deserve a place in the public square," said Mefferd, whose program airs on the Salem Radio Network.[31]

Tom Tradup, vice president of news and talk programming for Salem Radio Network, denounced the attack on the Benham brothers. "In the 1950s Senator Joseph McCarthy terrorized Americans whose views differed from his, resulting in the infamous Hollywood blacklists and people losing their jobs in the radio and television industry," he told me. "Sadly, thanks to 2014-style McCarthyism, history appears to be repeating itself."[32]

HGTV caved in to pressure from gay activists, making it a cowardly, bigoted network. Pardon me for saying that I would have loved to have been a fly on the wall in their offices the day after Trump was elected. It's not because the election will necessarily lessen the persecution people such as the Benhams are experiencing, though I hope and pray it does. But it's to see the looks on their faces when they realized how loudly those deplorable Americans could roar, even when persecuted.

THE PUBLIC SHAMING OF CHIP AND JOANNA GAINES

HGTV found itself involved in yet another exchange of cultural cross fire. *Fixer Upper* hosts Chip and Joanna Gaines not only have made Waco, Texas, a tourist destination, but also have educated us about the many uses of shiplap. If you haven't seen the show, you might want to google that.

Chip and Joanna are devout Christians, and viewers can see how their faith flavors not only their television program but also their family life. But not everyone appreciates those Christian beliefs, especially the militant LGBT crowd. And they went on the warpath.

The mainstream media and militant LGBT activists unleashed their fury over reports the Gaines family attends Antioch Community Church, a non-denominational megachurch. "Chip and Joanna Gaines's Pastor Preaches 'Homosexuality Is a Sin'" read a headline on *Cosmopolitan*.[33]

"Chip and Joanna Gaines' Church Is Firmly Against Same-Sex Marriage," screamed a BuzzFeed headline. "Their pastor considers homosexuality to be a 'sin' caused by abuse—whether the *Fixer Upper* couple agrees is unclear."[34]

What the shiplap, America! "Their pastor, Jimmy Seibert, is both staunchly against same-sex marriage and a strong believer that homosexuality is a 'lifestyle' choice and a 'sin'," *Cosmo* reported.[35]

This bit of news was more than their feeble journalistic minds could handle. "Given the diversity of *Fixer Upper*'s audience, this is a startling revelation that has left many wondering where Chip and Jo stand," *Cosmo* reported.[36]

BuzzFeed went so far as to investigate Pastor Seibert's sermons, which demonstrated nothing more than that what is preached from the pulpit at Antioch Community Church is the same kind of message being preached in nearly every evangelical church in America.[37]

NewsBusters tracked down this item originally published in *Us Weekly*:

> "As a *Fixer Upper* fan, I would love to know @joannagaines and @chippergaines's thoughts on their pastor's hateful, anti-LGBT beliefs," one [viewer] declared. Another went further, writing: "If Chip and Joanna Gaines end up being anti-LGBT, I am cancelling my mag subscription and ignoring their show."[38]

"So are the Gaineses against same-sex marriage?" BuzzFeed demanded to know. "And would they ever feature a same-sex couple on the show, as have HGTV's *House Hunters* and *Property Brothers?*"[39]

Why is that the business of BuzzFeed? Do they expect Chip and Joanna to inquire about the sexual proclivities of potential clients?

"*Fixer Upper* has fans of all stripes: Christians, feminists and LGBT viewers have all found something to love in the Gaineses," BuzzFeed's Kate Arthur reported. "So in the absence of a response from them or their representatives, it's worth looking at the severe, unmoving position Seibert and Antioch take on same-sex marriage."[40]

For the record, it's the same position taken by most evangelical churches in the nation, not to mention the Roman Catholic Church. Does BuzzFeed plan on investigating HGTV's Catholic home improvement hosts?

HGTV, probably looking at the substantial popularity (read: revenue) of the show, dispatched a spokesperson who told me in a statement they "respect the privacy of our show hosts and will not comment on matters related to their personal lives."[41]

Understandably neither the Gaines family nor the church wanted to comment. Nor should they have to comment.

"While fans shouldn't necessarily jump to conclusions about what this might mean, for many people who watch the show, their silence speaks volumes," *Cosmo* wrote. "Here's hoping they speak up about this soon."[42]

Well, here's a truth bomb for *Cosmo* and BuzzFeed: it's really none of your business where Chip and Joanna Gaines worship.

And for the record, where were their hysterical screeds when President Obama's pastor was asking God to damn America?[43] Anybody want to talk about those roosting chickens?

If anybody knows what Chip and Joanna are going through, it is the Benham brothers. "We were actually filming our show the exact same time the Gaineses were filming their first episode," David Benham told me. "We developed a great relationship."[44]

And the first telephone call the brothers received when they were given the heave-ho was from Chip. "He called to support us, to say, 'Guys, I'm in this with you, brother,'" Jason Benham said. "The Gaineses believe as we do—as millions of other Christians do—that marriage is between a man and a woman. That's not anti-anything. That's not hateful. Chip and Joanna don't hate anybody. It's ridiculous."[45]

The Benham brothers said they especially feel bad for HGTV being pushed into another faux controversy. "It's a mafia," David Benham said, referring to the militant activists. "They are going to go after the Gaines family. They are going to try and vilify them. They are going to try and vilify their church and their pastor. And if they can't get anyone to bend or concede, they are going to start vilifying HGTV and going after their advertisers."[46]

It's absolutely true that the Gaines family attends a church that believes marriage is between one man and one woman. Should that disqualify them from having a television program on HGTV?

Do the militant LGBT activists want to create a blacklist, banning individuals who attend evangelical Christian churches from working in television? Is that what they really want?

Friends, this is nothing more than a modern-day witch hunt. And it's time for all freedom-loving Americans to rise up and stand with HGTV and the Gaines family. To the militant LGBT mob we say stand down.

BuzzFeed quoted a rather appropriate statement from one of Pastor Seibert's messages:

> We're being called to a higher calling. A greater compassion and love, but a greater clarity than ever before. Because it is coming now. Starting Monday morning, we will not have the option anymore. And with that will come persecution.[47]

Prophecy fulfilled.

It's not exactly clear why BuzzFeed chose to pick on Chip and Joanna Gaines. Nor do we know why the online publication attacked the Christian couple's church. We may never know. Regardless their ugly attack on the Gaines family and Antioch Community Church in Waco cannot be undone.

"The real shame is not on the Gaines family but on this media inquisition of Christianity," National Religious Broadcasters President Jerry A. Johnson told me. "Fake scandals are as bad as fake news, and this is a fake scandal. In fact, millions of Americans go to tens of thousands of churches that teach in agreement with President Obama's original position against same-sex marriage."[48]

That's an excellent point.

"Unlike the president, most pastors have not changed their position," Johnson told me. "They know that the biblical pattern for sexuality is male-female, not same-sex relationships. If the Gaineses' church has that kind of pastor, they are in the mainstream of American Christianity, as well as many other religious traditions, on this issue. The real shame is not on the Gaines family, but on this media inquisition of Christianity." [49]

So let's cut to the chase. Is Antioch Community Church antigay? "Absolutely not," Pastor Seibert told me in an exclusive interview. "We are not only not antigay, but we are pro-helping people in their journey to find out who God is and who He has made them to be." [50]

The pastor told me he was surprised by the controversy surrounding a message he delivered more than a year ago, pointing out that people from all different walks of life attend the church. "For us, our heart has always been to love Jesus, preach the Word of God, and help people in their journey," he said.[51]

But what about the church's position on same-sex marriage? "Our definition is not the definition we made up. It's straight from the Scripture," the pastor said. "One man, one woman for life. That's how God created us. That's what he has for us." [52]

"The main reason for the sermon is for the confused middle, the majority of America. People don't know what the Bible says anymore on issues of sexuality," he added. "People don't know what God says on homosexuality or any other issue. I felt the need to say we are all a mess, but the fixed points were set by God, not us." [53]

Chip and Joanna have been members of the church for fifteen years and are dear friends with pastor Seibert. "This is who they have always been," he said. "They are tremendous people with tremendous values, and I've known them for many, many years." [54]

The pastor said over the past few days he's exchanged text messages with the Gaineses, but he declined to reveal the content of their conversations. He did, however, offer some words of encouragement to other Christians facing similar attacks. "Do we believe that God and His Word is right and enough? As a believer I need to do what's right and trust God with what's wrong. So when I have a biblical conviction about my lifestyle choices or how I should run my business or how I should run my home, we should be free to do that—to lovingly express our views to the world around us." [55]

He also called on fellow Christians to stand together in the face of adversity.

"Support one another when people make stands," he said. "Don't leave them out there alone. Let's get behind them and support them and love them and pray for them."[56]

And at the end of the day—no matter what—know that God is ultimately in control. "If we believe God and His Word is the answer to every problem on the planet, then we've got to live it out in our own lives," the pastor said.[57]

Those are great words of encouragement as we face an onslaught from a small, but vocal, mob of anti-Christian bullies. Perhaps next season Chip and Joanna can spend a few episodes refurbishing safe spaces for emotionally fragile snowflakes.

All three of our subjects had every right to be angry over their circumstances. They had every right to lash out and engage in a bit of righteous indignation. But they chose a different path.

Chip Gaines actually tweeted a message to his fans, urging them to be kind to the BuzzFeed and *Cosmo* writers.[58] After their ordeal the Benham brothers encouraged their followers to send positive notes to HGTV.[59] And Mrs. Stutzman told me she would gladly embrace the gay customer who is causing her such grief.[60]

They all were following the advice laid out in 1 Thessalonians 5:15–18: "See that no one renders evil for evil to anyone. But always seek to do good to one another and to all. Rejoice always. Pray without ceasing. In everything give thanks, for this is the will of God in Christ Jesus concerning you" (MEV).

These courageous believers would not be silenced. Like Paul and Silas, they sang hymns at midnight and let God do the rest. As Miss Bertha would've said, that's how you back up and bring it!

As deplorable Americans determined to stand our ground with grace the way these people have, what do we do? Here are some ideas:

MARCHING ORDERS

1. **Really dig into the passage in Acts 16,** and picture yourself in the kind of difficult circumstance Paul and Silas faced. Plan now how you would respond and how you would testify of the goodness of God in Christ so when that day comes, you will be prepared. Remember, probably none of the people written about in this chapter anticipated the battles they found themselves in either.

2. **Consider ways you can minister to those who are facing persecution.** Support local businesses that face religious liberty attacks. What better way to support your local Christian-owned flower shop

than to frequent the store? Encourage your friends and church members to do the same.

You might even start a ministry that comes alongside families that are facing adversity because of a public stand for morality. You could support them financially or personally with encouragement, prepare meals, or mow the grass as they deal with legal proceedings.

3. **Contact the Family Research Council, and learn how you can start a Culture Impact Team in your church.** This may be a great avenue through which you can serve your country and your culture using Christ-honoring methods that bring lasting results.

4. **Be intentional with your prayers.** Pray for people such as the Benhams, the Gaineses, and Stutzman. They are people too. Their reality is changed by prayer just like anyone else's. Let them know you are lifting them up to heaven. They will deeply appreciate it.

5. **Think before you tweet or blog or post something on Facebook.** Don't let the pain of being attacked cause you to use those same painful tactics and damage your ability to represent the gospel. Sing hymns at midnight. Let the joy of the Lord be your strength.

6. **Know your rights.** Contact law firms that specialize in religious liberty cases. Many of these organizations offer their services pro-bono. Among the law firms that have my stamp of approval are First Liberty Institute, Alliance Defending Freedom, Liberty Counsel, the Thomas More Law Center, and the Pacific Justice Institute.

Chapter 5

INDOCTRINATION 101

WHERE DID IT all start? How did America go so badly off track? I say America's classrooms had a lot to do with it. Parents and patriots must understand that our public school classrooms have been used against us. A stealth revolution is taking place using textbooks instead of firearms.

How else have we seen such a massive cultural shift on issues such as gay marriage and transgenderism? Why do you think so many young people were drawn to an avowed socialist like Bernie Sanders? Far Left educators have added a fourth "R" to their list. Now it's reading, writing, arithmetic—and radicalism.

Take, for example, Forest Hills Public Schools in Michigan. In 2016 the local school district deemed the Betsy Ross flag a symbol of hate after students displayed the flag at a high school football game. "To wave a historical version of our flag, that to some symbolizes exclusion and hate, injects hostility and confusion to an event where no one intended to do so," Superintendent Daniel Behm wrote in a letter to parents.[1]

Students at the predominantly white school were admonished for waving Old Glory during a red, white, and blue-themed football game.[2] The head of a Black Lives Matter group in nearby Grand Rapids accused the children of "overt, intentional racism."[3]

"For these white kids from a white school to bring out the flag of the colonies with the 'Make America Great Again' Trump flag to a game with black students on the field, it's all very obvious," Briana Urena-Ravelo told a local television station.[4] One parent went so far as to accuse the children of "brandishing these symbols of nationalism and white supremacy."[5]

That's as overt an attack on traditional American values as you're likely to see. Unless we begin to employ teachers and school administrators who promote American ideals, we could be living in a very frightening country in the years to come.

Let me share a few examples of indoctrination with you so you get a picture of what is happening in America's once-vaunted schools and colleges.

DROP-KICK ME, JESUS, THROUGH
THE GOAL POSTS OF LIFE

In the South faith and football go together like biscuits and gravy. That's especially true in a place like Laurens County, Georgia, where faith flavors everyday living far beyond the walls of the church house.

Those traditions were especially evident at West Laurens High School in Dexter, Georgia, where the marching band performed great songs of the faith and folks bowed their heads to pray before Friday night football games.[6] But those traditions are a problem, according to Americans United for Separation of Church and State, a Washington, D.C.-based group that loves to put its nose in other people's business, especially when it comes to public displays of the Christian faith. The group fired off a letter in May after someone complained about a pregame prayer and the marching band's performance of the Christian hymn "How Great Thou Art," which it said was "timed to accentuate the prayer."[7]

"The opening prayer and religious hymn at the football game were plainly unconstitutional," Americans United wrote to the school district. "The presentation of prayers at school sporting events violates the Establishment Clause of the First Amendment to the US Constitution."[8]

Now we don't know who complained, but I'd be willing to bet a bucket of chicken that we're dealing with one of those long-haired, hummus-eating, godless pedagogues who smell of patchouli. The offended party probably doesn't eat pork butt either.

After consulting with its legal counsel, the school board decided to replace the prayers with a "moment of silence," according to the Courier Herald, the local newspaper of record.[9] It should be noted that there have been no reported instances of football fans converting to Christianity as a result of the prayers or the playing of "How Great Thou Art."

Dr. Juliann Alligood is the school superintendent. She flat-out told me the decision to drop the prayers was made before she got hired. She also informed me in short order that she is a good Christian lady and a church pianist.[10]

That being said…

"I believe we should follow the law," she said. "And the moment of silence probably protects everyone's religious interests. We're doing what we have to do."[11]

Dr. Alligood said the now-banned invocations were just a part of the fabric of the community. "We're the Bible Belt," she said. "It wasn't something we were doing belligerently or to thumb our nose at anybody. It had been common practice."[12]

But a common practice no more. The school board decided to follow the demands of Americans United. So when the West Laurens Raiders started their season, instead of one person leading the invocation, the entire stadium led the invocation. Hundreds stood to their feet and recited the Lord's Prayer.[13]

And the marching band also complied with the demands of Americans United. They did not follow the prayer with a rendition of "How Great Thou Art." Instead they played "Amazing Grace."[14]

Will Americans United perceive that as a musical act of civil disobedience? Will it fire off another cease-and-desist letter?

If Americans United wants to ban "Amazing Grace," so be it. There are plenty of songs in the hymnal, songs such as "All Hail the Power of Jesus' Name" and "When the Roll Is Called Up Yonder."

So give it your best shot, Americans United. The rest of us are ready for a toe-tapping, hand-waving, all-night singing, armed with the Baptist Hymnal in one hand and the Church of God Red-Back in the other.

Finally, a word of advice to the hummus-eating, hymn-hating culprit who caused this kerfuffle. I sincerely doubt that our Lord appreciates your picking on a bunch of teenagers. So knock it off. Otherwise when the roll is called up yonder, you may not be there.

If you think liberals are strangely focused on marching bands and football games, you're right. Read on.

MARCHING BAND SILENCED IN DIXIE

A similar silencing happened at Brandon, Mississippi's Brandon High School, where there was no halftime show under the Friday night lights—because the marching band had been benched.

The band was ordered off the field because the Christian hymn "How Great Thou Art" was part of their halftime show, and performing it would violate a federal court order. "The Rankin County School Board and District Office are very saddened students will not be able to perform their halftime show they have worked so hard on this summer," the district wrote in a statement to the *Clarion-Ledger* newspaper.[15]

In 2013 a student sued the district over a series of Christian meetings that had been held on school property, the newspaper reported. The district later settled the lawsuit and acknowledged they had violated the student's First Amendment rights.[16]

Then-US District Court Judge Carlton Reeves ruled the district had violated the agreement after a Christian minister delivered a prayer at an awards ceremony. Judge Reeves, who was appointed to the bench by President Obama, came down hard on the school district, ordering it to pay thousands of dollars in fines. He also warned the district that future violations would cost it ten thousand dollars. "Defendants are permanently enjoined from including prayer, religious sermons or activities in any school sponsored event including but not limited to assemblies, graduations, award ceremonies, athletic events and any other school event," the order reads.[17]

Word about the band getting benched spread across the town quicker than kudzu. I must have received e-mails and Facebook messages from nearly the entire state, from DeSoto County to Yazoo City. Something must be done to right this wrong, people said. A message had to be sent to the likes of Judge Reeves. Locals gathered in coffee shops and garages to devise their plan.

And what they did would become known as the musical shot heard around the world.

During halftime at that Friday night's game a lone voice began to sing the forbidden song. "Then sings my soul, my Savior God to Thee," the singer sang.[18] Brittany Mann was there and witnessed the entire moment of defiance. "We were just sitting there, and then one by one people started to stand," she told me. "At first it started out as a hum, but the sound got louder and louder."[19]

She said it was a "truly incredible" moment to watch hundreds of people singing together in the stadium. "At that moment I was so proud of my town coming together and taking a stand for something we believe in," she said. "It breaks my heart to see where our country is going—getting farther and farther away from the Christian beliefs that our country was founded on."[20]

I suspect Brittany wasn't the only one who felt a sense of pride in the Magnolia State on that warm summer night. "We may be pictured as toothless, barefoot, uneducated people around the country, but we are far from it," nearby resident Mandy Miller told me. "I'm from Mississippi, and I'm not ashamed to take a stand."[21]

Oh, what a sight it must have been as hundreds and hundreds of people stood together and with one voice sent a message to Judge Reeves.

"This is the kind of thing that makes me proud to be from the South," Mandy told me. "We are getting tired of being told to sit down and shut up. People are ready to fight back."[22]

Mandy is absolutely right. The time has come to stand up to the secularists. The time has come to put an end to their cultural jihad.

The time has come to stop the godless indoctrination in our schools, even if it happens one dunking at a time.

MAYBE THEY SHOULD'VE USED SPRINKLERS

Asking a Baptist preacher to baptize is like asking Colonel Sanders if he wants a bucket of chicken. So when a football coach in Villa Rica, Georgia, asked to be baptized on the high school football field, the local First Baptist Church obliged.[23]

At the end of the school day somebody hauled out an old feeding trough, plopped it in the end zone near the field house, and filled it with water. A crowd of about seventy-five folks, black and white, young and old, gathered in the sweltering August heat to watch the coach take the Baptist plunge, an outward symbol of being washed anew.[24]

Perhaps inspired by their coach's public display of his faith, some of the players also asked to be baptized. One by one the teenage boys stepped into the trough as onlookers prayed and rejoiced and applauded.[25]

It was quite a moment in Villa Rica—all captured on video by a First Baptist Church staff member.[26] Little did anyone know a rite of Christian passage would soon spark national outrage.

The Freedom From Religion Foundation (FFRF), a group of perpetually offended atheists and free-thinkers based in Wisconsin, saw the video and fired off a nasty letter to the Carroll County School District superintendent. "It is illegal for coaches to participate in religious activities with students, including prayer and baptisms," attorney Elizabeth Cavell wrote. "Nor can coaches allow religious leaders to gain unique access to students during school-sponsored activities."[27]

They called the full immersion baptisms an "egregious constitutional violation."[28]

In hindsight, perhaps an Episcopal priest should've handled the baptisms. He could've just turned on the sprinklers and had the players run down the field. The Freedom From Religion folks would never have known the difference.

The godless bullies demanded the school district launch an immediate investigation "and take full action to ensure there will be no further illegal religious events, including team baptisms and prayer, during school-sponsored activities."[29]

Kevin Williams, the pastor of First Baptist Church, told me the football field baptisms were held after school and were completely voluntary. "We never meant to cause any problems for the school, and we never thought we would get this much media attention for baptizing kids," the pastor said.[30]

First Baptist Church has a long history of ministering to the community, including the football team. Just this past summer the church provided financial assistance so the team could attend a football camp. And the church recently held a football-themed worship service called "Gridiron Day." It was at that event one of the coaches asked if he could be baptized on the football field. Several players who had recently converted to Christianity also asked to be baptized.[31]

"It was their choice to do that," Pastor Williams told me. "We live in a free nation. People choose what they want. These people that got baptized freely chose at a church service to accept Christ, and this was a follow-up to that."[32]

Times have been tough in Villa Rica, especially for young people. Over the past few years several teenagers have committed suicide.[33] "We're trying our best as a community to reach out to these kids and love on them and show them there's a better way—there's hope," Pastor Williams said. "That's what we are providing through Jesus Christ to these kids."[34]

The question is whether the atheist carpetbaggers will bully the school district into silencing people of faith. "I believe we live in a free country," the pastor said. "These people that are trying to say you can't do that, well, they're taking away freedom. When did it become illegal to bow your head and pray? When did it become illegal to say, 'I'm a Christian'?"[35]

You need to watch the video to truly understand and appreciate what happened on the football field that warm Southern afternoon, the day a group of young black men and young white men decided to take a public *stand* for our Lord.[36] They emerged from the waters no longer just teammates, but brothers.

COLLEGE KIDS THINK JUDGE JUDY IS ON THE SUPREME COURT

There's really no way to sugarcoat this next anecdote, moms and dads: because of relentless anti-American indoctrination, your recent college graduate may be dumber than dirt.

There. I said it.

A survey showed that nearly 10 percent of recent college graduates say television star Judith Sheindlin is on the Supreme Court.[37] Yes, good reader. Our best and brightest seem to think that Judge Judy sits on the highest court in the land.

The American Council of Trustees and Alumni (ACTA) said its survey uncovered a "crisis in American civic education." Ya think? The ACTA describes itself as an independent organization "committed to academic freedom, excellence, and accountability at America's colleges and universities." Its findings reveal "that recent college graduates are alarmingly ignorant of America's history and heritage."[38]

That could explain why an avowed socialist like Bernie Sanders gave Hillary Clinton a run for her money.

The study reported that students could not identify the father of the US Constitution or name one of our First Amendment rights, which makes it no surprise that a frightening number of college students support curbing free speech.[39] Last November the Pew Research Center released a survey that showed 40 percent of Americans between the ages of eighteen and thirty-four believe the government should be able to ban any speech that is offensive to minority groups.[40]

That is the looming danger we face if anti-American indoctrination doesn't stop. And that brings us to the nearly 10 percent of American college kids who think Judge Judy is on the Supreme Court—holding forth with Justice John G. Roberts Jr. and Justice Clarence Thomas, et al.

Judge Judy said something during an episode that relates to this discussion. "I'm older, smarter," she told one of the simpletons in front of her bench. "If you live to be one hundred and twenty, you're not going to be as smart as I am in one finger."[41]

To be honest, it doesn't seem like a bad idea, appointing Judge Judy to the highest court in the land. They could use a good dose of common sense in that courtroom.

I only wish that was the worst of it. Not only are our taxpayer-funded universities and colleges churning out boatloads of ignoramuses, but our educational system wants to whitewash America's recent history as well.

SCHOOL SUPERINTENDENT: 9/11 HAD NOTHING TO DO WITH RELIGION

The vocabulary list at High Mount School in Swansea, Illinois, included words such as jihad, Islam, Muhammad, and Koran, according to the *Belleville News-Democrat*. That caused one mom to take notice.[42]

"She said, 'What's *Koran* mean?' and I flipped out," Rachel Seger said, shocked that her twelve-year-old daughter's public school history class was teaching Islam 101. "I said, 'Excuse me?' and I looked at them, and I said, 'Oh my God.'"[43]

Superintendent Mark Halwachs said the lessons on Islamic vocabulary words was all about teaching tolerance. But get a load of what he told the newspaper about what happened on September 11, 2001: "It wasn't a religion that did that. It was bad men that did that."[44]

Well, I hate to break it to the superintendent, but the radical Islamic extremists were not hollering, "Jesus Saves" when they flew the jetliners into those buildings.

The superintendent explained that it's important to teach "the difference between a large group and a fanatical faction." He told the newspaper, "I think you have to take moments like that and use them as teachable moments. You have to look at the age group and your students, and to me you can talk about different things in the world and teach about tolerance."[45]

However, the school district's definition of *tolerance* does not seem to include in-depth, theological discussions about Christianity. "You can teach about religion, you just can't…endorse or support a religion over another," he told the newspaper. "You can't say [Jesus] is the one and only, or he's the best; you can explain about and teach about the religions of the world."[46] Sounds to me like the folks at High Mount School need to add another word to their vocabulary list: *indoctrination*.

SCHOOL SENDS SHERIFF TO ORDER CHILD TO STOP SHARING BIBLE VERSES

As you may have guessed, the only approved indoctrination in public schools these days is non-Christian or anti-Christian. In fact, your child is in greater danger of discipline by bringing a Bible to school than bringing a peanut butter sandwich.

One public school in California ordered a seven-year-old boy to stop handing out Bible verses during lunch—and dispatched a deputy sheriff to the child's home to enforce the directive.[47] "This is a clear, gross violation of the rights of a child," said Liberty Counsel, the legal group representing the first-grader, who attends Desert Rose Elementary School in Palmdale. Liberty Counsel is also representing his parents, Christina and Jaime Zavala.[48]

Christina Zavala made it a practice to include a Bible verse and encouraging note in her son's lunch bag. The boy would tell his friends about the notes and read them aloud at the lunch table. It wasn't long before children asked for copies of the notes, and Christina obliged, including a brief note to explain the daily Bible verse.[49]

A few days later a teacher called Christina and said her son would no longer be able to share the Bible verses because he was "not allowed to share such things while at school." Liberty Counsel said the school would only allow the child to distribute the Bible verses outside the school gate after the bell rang.[50]

Liberty Counsel said the teacher told Christina her son "could no longer read or share Bible verses or stories at lunch," citing "separation of church and state." So the Zavalas complied with the school's clearly unconstitutional edict and started giving out the Bible verses outside the school after the bell rang. But a few weeks later the school's principal implemented a complete ban on the Bible verse sharing. He told the boy and his father to move to a public sidewalk. They complied with the principal's demand. Then a few hours later the Zavala family heard a knock at their front door.[51]

"The deputy sheriff said he had been sent by the school," Liberty Counsel attorney Richard Mast told me. "The deputy went on to tell the parents that the school was worried that someone might be offended by the Bible verses."[52]

Liberty Counsel said the deputy sheriff was not belligerent or threatening. The family was not served with any sort of legal documents. It appeared to be a "friendly" warning. "It was outrageous and should shock the conscience of every freedom-loving American," said Liberty Counsel attorney Horatio Mihet, who is representing the first-grader. "Apparently all the real criminals have been dealt with in Palmdale—and now they're going after kids who share Bible verses during lunchtime."[53]

It appears to me that the deputy sheriff was dispatched to the home as part of a strategy to intimidate the Zavala family. "I would expect something like this to happen in Communist Romania, where I went to elementary school, but cops don't bully seven-year-olds who want to talk about Jesus in the Land of the Free," Mihet said.[54]

Not unless they're empowered by a broader agenda to remove God from the nation's classrooms. Thankfully there are times when students take it into their own hands to stop the indoctrination. This next story will warm your heart—and give you hope.

HIGH SCHOOL STUDENTS DEFY ATHEISTS, RECITE LORD'S PRAYER AT GRADUATION

At East Liverpool High School in East Liverpool, Ohio, just moments before the graduation ceremony the senior class gathered in a nearby auditorium. Together they decided to do something that would make national headlines.

The week before, students learned they would no longer be allowed to sing "The Lord's Prayer," a graduation tradition dating back some seventy years.[55]

The school district banned the song after—guess who?—the Freedom From Religion Foundation complained that "The Lord's Prayer" violated the US Constitution and promoted religion.[56] Fearing a possible lawsuit, the district dropped the tradition, which seemed to appease the perpetually offended atheists, agnostics, and free-thinkers from Wisconsin. (You can read more about these loathsome bullies in my best-selling book *God Less America*.)

The school district's decision devastated the entire community, especially students in the high school's esteemed music program. "It breaks my heart," choir director Lisa Ensinger told me at the time. "Our students are really sad."[57]

It appeared a cherished tradition would be eradicated to satisfy the bloodlust of a bunch of out-of-town harassers. But then the senior class gathered in that room. They were lining up to march when some of them began talking about that longtime tradition that was now outlawed. "Pretty much everyone was in agreement," senior Bobby Hill told me.[58]

The graduating class had decided to defy the Freedom From Religion Foundation. "The class thought it was wrong that we were being forced to remove it," Bobby said.[59]

Bobby's father was sitting in the bleachers inside the gymnasium when he received a text message from his son. "He told me when and how they were going to do it," Mr. Hill told me. "I was thrilled to find out."[60]

Just after the valedictorian welcomed the crowd the seniors stood to their feet and began committing an act of disobedience.

"Our Father, which art in heaven..."

"I was very proud to see the youth, our future leaders, decide to stand up for what they believed in," Mr. Hill said. "I can't lie—I teared up."[61]

It was an emotional moment, a poignant example of Americans standing up for what they know to be true and right. "I've always taught my two boys to stand up for what you believe is right," Mr. Hill said. "The same lesson my parents taught me. It doesn't matter if it's over religion or something else—take a stand."[62]

Technically the graduation class did not break any rules. They were ordered not to sing "The Lord's Prayer." The school district did not say anything about reciting "The Lord's Prayer."

Clever, kids. And courageous.

Can we get a million other students to do the same? Because if we don't, Christians might actually find themselves marginalized in their careers, as the next example demonstrates.

MISSOURI STATE BOOTED STUDENT FROM COUNSELING PROGRAM FOR CHRISTIAN BELIEFS

Indoctrination is not just about what we believe. It's being used as a tool to shut people out of entire professions.

Andrew Cash, a former student at Missouri State University, claims he was kicked out of a master's program in counseling because of his religious beliefs. Cash says he was "targeted and punished for expressing his Christian worldview regarding a hypothetical situation concerning whether he would provide counseling to a gay/homosexual couple."[63]

MSU spokeswoman Suzanne Shaw told the *News-Leader* that the "university strictly prohibits discrimination on the basis of religion or any other protected class." She would not comment on specifics of the case.[64]

According to the lawsuit, Dr. Kristi Perryman, the counseling department's internship coordinator, confronted Cash about his views toward counseling gay people. Cash told her he would counsel them individually on a variety of issues but not as a couple. He said he would refer them elsewhere.[65]

Cash explained to Perryman that his approach to counseling is centered on his "core beliefs, values and Christian worldview and these would not be congruent with the likely values and needs of a gay couple, who, for these reasons, would be best served by a counselor sharing their core value system and core beliefs," the lawsuit filed in federal court states.[66]

Perryman then told Cash that he "could not hold these views, which she deemed to be unethical, and which, she asserted, contradicted the American Counseling Association's code of ethics as discriminatory toward gay persons."[67]

"It made me angry," said attorney Tom Olp of the Thomas More Society, a law firm that specializes in religious liberty issues. "She took offense at his religious beliefs and then essentially kept dwelling on those until he was drummed out of the program."[68]

Cash is suing Perryman and a host of other university officials, including Tamara Arthaud, the head of the counseling department, and faculty member Angela Anderson. "We have this very dangerous trend towards allowing the government to shut down religious expression," Olp told me. "That is contrary to the First Amendment. A democracy requires vibrant expression of various points of view, and it really needs robust religious expression."[69]

Cash's troubles began in the spring of 2011 when he began a university-approved internship at the Springfield Marriage and Family Institute, a Christian organization. It was during a classroom presentation that the director of the Christian group was asked about counseling gay persons.[70]

A week later Cash was informed he would no longer be allowed to intern at the institute. He was also grilled about his personal views regarding counseling homosexuals, the lawsuit states.[71] In 2014 Cash was just a few courses shy of graduating with a master's degree in counseling. He had a 3.81 grade point average and was a student in good standing with the school.[72]

Olp told me it's not the first time Christians have been thrown out of counseling programs in public universities, citing cases in Michigan as well as Missouri. "It's an extremely intolerant and almost puritanical approach and more and more prevalent in secular universities," he said.[73]

Cash wants to be readmitted to the program so he can finish his studies and obtain his degree. He is living proof that we live in a nation where faith in Christ is now considered by some to be a career-killer.

WANT TO TALK ABOUT JESUS? YOU'LL NEED A PERMIT FOR THAT AT NC STATE

At North Carolina State University you can't even talk about Jesus without a permit, according to a lawsuit filed in federal court.[74] Grace Christian Life, a registered student group at NC State, filed suit over a policy requiring a permit for any kind of student speech or communication anywhere on campus, including religious speech.[75]

In September 2015, the student group was told that without a permit it must stop approaching other students inside the student union to engage in religious discussions or invite them to attend group events.[76] "It's an amazingly broad speech restriction," Alliance Defending Freedom attorney Tyson Langhofer told me. "Public universities are supposed to be the marketplace of ideas, not places where students need a permit just to exercise their constitutionally protected freedoms."[77]

Alliance Defending Freedom (ADF) is a law firm that specializes in religious liberty cases. It alleges the Christian group has been singled out by the university. "The University has not restricted the ability of other students and student groups to engage in expressive activity," the lawsuit states. "Grace has witnessed other students, student groups, and off-campus groups handing out literature either without a permit or outside of the area reserved by their table permit."[78]

NC State's rules were so draconian that the Christians were not even allowed to step from behind their table in the student union.[79] "Colleges are supposed to be places where ideas are freely shared, not gagged," Grace Christian Life President Hannalee Alrutz told me. "The only permit a student needs to speak on campus is the First Amendment."[80]

It's true that the university does regulate student speech—written, oral, or graphic. ADF points to Regulation 07.25.12, which "requires a permit for any form of commercial or non-commercial speech, which the policy broadly defines as 'any distribution of leaflets, brochures, or other written material, or oral speech to a passersby (sic).'"[81]

"The policy specifies that any person 'wishing to conduct any form of solicitation on University premises must have the written permission of the Student Involvement [Office] in advance," ADF noted.[82]

According to the lawsuit, a university official sent an e-mail to another official concerned about the Christian club. "There is an individual named Tommy who works with Grace who is essentially soliciting throughout the building," the e-mail reads. "He walks up to a single person or duo of persons, starts with a hello, and then starts the conversation into religion, ending with giving them a card." [83]

The e-mail goes on to explain how they've stopped other groups from engaging in similar behavior in order to "create that inclusive, welcoming environment."[84] In other words, the only way to be truly inclusive and welcoming is to shut down the Christians and shove them into a closet.

"The courts have well established that a public university can't require permits in this manner for this kind of speech—and certainly can't enforce such rules selectively," ADF Senior Counsel David Hacker said. "Unconstitutional censorship is bad enough, but giving university officials complete discretion to decide when and where to engage in silencing students makes the violation even worse." [85]

Kudos to Grace Christian Life for standing up to a bunch of academic bullies who want to silence Christian voices. And thank goodness for bold believers such as Alrutz. "I think this is an attack on my liberty as a citizen of the United States," she told me, warning that every freedom-loving American should be concerned. "If they could do it to us, they could do it to anybody," she said.[86]

NO COWBOYS OR INDIANS AT THE UNIVERSITY OF TEXAS IN AUSTIN

Some attempts at indoctrination are simply laughable. Students at the University of Texas at Austin were actually advised not to wear cowboy boots or cowboy hats on Halloween.[87] Telling a Texan not to wear cowboy boots is like telling a Minnesotan to avoid lakes. It's almost physically impossible.

Nevertheless fraternities and sororities at UT Austin were instructed to avoid Halloween party costumes and themes that might "appropriate another culture or experience." Students were issued a twenty-one-point checklist to ensure they avoid any controversial or offensive trick-or-treat regalia. The helpful guide read, "You don't have bad intentions, but your social theme or costume idea could have negative impact. Themes and costumes may intentionally or unintentionally appropriate another culture or experience." [88]

The guide urged students to ponder how their costume might be perceived by others and whether they would be proud if a photo of their party was sent to their parents. Here's a brief list of the costumes and themes considered harmful by the University of Texas—you're going to love this:

+ "Cowboys and Indians"/anything "Squaw" or any generalized depiction of an Indigenous person or peoples

+ "South of the Border"/"Fiesta"

+ "Ghetto Fabulous"/"Urban"

+ "Pimps & Hoes"

+ "Trailer Trash"

+ "Chicks and Hicks"/"Rednecks"[89]

In other words, no tacos, teepees, or Daisy Dukes. The university also urged partygoers to avoid sensationalizing transgender celebrities such as the Jenner formerly known as Bruce.[90]

UT Austin isn't alone by any stretch. Schools across the fruited plain have been warning students that Halloween is less about trick-or-treating and more about not triggering microaggressions among overly sensitive and easily offended millennials.

The University of Florida offered bona fide counseling for any student offended by a Wonder Woman, zombie, or Papa Smurf costume. "Some Halloween costumes reinforce stereotypes of particular races, genders, cultures, or religions," school administrators wrote in a blog post. "Regardless of intent, these costumes can perpetuate negative stereotypes, causing harm and offense to groups of people."[91]

Yale University lectured students on the horrors of wearing "feathered head-dresses, turbans, wearing 'war paint' or modifying skin tone."[92] Tufts University warned its Greek community that those wearing offensive costumes could be subjected to a police investigation and "serious disciplinary sanctions."[93]

"There are consequences for wearing an offensive costume," read a letter to Greek club presidents.[94]

And while superheroes and war paint might send millennials into an existential crisis, maybe the most offensive person of all is Jesus Himself.

MISSOURI SCHOOL DISTRICT EXPELS JESUS

The Tipton R-VI School District in Missouri cleansed itself of anything remotely affiliated with Christianity after being bullied by—do I have to type its name again?—the Freedom From Religion Foundation. Tipton even pulled down a giant portrait of our Lord that was displayed in the grade school's library.[95]

For as far back as anyone can remember, students at Tipton High School always concluded their annual awards program with a candlelight ceremony. Teachers and students would get in a circle and sing "Blest Be the Tie That Binds," a familiar hymn to churchgoers.[96]

Blest be the tie that binds
Our hearts in Christian love;
The fellowship of kindred minds
Is like to that above.
When we asunder part,
It gives us inward pain;
But we shall still be joined in heart,
And hope to meet again.[97]

Cue the manufactured offense from the FFRF. "The singing of a hymn as part of the candlelight ceremony is on par with other religious practices that courts have ruled are unconstitutional," FFRF attorney Patrick Elliott wrote. "The hymn declares that participants are bound together as part of a Christian community." [98]

Elliott went on to complain that singing the hymn would lead to hurt feelings and the sense that non-Christians "are outsiders, not full members of the political community." The FFRF also took offense at the school board's practice of conducting a prayer during its meetings. "School-sponsored religious exhibitions, such as singing a hymn signifying the group is part of a Christian community, are unconstitutional," the attorney wrote. "Calling upon Board members, parents, students and members of the public to pray is similarly unconstitutional." [99]

Faster than you could sing all the verses to "Amazing Grace," the school board capitulated to the outrageous demands. "In response to the letter, the District reviewed its practices in order to ensure compliance with both state and federal constitutional law," Superintendent Daniel Williams told me in a statement. "After this review the District discontinued practices that could be construed as an endorsement of religion." [100]

"The District's goal is to provide a positive learning environment for all its students and staff," he went on to write. "The District strives to carefully balance individual rights under the Free Exercise Clause while ensuring it complies with its obligations as a public entity under the Establishment Clause of the First Amendment. The District will continue to monitor its practices going forward in an effort to ensure continued compliance—and a safe, welcoming environment for all students." [101]

Now it turns out the portrait of Jesus that hung in the library was not included in the FFRF's complaint letter. But seeing how the district caved on the hymn and the intercession, it was pretty obvious Jesus didn't stand a prayer.

Locals say the portrait was originally donated years ago as a memorial to a young man who had passed away.

Don Hinkle, the director of public policy for the Missouri Baptist Convention, first alerted me to this story, and he was fired up. Let's just say that the good Baptists in Missouri don't take kindly to out-of-state atheists stirring up a stink. "The atheists just swoop in and with a simple letter written by a threatening lawyer, they win," Hinkle told me. "They kick Christ and Christianity and the First Amendment right out of a public school."[102]

Sadly the atheists successfully got rid of Jesus, the hymn, and the prayer. Say what you will, but the Freedom From Religion Foundation pulled off one mighty impressive hat trick.

If these instances of indoctrination, bullying, and silencing don't paint a portrait of what we're up against, nothing will. Fellow Deplorables, if we want to make America great again, we must find a way to stand our ground at the local level in our public schools and universities. While you're praying that the White House and Congress abolish the Department of Education, eradicate Common Core, and yield back control of our public school systems and universities, I want you to think good and hard about what you can do from the marching orders below.

It's time to take America's classrooms back!

MARCHING ORDERS

1. **Get involved in your child's school.** While many people of faith are opting for home schools and private schools—great options I'll address below—lots of good people are staying in the ring and duking it out in public schools, and that's an honorable and patriotic path as well. If that's you, get involved immediately in your child's public school. As in war, it all starts with boots on the ground. There is no substitute for involvement. The easiest way is to simply volunteer in your child's class. Being there once a week, in the classroom, makes your presence felt by the teacher. Suddenly you are not a nameless, faceless parent, but a flesh-and-blood person with interest in your child's education.

    You will learn a lot just being in the classroom. You will get a feel for the teacher's perspective on life. You will see what posters and inspiring quotes the teacher has used to adorn the walls. You will observe the privately meaningful things she puts on her desk. Are there quotes from liberal politicians? Social reformers you find troubling? Desk calendars with humanistic or even antireligious sentiments? Photos of her family at liberal causes and events?

You will also get a vibe for what is being taught in "social studies" and other subjects just by being present. Sometimes you might be asked to grade papers, quiz students, or lead them in reading through the textbook. You might be amazed at what they are teaching your kids when you dive into the particulars.

That's a big point: read your kids' textbooks. There's no excuse for a parent to be ignorant of what a school is inculcating into your progeny. If you can't take the time to look through your child's American history or government book, you're really falling down as a parent and surrendering that part of his brain to the tender mercies of his teachers. And I think most of us know that teachers aren't necessarily a conservative bunch.

Much of the indoctrination happening in schools is stealth. Pay close attention to history books and world geography books. If you see something, say something.

2. **Assist with an extracurricular activity.** If the classroom environment freaks you out—if being around graded tests and homework gives you hives and nightmares—jump in elsewhere in the school community. As the stories in this chapter illustrate, craziness can creep in just about anywhere. Volunteer to help with a sport, cheer team leadership, or the debate club. Be present on campus. In a kind and confident way let your stance be known. Many problems can be avoided before lunacy ensues just because they recognize that someone sane is in the mix.

3. **Go further if you can.** Join the PTA, attend school board meetings, and form a committee of like-minded parents to be watchdogs. Be willing to mobilize. Remember, our tax dollars are paying for whatever our kids are learning. We have a say.

4. **Befriend the principal.** These people are often truly under-appreciated. Drop off a coffee gift card now and then. Stick your head in his office and tell him you're praying for him—if you really want to see an interesting reaction. Get to know the people in leadership. You may forge true friendships. And if not, at least they'll be on notice that you're observing what's going on and are interested in learning outcomes—and freedom—just as they are.

5. **Equip your child with the information and convictions to speak up.** This is simply called *parenting*. By living a credible example and making your views on American society part of that example, you embolden your child to stand for those things. It may

not always be comfortable, but your child will learn to be a little patriot, and even a revolutionary, right where he is.

6. **Encourage your child to start a God-honoring club.** If your child is ambitious, encourage him to start a club that promotes God-honoring activity. It might be an American history club, a Bible study, a book-of-the-month type thing, a political club, or a civic-minded group. Whatever it is, have him plant his stake in the ground so others can rally to it.

7. **Consider running for the school board.** The best way to facilitate change is from the inside.

8. **Teach your kids yourself.** This is perhaps the easiest way to shield them from indoctrination. Homeschooling can be done individually or as part of a community. States have different rules about how homeschooling happens, so contact the Home School Legal Defense Association for information on how you can teach your children at home. It's a great alternative if you don't want to spend much of your time fighting the opposition in the public arena or if you don't feel that's the best path for you or your kids.

9. **Consider private school.** If you can manage the expense, private schools are another way to make sure your kids are getting the right kind of learning and are shielded from an increasingly godless and vulgar public school culture.

10. **Speak up if necessary.** If you see wrongdoing in your public schools and your school is unresponsive, contact the news media. And if they don't respond, contact me. My e-mail address is on my website, toddstarnes.com.

Chapter 6

SAFE SPACES, MICROAGGRESSIONS, AND SNOWFLAKES

★ ★ ★ ★

WHEN I FIRST heard the term *microaggression*, I reached out to the Centers for Disease Control, thinking we had a massive disease outbreak on our hands. In fact, I was right—it is a type of disease, a social disease, and the outbreaks appear to be limited to academic institutions—mostly public university and college campuses. This new "disorder" seems to infect only members of the perpetually offended generation—the ones the media have helpfully dubbed "generation snowflake" because they are so delicate.[1] The only known cure seems to involve securing infected students in "safe spaces."

The University of California, Los Angeles provided the world with a working definition of *microaggression*. They say it's "everyday verbal, nonverbal, and environmental slights, snubs, or insults, whether intentional or unintentional, that communicate hostile, derogatory, or negative messages to target persons based solely upon their marginalized group membership."[2]

Sweet mercy. That has to be the biggest pile of politically correct nonsense I've read all year.

So, for example, if you ask someone where she is from, you are really telling that person she is not a true American. If you ask someone of color how he became so proficient in math, you are implying that people of color are generally not as intelligent as white people. And, according to this thinking, if you're walking down the street and you clutch your purse if you see a person of color approaching, that signals you think the approaching person is either dangerous or a criminal.

As near as I can tell, white, evangelical Christian men from the Deep

South who eat barbecue, drink sweet tea, and drive pickup trucks are immune. Apparently we are the carrier for the disease.

The University of California Board of Regents is so concerned about the fragile nature of its student population that it is considering a policy to make the entire university system "free from acts and expressions of intolerance."[3]

I was able to get my hands on a copy of the policy, and it's a loaded with all sorts of liberal lunacy. "The University of California is committed to protecting its bedrock values of respect, inclusion, and academic freedom," the policy states.[4] (How about educating students? Is that part of their bedrock values?) "Free expression and the open exchange of ideas—principles enshrined in our national and state Constitutions—are part of the University's fiber," the policy continues.[5]

Brace yourself for a great big "but," folks.

"So, too, is tolerance, and University of California students, faculty, and staff must respect the dignity of each person within the UC community," the policy states. "Everyone in the University community has the right to study, teach, conduct research, and work free from acts and expressions of intolerance."[6]

We know what this is code for: free expression is great *unless* it violates our concept of tolerance, the definition of which is longer than an online dictionary.

And yet universities across the country are, with a straight face, implementing these draconian policies to combat perceived offenses. The University of Michigan, for example, launched an "Inclusive Language Campaign." This turned out to be a fancy way of saying "censorship." The university declared words such as *crazy*, *ghetto*, *gay*, and *retarded* unacceptable.[7]

During the 2015 Christmas season, the University of Mississippi actually renamed its annual Christmas party because the university determined there was just too much Christianity on campus. The party formerly known as "Grand Ole Christmas" became the "Hotty Toddy Holiday."[8] Couldn't stand your ground, could you, Ole Miss?

James Madison University banned a vocal group from performing "Mary, Did You Know?" at a Christmas carol concert. Instead the group was given a list of government-approved songs, which included "Frosty the Snowman" and "Jingle Bells."[9]

And Ohio State University urged students to avoid decorating their dorm rooms with the colors red and green, fearing some poor soul might take offense.[10] The University of Tennessee's Office for Diversity and Inclusion, a department funded by your tax dollars, directed students to have inclusive holiday celebrations.[11]

What in the name of *Animal House* is happening to free speech and freedom of religion on our public university campuses?

As I mentioned earlier, and mention again because it's so disturbing, a survey from the Pew Research Center revealed that 40 percent of Americans between the ages of eighteen and thirty-four believe the government should be able to ban any speech that is offensive to minority groups.[12]

Mamas and daddies, let's get real. We have raised a generation of snow-flakes so fragile that their psyches can't handle conflict or disagreement. Call it PTS Kids, *PTS* standing for participation trophy syndrome. There's no such thing as winners or losers anymore. There's only the desperate need to main-tain a child's comfort and feeling of acceptance. A public school district near Louisville, Kentucky, actually considered a plan to eliminate the valedictorian system because it created "unhealthy competition."[13]

Unhealthy competition? For encouraging students to be the best they could be?

This attempt to protect children from all forms of harm, including the emo-tional variety, is perhaps unwittingly training a generation to think their feelings should never be hurt, their ideas never opposed. And so a dissenting opinion does more than just upset them as young adults—it leaves them feeling traumatized.[14]

In the face of this reality the last thing we need to do is drop all standards and homogenize our children into one big pot of mediocrity so everyone will feel OK. The next generation needs to be encouraged to achieve, excel, do their best, and spur one another on to greatness.

But those ideas are not the order of the day. The University of California, Berkeley, is creating safe spaces to protect persons of color and those who iden-tify as gender queer.[15] The University of Michigan added a three-year diversity requirement to its undergraduate curriculum in the school of business. It will teach students how race, gender, and sexual orientation "connect to larger sys-tems of power, privilege and oppression."[16]

Warning: microaggressions are spreading faster than a case of gangrene.

WARNING WHITE PEOPLE: SINGING RIHANNA SONGS COULD BE A MICROAGGRESSION

In one example of how far this has gone, a human relations theory class at the University of Oklahoma made it clear that if you're white, you can't be singing Rihanna's "Umbrella."

Ah, yes. There's nothing quite like a bit of white-shaming paid for by the American taxpayers.

"I was told as a white woman it's insulting and a microaggression for me to cover or sing a Rihanna song because I'm not from Barbados," a student who was in the class told me. "I was literally told to go sing 'The Star-Spangled Banner.'"[17]

The student, who asked not to be identified, sent me copies of two of her class assignments, including a one hundred-item checklist to determine how much "privilege" you have.

For example, you have privilege if "a stranger has never asked to touch my hair, or asked if it is real." Straight, white guys who have a job, vacation in Cabo, Mexico, and go to church on Sunday are "very privileged." Atheists, Muslims, and anyone who works at a fast-food joint would be considered underprivileged.[18]

The student who reached out to me wants to work in human resources, and the class is mandatory. "They teach you that if you are not part of the minority, you cannot be discriminated against," she said. "A black person cannot be racist to a white person. A female cannot be sexist towards a man because men are the majority."[19]

Here's a sampling of the one hundred-question privilege checklist:

- I am white.
- I have never been told I would "burn in hell" for my sexual orientation.
- I still identify as the gender I was born in.
- I work in a salaried job.
- I have never done my taxes myself.
- I have had an unpaid internship.
- I don't know what "Sallie Mae" is.
- I have frequent flier miles.
- I spend spring breaks abroad.
- My parents are heterosexual.
- I can afford a therapist.
- I've used prescription drugs recreationally.
- I have never been called a terrorist.
- I have never questioned any of my identities.
- I had a car in high school.
- I've always had cable.[20]

The students were also asked to determine whether thirty-two scenarios were either harmless conversations or microaggressions. But it turned out to be a trick assignment because the professor and the class mutually agreed that all the scenarios were examples of microaggressions. Here are some of the items they deemed conversational no-nos:

+ "That's so gay." (When calling something/someone stupid)
+ "I need a new gay." (A girl talking about finding a new gay best friend)
+ "They have gay marriage, so they should be happy now." (A straight person talking about the Marriage Equality Act)
+ "I think true marriage is between a man and a woman because that's what the Bible says, but I respect everyone's choices." (A woman discussing marriage equality in a classroom discussion)[21]

"That blew my mind," the student told me, referring to the gay marriage question. "If I'm asked my opinion, I can't say it because it's offensive?" [22]

The student said there was a "huge" classroom discussion about the issue. "The professor said if it [your opinion] hurts others, you should question those views, specifically the Bible," she said. "The professor said we should question the Bible and question where those views came from." [23]

The student was smart enough to determine that the professor was advocating for putting limitations on free speech. "If we can't express differing views, how can we learn?" she wondered. "Christian students are being taught to question their values. They're being told their values are wrong." [24]

The student said it's beyond frustrating because she just wants to learn how to be a good human resources person. "I don't have time to play games with professors who are trying to push their agenda on me," she said. [25]

And unfortunately what happens at the University of Oklahoma won't stay at the University of Oklahoma. Here's the scary part, America: one day these privileged snowflakes with their lists of microaggressions will be in charge of HR departments all across the nation. Did I just feel a collective shudder?

PRIVILEGE QUIZ RILES FLORIDA PARENTS

Obsession with microaggressions drives instructors to take their secular gospel to ever-younger groups of kids in every possible setting. For example, at Monroe Middle School in Tampa, Florida, students got a lesson on privilege—in their Spanish class.[26]

"How much privilege do you have?" was the name of the survey administered to seventh-and eighth-grade students. It wasn't quite as bad as the white-shaming exercises we've seen on university campuses and in the Armed

Forces.[27] But it was certainly inappropriate for a bunch of twelve-, thirteen-, and fourteen-year-olds.[28]

The youngsters were asked about religion, skin color, and sexual orientation.[29] The teacher wanted to know if the children identified as straight, homosexual, bisexual, asexual, or pansexual.[30] They were also queried on their gender. They had to choose whether they were transgender, cisgender, or gender queer.[31] Sweet Lord Almighty! Don't even get me started, folks.

Many moms and dads were mucho angry that their kids were asked such probing questions—in a Spanish class. "Her sexuality has nothing to do with school," parent Regina Stiles told television station WTSP.[32]

Thankfully in this instance Hillsborough County Public Schools wholeheartedly agreed with the outraged parents. Spokesperson Tanya Arja told me the teacher had been removed from the classroom pending the outcome of a district investigation. "We expect our teachers to create a safe learning environment for our students, and this assignment could put students in an uncomfortable position or could compromise a safe environment for them," Arja told me.[33]

The school district says the privilege lesson was not approved or appropriate for the students. "This was a teacher-generated assignment without any type of principal approval," the spokesperson said. "It's absolutely something we would not want our teachers to use."[34]

Sanity prevailed this time, but the damage was done to those particular kids. It's a classic example of how a public school classroom has been turned into a social engineering petri dish.

MACROAGGRESSIONS

The amazing thing is how violent and aggressive some leftists become in opposition to microaggressions. Carol Swain, a renowned conservative professor at Vanderbilt University, was the victim of an anti-free-speech mob. Students demanded she be fired after she defended religious liberty by writing about her opposition to radical Islam.[35]

Would we call that a case of macroaggression against Carol Swain?

How about the left-wing students at Yale University who disrupted a gathering of conservatives by shouting at them, calling them racists, and spitting on one of them?[36] Or what about the Black Lives Matter protestors who invaded the Dartmouth library and verbally assaulted white students, screaming obscenities at "filthy white" people, as they called them?[37] How about the white students at the University of Vermont who were carted off to the woods for a three-day retreat on white privilege?[38]

What nonsense is being unleashed on our great nation! Progressives are raising an army of radicalized students to silence any speech they disagree with. In the name of microaggressions they are creating a generation of intolerance—a generation that is OK shutting down free speech and purging dissenting viewpoints, a generation that would seem fine with shuttering churches and burning books that violate any person's feeling of safety.

The other day I received a disturbing phone call from a friend of mine who is a journalism professor at a conservative Christian university. He was deeply concerned about the results of an assignment he had given on hate speech. Nearly half of his students—at a Christian university, mind you—believed that Donald Trump's views on immigration should be labeled hate speech. More than a third said a pastor's view that homosexuality is a sin should be called hate speech.

Microaggressions have infected even our Christian institutions.

CHRISTIAN CLUBS NOT WELCOME

Those preaching tolerance and diversity are obviously not so tolerant and diverse, especially when it comes to respecting Christians. Just ask the Chi Alpha fraternity at California State University, Stanislaus. They were kicked off campus, not for hosting wild parties or racial insensitivity. They were kicked off campus because of Jesus.[39]

Chi Alpha is a Christian student group, and for the forty years it's been on campus, it's required its leaders to be Christians. At face value that seems fairly reasonable—a Christian group with Christian leaders.[40]

But Cal State said that kind of behavior was discriminatory. The university's administration said Christian groups cannot ban non-Christians from holding leadership positions.[41]

I see. So does that mean gay groups must accept antigay leadership? Should Muslim groups accept non-Muslim leaders? And for that matter, why doesn't Cal State allow women to play on the men's basketball team or vice versa?

SOLOMON'S SNOWFLAKE ADVICE

This is where we find ourselves, fellow Deplorables. We're being attacked by the very generation we raised. The Bible predicted this kind of stuff. Solomon, a very wise guy, wrote that undisciplined children bring shame and disgrace to their parents (Prov. 29:15). And how, friends. And how.

May I humbly suggest that the Bible might have spared us all these snowflakes? Proverbs alone is chock-full of good, sound, and what used to be everyday advice that millions of Americans took to the bank for centuries. Here are some choice cuts:

My son, do not despise the LORD's discipline or be weary of his reproof, for the LORD reproves him whom he loves, as a father the son in whom he delights. .

—PROVERBS 3:11–12, MEV

A wise son heeds his father's instruction, but a scoffer does not listen to rebuke.

—PROVERBS 13:1, MEV

Train up a child in the way he should go, and when he is old he will not depart from it

—PROVERBS 22:6, ESV

Foolishness is bound in the heart of a child, but the rod of correction will drive it far from him.

—PROVERBS 22:15, MEV

Discipline your son, and it will bring you peace of mind and give you delight.

—PROVERBS 29:17, HCSB

Solomon says that people who don't discipline their children actually *hate* them. The Good Book reverses the modern understanding of "hate" speech and says instead that when we refuse to discipline our children, we are acting in hatred toward them. Why? Because by withholding discipline, we refuse to grow them into functioning, productive, loving, mature adults. Then when trouble comes—say, when a young adult's preferred presidential candidate loses—they have a meltdown and flee into the arms of a university counselor.

We are seeing before our very eyes the cause and effect of hateful parenting, inflicted on a generation by parents who didn't have the diligence (another good word from Proverbs) to discipline and train their tender young shoots.

What we're left with are roving gangs of young people either group-crying in their dorm rooms or setting cars and shops on fire.

How do we retroactively parent through this to a more successful place? How do we give our kids the confidence to recognize that hair-trigger offenses, micro-aggressions, and so-called safe spaces don't add up to actual maturity but are in fact a form of self-centered childishness? It may be our hardest task yet, friends. But if we don't get this right, we're in trouble. These are the people who'll care for us in our old age—if they can manage to stay un-offended.

Here's the game plan:

MARCHING ORDERS

1. **Raise a ruckus.** The most effective approach to impacting university culture is to speak with your voice and your dollars. Threaten the school's alumni donations. Make the school look bad. If you are an alumnus of a college that coddles young people, call your alumni relations office and make your opinion clear. Tell the school you are organizing other alumni to withhold donations if you get wind of any nonsense.

2. **Consider steering your child to a Christian college or university.** It might be a bit more expensive, but at least you have a better chance of avoiding left-wing indoctrination. Liberty University and Truett McConnell University are two rock-solid schools of higher learning.

3. **Participate in student ministry.** Launch a college ministry through your church, or volunteer in a campus ministry such as InterVarsity or Cru. These groups can use all the help they can get, and you can impact lives forever by offering Christ, a solid rock, in the midst of shifting sands of secular culture.

4. **Make some noise.** If there is a public university near you that is engaged in political correctness, contact your local state representative and state senator. Then contact the media. As you'll see in chapter 11, that works. In Tennessee a university backed down when the public expressed outrage at a ridiculous school policy that called for the use of gender-neutral pronouns such as ze, hir, zir, and xem.

5. **Raise kids who know better.** Take Solomon's advice to the woodshed if you need to—or give your kids some form of discipline that truly speaks to their hearts and changes their behavior. Everyone they come in contact with later in life will thank you for it.

6. **Get involved in a conservative student movement.** Turning Point USA and Young Americans for Freedom are doing a tremendous job in advancing the conservative agenda on college and university campuses. These groups are staging debates, bringing conservative speakers onto campus, and challenging liberal bias in the classroom. But more importantly, they are giving conservative students a voice.

Let's say it together: no more snowflakes!

Chapter 7

MEET THE DEPLORABLES

★ ★ ★ ★

A S SHOULD BE obvious by now, I'm originally from the Deep South. My father, who passed away in 2006, was a blue-collar worker. We lived paycheck to paycheck. We went to church on Sundays. We lived a quiet life, just like many families in so-called "flyover country."

My father was a member of the silent majority. Had he lived ten years longer, I know he would've cast his vote gladly for Donald J. Trump. That would have made him a Deplorable, according to Hillary Clinton and her ilk.[1]

I've lived in New York City for more than a decade now, and as I wrote in my book *God Less America*, I feel like a Duck Dynasty guy living in a Miley Cyrus world. Right is said to be wrong; wrong is called right. Our values have been turned upside down. I've seen firsthand the contempt for country folks such as my father, people from rural America.

I call it a war on the Deplorables.

President Obama labeled us bitter Americans—the kinds of people who cling to guns and religion.[2] Well, I'm proud to call myself a gun-toting, Bible-clinging, flag-waving, patriotic American. Maybe you are too.

President Obama was the four-star general in the war on Deplorables during his eight-year tenure in the White House. I'm convinced he thinks most of America is deplorable. Time and again he stood on foreign soil and apologized for our nation. To this day it remains unclear whether he believes, as our leaders should, that the United States is the most exceptional nation on earth. When he wasn't apologizing for America, he was lecturing Christians and telling anyone who would listen that the United States is "no longer just a Christian nation."[3]

Hillary Clinton wasn't far behind him. During the 2016 presidential campaign she stood before a raucous crowd at an LGBT campaign fundraiser and called us deplorable—irredeemable. I'll let her speak for herself: "To just be grossly generalistic," she declared, "you can put half of Trump supporters into what I call the 'basket of deplorables.' Right? The racist, sexist, homophobic, xenophobic, Islamophobic—you name it." [4]

The only thing deplorable was Hillary Clinton's basket of grossly generalistic comments. Did she even dream that Americans were just about to hand her opponent the White House? But she continued: "And unfortunately there are people like that. And he has lifted them up. He has given voice to their websites that used to only have 11,000 people—now have 11 million. He tweets and retweets offensive, hateful, mean-spirited rhetoric." [5]

She later suggested that every red-blooded American is racist, whether he knows it or not. "I think implicit bias is a problem for everyone, not just police," she said. [6]

Her campaign never backed away from her *deplorable* accusation but instead doubled down on it. "I think a lot of people that stand by Donald Trump are deplorable, and the things they say are deplorable," campaign manager Robby Mook told NBC's *Meet the Press*. [7]

CHRISTOPHOBIC

To use similar language to what Hillary pulls out of her Big Bag of Smears, would it be accurate to portray some of her followers as a bunch of anti-American, heterophobic, basement-dwelling Christophobes? After all, her campaign portrayed conservative Catholicism as a "bastardization of the faith" and seemed to imply that evangelicals are a bunch of impoverished country bumpkins who wouldn't know the Hudson River from the Nile. [8]

Throughout the campaign we Christians were mocked by Hollywood and dismissed by academics. We were marginalized by the media—bullied and belittled by sex and gender revolutionaries.

Hillary's top campaign staff appeared to have deep reservoirs of contempt for Catholics and evangelical Americans, according to one batch of WikiLeaks e-mails. In a 2011 e-mail exchange among campaign chairman, John Podesta; communications director, Jennifer Palmieri; and John Halpin from the Center for American Progress, Halpin referenced a *New Yorker* article written by Ken Auletta. The article pointed out that Rupert Murdoch, 21st Century Fox chairman and Fox News executive chairman, and Robert Thomson, chief executive of News Corp, raised their children Catholic. [9]

That bit of news was just too much for Halpin's delicate psyche to handle. "Friggin' Murdoch baptized his kids in Jordan where John the Baptist baptized Jesus," Halpin fumed. [10]

Getting dunked like a Mississippi revival attendee seemed wildly uncultured to precious Halpin. "Many of the most powerful elements of the conservative movement are all Catholic (many converts) from the [Supreme Court] and think tanks to the media and social groups," he went on to say.[11]

Palmieri piled on with a nasty slap at evangelicals. "I imagine they think it is the most socially acceptable politically conservative religion," she replied. "Their rich friends wouldn't understand if they became evangelicals."[12]

Well, bless your heart, darlin'.

Halpin went on to call the conservative movement within the Catholic Church "an amazing bastardization of the faith."[13] He wrote, "They must be attracted to the systematic thought and severely backwards gender relations and must be totally unaware of Christian democracy," he wrote.[14]

Outrage came fast and furious when these e-mails saw the light of day. The Catholic League's Bill Donohue called on Clinton to immediately sanction the campaign staffers. "Hillary Clinton is not responsible for this Catholic bashing, but she has a moral obligation to sanction Mr. Podesta and Ms. Palmieri immediately," Donohue said. "Their contempt for Catholicism is palpable."[15]

Tony Perkins, president of the Family Research Council, told Fox News the e-mail exchange was troubling. "They believe that people who want to live by their faith are backwater people," he said. "Hillary and her team hold evangelicals in disdain."[16]

If the Clinton campaign wanted to address the issue of bastardizing faith, perhaps they should have had a coffee klatch with their boss. In 2015 Clinton suggested that Christians should change their religious beliefs to expand abortion. "Laws have to be backed up with resources and political will," she said. "And deep-seated cultural codes, religious beliefs and structural biases have to be changed."[17]

Hillary Clinton wasn't just running for president. She also wanted to be pope, to continue the holy war against deplorable Americans.

I'm not terribly surprised that this sort of anti-Christian bigotry came to infest Clinton's campaign. She's cut from the same cloth as former president Obama. Can you imagine either of them tolerating anyone on their staff uttering a cross word about Muslims? Me neither.

And yet they think we're irredeemable.

Thankfully all that changed on Election Day, when Donald Trump became a champion for deplorable Americans. He gave us a voice. And now the silent majority is silent no more.

"We the People" decided it was time to drain the swamp. It became time to restore traditional values. To protect the Constitution. To defend our sovereignty. To save unborn babies. To stand up for the American working man and bring jobs back from China and Mexico. It is time to eradicate the scourge of

Obamacare and to hire the bricklayers so they can start building that giant wall. "Now some of those folks, they are irredeemable. But they are not America," Hillary had said.[18]

Don't want your malls and churches turning into terrorist targets? Well, folks, Hillary and her followers thought you were Islamophobic.

Do you believe all lives matter, no matter the ethnicity? Hillary said you were racist.

Trump campaign spokesman Jason Miller pounced on Hillary's ugly remarks. "She ripped off her mask and revealed her true contempt for everyday Americans," he said.[19] "Tonight's comments were more than another example of Clinton lying to the country about her emails, jeopardizing our national security, or even calling citizens 'super-predators.' This was Clinton, as a defender of Washington's rigged system—telling the American people she could care less about them."[20]

No wonder America decided it was time to drain the swamp.

In a post-election confab at Harvard University, Clinton's campaign doubled, tripled, and quadrupled down on that notion, arguing that Donald Trump gave a platform to white supremacists and white nationalists.[21] It was an absurd accusation. It sounded desperate, petty, absurd.

Congresswoman Nancy Pelosi, the Democrat from California, told PBS one of the reasons Clinton was having a hard time attracting white male voters was because of the "three g's"—God, gays, and guns.[22]

These are the kinds of people running the Democratic Party. These are the kinds of people teaching in our universities and producing films in Hollywood. They simply despise the land that we love, which for them is nothing but a vast wilderness beneath them on their coast-to-coast airplane rides.

In the end the Deplorables didn't think too highly of Hillary Clinton either or the country that had been transformed by the former president. A Fox News poll taken before the election revealed that barely 50 percent of Americans said they were proud of their country. Fifty percent![23]

But that was before we had our say on November 8.

BARBECUE, BISCUITS, AND TEXAS RESTROOM RULES

The war on Deplorables had begun much earlier, of course. I have watched the battle lines shift in the South, which is suffering from "culture creep" that's spreading across Dixie like kudzu. One day your local meat-and-three is serving unsweetened tea, the next day your neighborhood is home to a yoga shop, a

Prius dealership, and a farm-to-table restaurant serving eggs delivered by an Amish midwife.

It's not that surprising the Left would target the South. They think it is the birthplace of the irredeemable Deplorables—where we were dipped in batter, deep-fried, and served with a side of bigotry.

The cultural cleansing of the Southern states has meant the eradication of untold numbers of Southern traditions and icons in the name of tolerance and diversity. The NAACP wanted to sandblast Confederate generals off the face of Stone Mountain in Georgia.[24] The Memphis City Council wanted to dig up a dead Confederate Civil War hero and remove his remains from a city park.[25] And the University of Mississippi stopped flying the state flag, which includes the Confederate battle emblem.[26]

Anti-Southern hate groups rationalized the cultural cleansing by explaining that the icons were offensive. Somebody forgot to tell them the Constitution of these great United States does not guarantee you the right to freedom from offense.

I am a son of the South, born in Tennessee and raised in Mississippi. And even though I've lived in New York City for the past decade, I still take my tea sweet, my chicken fried, and my biscuits buttered.

I'm proud to call myself a Tennessee Volunteer. So you can imagine my befuddlement when I learned the Oak Ridge National Laboratory wanted to crack down on workers who have Southern accents by holding a Southern Accent Reduction course.[27] In other words, them government folks want to learn all of us rednecks how to talk right. Bless their hearts.

The *Knoxville News Sentinel* reported the government-managed facility wanted to bring in a "nationally certified speech pathologist and accent reduction" instructor.[28] "Feel confident in a meeting when you need to speak with a more neutral American accent, and be remembered for what you say and not how you say it," read a notice that was sent to workers.[29]

A neutral American accent? That sounds about as appealing as a fermented soy sandwich with a side of bean curd. Needless to say, Oak Ridge's edict stirred up a mess of trouble, and they eventually called off the class. "Given the way that it came across, they decided to cancel it," lab spokesman David Keim told the newspaper.[30]

So what's wrong with a Southern drawl? *Scientific American* reported in 2012 that some Americans say a Southern accent sounds ignorant.[31]

"Studies have shown that whether you are from the North or South, a Southern twang pegs the speaker as comparatively dimwitted, but also likely to be a nicer person than folks who speak like a Yankee," the publication reported.[32]

Folks, if Southern-fried stereotypes like that don't grip your grits, I don't know what will. For the record, Southerners do not talk funny. We just like to savor our vowels, let them linger for a bit.

I believe these are skirmishes in the war on Deplorables, part of a much larger crusade to erase our way of life. Recently a liberal reader took me to task for mentioning that Tennesseans enjoy eating catfish and hush puppies. The reader accused me of stereotyping. I tried to explain that I happened to be from Tennessee, and I enjoy eating both fried catfish and hush puppies. It's not stereotyping. It's just good eatin'.[33]

I mentioned that encounter on my Facebook page, and soon my newsfeed lit up with irate readers—who sided with me (and catfish). A fan from New York mentioned that he loved catfish. Some church ladies from Alabama said they eat their fish with a side of white beans. And a guy from Dallas reminded us that the catfish are actually bigger in Texas.[34]

Southern traditions are under assault, and people sense it. Restaurants are serving barbecue tofu in Asheville, North Carolina, and tuna tartar at the Opryland hotel. It won't be too long before aspiring country music stars use spray-on tan.

Just the other day I was in Texas and ordered a glass of sweet tea and a buttermilk biscuit. The waitress told me they stopped serving sweet tea—and the only bread product they had was something called a bran muffin with flax seed. I'm sure it's quite tasty, if you happen to be a constipated bird.

Earl Clodnocker of the Mississippi Clodnockers (and my second cousin twice removed) is the resident expert on Southern culture. "There is a proper way for Southerners to barbecue tofu," he told me. "First you need to bury the tofu in the backyard. Then you should put a slab of ribs on the smoker."

He also tried to open a chain of barbecue joints in Dearborn, Michigan. Cousin Earl learned a very difficult financial lesson: you can't eat barbecue wearing a burka.

THE CROSS-DRESSING COWBOY

While we're on the subject of barbecue, which is a primary food group for many Deplorables, there's an unspoken code of conduct when you enter a barbecue joint. You don't order salad, you don't use a fork, and if you're a cross-dressing cowboy with an affinity for stilettos, you don't use the ladies room.

That last story came to light in the *Fort Worth Star-Telegram*. Apparently a small-town barbecue joint inadvertently found itself right smack in the middle of the big debate over transgender bathrooms.

John Sanford owns BBQ on the Brazos, located about thirty minutes or so southwest of the stockyards in Fort Worth. It's the place to go for brisket in Cresson, population 741.

A few years back a truck driver, who also worked as a rodeo cowboy, would show up to order a plate of barbecue. Now that in and of itself would not be terribly unusual or newsworthy. But this particular cowboy was partial to wearing ladies garments. He was a cross-dresser.[35] "Sometimes he'd have on hot pants, a miniskirt, and six-inch stilettos," John told me matter-of-factly.[36]

It really wasn't that big of a deal until the cross-dressing truck driver and rodeo cowboy used the ladies room. Let's just say his powder room preference went over about as well as a plate of barbecue tofu. "I have no problem [with cross-dressers]—doesn't bother me a bit," John said. "But he can't go into the ladies room."[37]

"We just prefer that everybody use the right restroom," he added. "That's the nicest way to say it."[38]

So they put a sign on the bathroom door clearly explaining bathroom etiquette at BBQ on the Brazos: "No men allowed in women's bathroom please."[39]

The cross-dressing trucker told the staff that he felt uncomfortable using the men's room but agreed to comply with their wishes. "If you are a man, you can't go into the ladies restroom," John said. "I don't know if it's a Texas thing, [but] it should be a world thing. I don't know what all the debate is about."[40]

That's because folks who live in the Lone Star State were blessed with a double dose of common sense. They understand that you're supposed to use the bathroom that corresponds to your God-given plumbing.

Meanwhile New York City liberals have been so confused over politically correct potties that they can't figure out if they're supposed to stand, squat, or lift their leg. The NYC Commission on Human Rights recently spent $265,000 in tax money to let folks know they should "Look Past Pink or Blue" and use whatever restroom they so choose.[41]

So how did the BBQ on the Brazos bathroom policy become national news?

Well, it turns out a reporter for the *Star-Telegram* is a regular customer, and one day he noticed the bathroom sign. Questions were asked. Stories were told. And before you could say, "Pass the barbecue sauce," the tiny barbecue joint in Cresson became the lead story around the watercooler. "Cross-Dressing Cowboy Not Welcome in Ladies' Room at North Texas Barbecue Joint," the headline screamed.[42]

John said the sign had nothing to do with politics and had absolutely nothing to do with the transgender controversy. "It's not whether you are gay or transgender or black or white or yellow or pink. To me it doesn't matter," he said. "If you walk through my door, I'll be happy to fix you a plate of barbecue. But if [you] come, be sure to use the right restroom." [43]

AN UNWHOLESOME ATTACK ON SOUTHERN FOOD

Meanwhile, *the New York Times* has declared down-home Southern cooking undignified in a story that heaped praise on a new generation of Southern chefs while denigrating fried chicken, Cracker Barrel restaurants, and the queen of Southern food: Paula Deen. [44]

The food snobs at the *Times* attacked Deen in the second sentence of their lengthy diatribe, calling her a "so-called queen of Southern food, who cooks with canned fruit and Crisco." [45] The *Times* bemoaned the "hayseed image" of Southern cooking while praising "a new generation of chefs who have pushed Southern cooking into the vanguard of world cuisine." [46]

The *Times* headline proclaimed: "Vanquishing the Colonel—Farmers Work With Chefs to Restore Southern Cuisine's Dignity." [47] The *Times* whined, "Today, purists believe, Southern cooking is too often represented by its worst elements: feedlot hams, cheap fried chicken and chains like Cracker Barrel." [48]

Perhaps the *New York Times* should consider first restoring its own dignity before launching a crusade against shrimp and grits.

It seems to me that the "so-called" queen of Southern cooking should fly up to New York City and take a cast-iron skillet to the backside of the "so-called" newspaper that printed such nonsense. But Deen is a genteel Southern lady and would probably just shake her head and say, "Oh, Lord, y'all."

So as a proud son of the South I believe it is my duty to defend the honor of our skillet-fried chicken, our ham hocks, and our sweet potato pies. Nobody speaks ill of butter and gets away with it.

For the record, I happen to have a Cracker Barrel rocking chair in my office at the Fox News corner of the world, along with several copies of Paula Deen's cookbooks. That being said, I'm really not quite sure why the *New York Times* felt compelled to launch a broadside against the traditional cuisine of the Southern states.

I'll take a Cracker Barrel meatloaf sandwich and a slice of the restaurant's double chocolate fudge Coca-Cola cake any day of the week over the slop they serve at those five-star New York City restaurants.

Does the "Old Gray Lady" [49] really want to pick a food fight with Alabama or Mississippi? There's a reason the Magnolia State is the plumpest in the nation—it's called banana pudding.

As an expatriated Southerner living in Brooklyn, I've come to realize that this quest to redefine Southern cuisine has taken root in the Big Apple. Chefs who couldn't succeed in Dixie have moved north to ply their trade. It's a movement called "New Southern Cuisine."

To be fair I decided to visit one of those so-called "New Southern Cuisine" restaurants the other day. To its credit it served sweet tea. But that was the only Southern thing in the building. The first item on the menu was black-eyed-pea hummus. I threw up a little inside my mouth.

The waiter brought my iced tea and suggested I try something they called *arugula smear*. I wasn't sure if I was supposed to eat it or wipe it. I paid for my sweet tea, went home, and whipped up a batch of Paula Deen's macaroni and cheese. And as I sat down at my table, I prayed this prayer: "Dear Jesus, thank You for butter. Amen."

PURGING THE GENERAL LEE

The latest victim of cultural cleansing in the Southern states is the General Lee. If you're under forty, you have no idea. Let me explain.

The General Lee is simply one of the most famous cars in television history. It's orange and beautiful and drives like an angry bull. Watch old *Dukes of Hazzard* episodes, and you'll see what I mean. It went tearing around the backwoods and hollers, often flying through the air as the boys inside whooped. Of course, painted on the roof of the car, as everybody knows, is the Confederate flag.

Not anymore.

Warner Brothers announced it will remove the Confederate flag from the General Lee's top. It will also ban any *Dukes of Hazzard* merchandise that once sported the Confederate flag. Sears, Walmart, and eBay have also announced they will no longer sell Confederate merchandise.[50]

Maybe they could just paint a rainbow flag on top and rename it the General Sherman. He culturally cleansed the South too. Just ask the good people of Atlanta.

It's just another step away from an aspect of our American heritage. As lawmakers debate whether to remove state flags and rename schools, parks, and streets named after Confederate war heroes, in Washington they're talking about removing Confederate statues from the US Capitol.[51]

Senator Mitch McConnell wants a statue of Jefferson Davis evicted from the Kentucky statehouse.[52] And Senator Harry Reid wants the University of Nevada, Las Vegas to rename its Runnin' Rebels mascot.[53]

Get ready, Ole Miss. They'll be coming after you folks next.

It's only a matter of time before the cultural revolutionaries destroy films such as *Gone With the Wind* and *Forrest Gump*, and burn copies of *Tom Sawyer* and *Huckleberry Finn*.

Stalin and Lenin would be bursting with pride.

You know who else has been doing some cultural cleansing? The Islamic State. It's been bulldozing its way through history, turning Iraq's heritage into rubble.

Mark my words; the Left's cultural crusade will not stop with the Confederate flag. They will use the perception of racism and hatred to whitewash history and silence dissent. One day—very soon—I predict they will come after another flag, the one with broad stripes and bright stars. After all, it probably makes some Americans feel "unsafe."

What a troubling time in America.

My forefathers fought in the Civil War. One of my great-great-great-grandfathers was killed at Reams Station, Virginia. Another was killed defending Richmond, Virginia. Many others fought and died for the Confederacy. My people did not own slaves. They were farmers, and at least one ran moonshine. (He was Methodist.)

I am proud to call myself American by birth but Southern by the grace of God. And if you have a problem with that, well, in the words of Rhett Butler, frankly, my dear...

The war on the South is really an arm of the war on Deplorables. We are all involved, not just those hailing from south of the Mason-Dixon line.

What should we do as responsible deplorable Americans to push back this terrible assault on liberty? Eat more catfish obviously. And here are some other valuable ideas:

MARCHING ORDERS

1. **Never forget.** Let's never forget the terrible harm done to America during the eight years of the Obama administration. We must speak plainly about that dismal chapter in our history so we are less likely to repeat it. Tell your kids and talk to your friends about what went wrong and why. Point to the obviously destructive results. Be part of the national conversation. Do your part right where you are.

2. **Repair what was broken.** By rebounding strongly with the right solutions for problems created under the liberal reign, we not only strengthen our country, but also we continue the American story. We show we are a people who can bounce back from bad situations and truly epic disasters—World War II, the Civil War, and

the Obama administration. American pride is built by overcoming bad things and making our nation great again. It's in our DNA as Americans.

3. **Grow strong roots in our children.** Kids who are connected to and appreciative of this country's magnificent founding won't quickly abandon it. Keep the roots intact, and the fruit of American freedom and ingenuity will continue to grow. Let's never let the liberals redefine our American culture again. Let's raise generations of historically literate children who won't be fooled by airy and ultimately damaging visions of a different kind of American future.

4. **Complain.** Yes, complain. Make noise about bad history books. Tell your kids' school and school district that you're done with America's heritage being purged from curriculum. You're tired of Easter break becoming spring break, Columbus Day being ignored or mourned, Christmas being handcuffed and replaced with winter break, and the spiritual aspects of Thanksgiving being exchanged for Native American Appreciation Day.

You don't have to kowtow to the so-called arbiters of public morality. Don't bend the knee to these people anymore. If someone as brash and occasionally offensive as Donald J. Trump could win the White House, surely you can speak up in your house, your neighborhood, your school system, your city. Remember, this country can't be saved by one man on Pennsylvania Avenue. It takes all of us rowing in the same direction.

Deplorables, git 'er done, y'all.

Chapter 8

THE RISE OF RADICAL ISLAM

I DON'T KNOW ABOUT you, Deplorables, but I've been sleeping pretty soundly knowing there's a guy named "Mad Dog" in charge of protecting us from the Islamic radicals. "Find the enemy that wants to end this experiment [in American democracy], and kill every one of them until they're so sick of the killing that they leave us and our freedoms intact," he once said.[1]

President Trump's decision to nominate retired US Marine Corps General James "Mad Dog" Mattis as the new Secretary of Defense was a stroke of genius. He is the real deal—known for his candor, his tough talk, and his ability to kill the enemy. I have no doubt the Islamic radicals are at this very hour trembling in their caves. Soon—very soon—Secretary Mattis will dispatch every last one of them to their Maker. And once they arrive at the hereafter, they will discover an unfortunate error in their religious texts—meaning the radicals will be spending eternity with seventy-two vegans.

Former president Obama (oh, how I do enjoy writing those words) had a very different philosophy when it came to dealing with the Islamic radicals—namely by not even mentioning their name. He seemed to think the best way to fight the war on terror was to invite the radicals over for an evening of appletinis and Iranian chick flicks.

But not General Mad Dog Mattis. He's not an appletini kind of guy. Don't get me wrong. The general is a man of peace, but he's not one to be trifled with. Marines, he once said, don't know how to spell the word *defeat*.[2]

"Be polite, be professional, but have a plan to kill everybody you meet," he once said.[3]

And there's this gem: "We've backed off in good faith to try and give you a chance to straighten this problem out. But I am going to beg with you for a minute. I'm going to plead with you, do not cross us. Because if you do, the survivors will write about what we do here for 10,000 years."[4]

Secretary Mattis is a good man with a good heart and a fierce determination to protect our nation—so that boys and girls and men and women might be able to breathe free.

Our former commander in chief seemed to hold the Armed Forces in contempt. And he certainly advanced a narrative of appeasement when it came to the Islamic enemy. It's important for us to remember what has transpired over the past eight years to truly appreciate what President Trump and Secretary Mattis are about to do.

The ink had barely dried on the nuclear deal with Iran when protesters surged into the streets of Tehran shouting, "Death to America."[5] You would think that might give the diplomats within the Obama administration cause for alarm. But the president simply dismissed public concerns, as if shouting, "Death to America," is the Muslim way of saying, "Hey, y'all."

I'm not an Ivy League-educated diplomat, but I'm not so sure we should trust the Iranians to keep their end of the pinkie promise.

The president defended the Islamic Republic of Iran by explaining that the threats were meant for a "domestic political audience."[6] In other words, the ayatollah was just yanking our chain. Yes sir. That ayatollah is a real rib tickler.

The administration's laissez-faire attitude with the Iranians is symbolic of their carefree attitude toward radical Islam, a phrase that at the time of this writing had yet to cross President Obama's lips.[7] Homeland Security Chief Jeh Johnson told ABC News that it was critical to stop using the word *Islamic* when referring to terrorist attacks, as if that is somehow going to make us safer.[8] The Hindus aren't trying to blow us up.

Mr. Johnson said it was not about being politically correct. He said it was about building trust with Muslim community leaders. He said the phrase *Islamic extremism* played right in the hands of ISIS. And he said the only way to keep the Islamic State from radicalizing Americans is by avoiding using the "I" word to describe their brand of terrorism.

Of course this is the same Obama administration official who told a Muslim group that the teachings of the Quran reminded him of quintessential American values.[9] Oh, really? And which values might those have been?

The Federal Bureau of Investigation admitted there are open investigations involving terrorists in all fifty states. But what they won't tell us is how many investigations there are. The Islamic State says they have seventy-one trained soldiers in fifteen states waiting to commit acts of jihad.[10] By now there may be more. Now, they could be blowing smoke out of their hookahs. But what if they are telling the truth? What if just one of the seventy-one is really a trained soldier, a jihadist?

New York Times best-selling author Joel Rosenberg tells me there's an even greater danger lurking in the shadows. It's a hybrid of Islamic radicalism that even scares al Qaeda. Rosenberg calls it "apocalyptic Islam."

"Apocalyptic Islam doesn't want to simply attack us; it wants to annihilate us," Rosenberg told me during an interview for this book. "Apocalyptic Muslims like the leaders of Iran and the leaders of the Islamic State believe that we are living in the end times and that it's their mission from Allah to bring about the end of the world as we know it."[11]

Rosenberg describes apocalyptic Islam as a subset of radical Islam. "We're not talking about 1.6 billion Muslims," he said. "We're talking about 10 percent or less who are radicals."[12]

But 10 percent of 1.6 billion is still a mighty big number—and they want to destroy Christians, Jews, and anyone else they consider to be an infidel. Now, that ought to make your Jell-O jiggle. "They want to establish their global Islamic kingdom where everybody has to follow Islam," he said. "And that is a substantively, significantly different and much more dangerous form of radical Islam than even al Qaeda and Hamas and the Taliban."[13]

"This is not just about attacking us," Rosenberg warned again. "This is about annihilating us."[14]

Even al Qaeda has denounced the apocalyptic Muslims as bloodthirsty. "When al Qaeda thinks you're crazy, you're really crazy," Rosenberg said. "And these people are not just crazy—they're demonic."[15]

And yet former president Obama and his administration tried to appease the Islamists, including the ones currently in charge of the Islamic Republic of Iran, the same ones he reached a nuclear deal with. Rosenberg called the nuclear deal foolish, dangerous, and insane.

"Once you understand apocalyptic Islam, you understand just how dangerous it is to give Iran not just one path to nuclear weapons, but two," he said. "[Former president Obama] doesn't understand the threat of radical Islam. He won't even define that, much less apocalyptic Islam."[16]

It's not so much that the world is facing a future threat—the threat is already here. "These people are crucifying Christians; they're beheading people," he said. "They are creating mayhem and really genocidal conditions in Syria and Iraq." And yet former president Obama used half measures to run a public relations war against them, he added.[17]

Consider what happened when former president Obama decided to move tens of thousands of Syrian refugees into American neighborhoods. The possibility that Islamic radicals might be able to slip across the border frightened both Republican and Democratic governors.[18]

Donald Trump suggested a temporary moratorium on immigrants arriving from places such as Syria. I thought it was a prudent measure to take, especially in the aftermath of the Islamic terrorist attack in Paris in November 2015.[19] And it was especially prudent after ISIS warned that America would be next.[20]

"We need to take ISIS at their word," Franklin Graham wrote on his Facebook page. "Their goal is world domination. They want to control us—they want to destroy us."[21]

However, former president Obama and the Council on American-Islamic Relations (CAIR) called the moratorium on Syrian refugees un-American. "That's shameful," the former president said, referring to suggestions that only Syrian Christians be allowed to enter the United States. "That's not American. That's not who we are. We don't have religious tests to our compassion."[22]

CAIR went on to say that such actions were "driven by fear and Islamophobia."[23] Well, if wanting to keep the radical Islamists out of our nation makes me an extremist, then so be it.

Governor Mike Huckabee delivered the harshest critique of former president Obama's response to the Paris terrorist attacks, calling it wimpish. "We have a Cub Scout for commander in chief," he said. "It's embarrassing when a left-wing socialist French President shows strength and determination to eradicate animals who are slaughtering innocent civilians while our president lectures us on the moral necessity to open our borders to tens of thousands of un-vetted people from the Middle East."[24]

Former president Obama piously prattled that any objections to his plans to relocate Muslims to America would be counterproductive and demanded it stop. And yet his minions had no problem calling those of us opposed to the plan every name in the book: bigots, Islamophobes, un-American. The cold, hard reality is that Protestants, Catholics, and Jews are not the ones beheading people. The Lutherans and Nazarenes aren't gunning down young folks at concert venues. The Baptists aren't throwing people off buildings because of their sexuality. Nevertheless the president remained steadfast. The Muslims will come. Period.

Yet again, "We don't have religious tests to our compassion," he told journalists from atop his soapbox.[25]

But that's not entirely accurate. In 2014 the Obama administration waged a fierce legal battle to have a German Christian family thrown out of the United States. I wrote about their plight in *God Less America*. The Romeikes fled their homeland in search of a nation where they could homeschool their children. A judge initially granted them asylum in the United States, believing they were escaping from religious persecution. However, the Obama administration demanded they be returned to Germany.[26]

Immigration and Customs Enforcement also tried to deport 120 international students studying at a Christian college in Ohio.[27] And in early 2015 a federal immigration judge ordered a dozen Iraqi Christians deported from a facility in San Diego.[28]

And all of this while former president Obama remained steadfast in his defense of the Muslim faith, saying the world has a terrorist problem, not a Muslim problem. "The overwhelming majority of victims of terrorism over the last several years, and certainly the overwhelming majority of victims of ISIL, are themselves Muslims," he said. "ISIL does not represent Islam. It is not representative in any way of the attitudes of the overwhelming majority of Muslims."[29]

MODERATE MUSLIMS?

I really want to believe that Islam is a religion of peace. I really do. But it's hard to do when there is not overwhelming condemnation of the terrorist attacks from the majority of Muslims.

Where are the voices of the Muslims outraged that their faith has been hijacked? Where are the thousands of Muslims marching in the streets denouncing the terrorists? Where are they? Why have they chosen to remain silent?

I'm all for welcoming the huddled masses yearning to be free. It's the ones yearning to wage jihad that I'm worried about.

What's going to happen when one of those Syrian refugees opens fire in a Chick-fil-A or launches a chemical attack at Disney World or explodes a pressure cooker at Café Du Monde in the French Quarter of New Orleans? We are not Islamophobic. We are not un-American. We just don't want our kids to get blown up.

But that simple belief invites scorn. Consider the case of Jerry Falwell Jr., the president of Liberty University.

President Falwell fielded criticism from Democrats and jihadist sympathizers after he urged students at the nation's largest Christian university to carry concealed weapons on campus to counter any possible armed attack from jihadists. "Let's teach them a lesson if they ever show up here," Falwell told thousands of cheering students during convocation. "I've always thought if more good people had concealed-carry permits, then we could end those Muslims before they walked in."[30]

He told *the Washington Post* he was specifically referring to those behind the November 2015 terrorist attack in Paris, and Syed Farook and Tashfeen Malik, the couple who shot and killed fourteen people during a holiday party in a Southern California office building in December 2015.[31]

Virginia governor Terry McAuliffe criticized Falwell's remarks, calling them "rash and repugnant" in a statement to *the Washington Post.* "My administration is committed to making Virginia an open and welcoming Commonwealth, while also ensuring the safety of all of our citizens," McAuliffe said. "Mr. Falwell's rash and repugnant comments detract from both of those crucial goals." [32]

Hillary Clinton went so far as to accuse Falwell of giving "aid and comfort" to the Islamic State. "This is the kind of deplorable, not only hateful, response to a legitimate security issue," Clinton told ABC News. "But it is giving aid and comfort to ISIS and other radical jihadists." [33]

Pardon me, but if a terrorist opened fire on the Liberty University campus while I was visiting there, I would be hoping to God that everyone around me had concealed carries—and was up to speed on their target practice.

WASHINGTON POST: LAY DOWN YOUR GUNS, CHRISTIAN SOLDIERS

What is the Christian response to radical Islam's threat? Get a load of the crackpot theory offered up by the *Washington Post*: "Some theologians believe that Jesus would call on Christians to put down their weapons in the face of violence." [34] I only wish the *Washington Post* had named the lunatic theologians who believe Christians should gladly offer themselves to the Islamic radicals as sacrificial lambs.

Does the mainstream media suggest that Christians should not protect their families from harm? Do they suggest that Christians should not serve in the military or law enforcement? In the warped world of American journalism is there any instance in which people of faith would be allowed to defend themselves against the sword of the radical Muslims? Sometimes I wonder who hates Christians more, the mainstream media or the Islamic jihadists.

Let's compare track records of Christians and Islamic radicals briefly. Christians are a good-hearted people. If you are down on your luck, there's always a church willing to lend you a helping hand. If you get hungry, we'll fix you a plate of chicken. If you're thirsty, we'll pour you a glass of tea. If you need some clothes or gas money to get you where you're going, we'll take care of that too.

We rebuild homes washed away by the floods. We look after the widows and orphans. We tend to the sick and afflicted. We are slow to anger. We give billions of dollars to charities that operate overseas.

On the other side, over the past eight years we have seen Islamic radicals wage jihad across the fruited plain. We have seen jihadists spill American blood on American soil. They have terrorized our people—from Boston to Fort Hood to Chattanooga to San Bernardino to Orlando. We have watched as the jihadists beheaded our brothers and sisters in foreign lands. We have watched as churches have been destroyed, parishioners crucified.

American Christians should be slow to anger indeed. But not stupid.

The enemy is now beyond the gate. The enemies live among us. So what do we do as peace-loving, family-protecting, God-honoring believers? Following are some serious ideas.

MARCHING ORDERS

1. **Serve in the military.** This is an honorable calling, and our young people should know that. Let's encourage those who want to defend our freedom overseas so the battle doesn't make it to our shores. Honor veterans and those currently serving in the Armed Forces. If you are a young person, put military service alongside your professional considerations. It's possible to serve for several years and return to civilian life with greatly enhanced skills of many kinds. Your country would thank you for it.

2. **Own a gun.** There's nothing that promotes community safety like a firearm in the hands of a peace-loving person. Look into your local laws to see what you're allowed to do. Then lock and load, and start target practice at the local shooting range.

3. **Talk to your kids about the Second Amendment.** Guns used to be standard in most homes in America, back when home and crop protection fell to each family. But now many households have never owned or even handled a gun. Instruct your kids on the history of an arms-bearing citizenry in the United States and why it's so important that the government not take away our ability to defend ourselves against threats from within and without. Change the perception of guns from tools of violence to tools of peacekeeping so your children appreciate both the seriousness of the weapon and the seriousness with which the founders protected our rights to own them. And be sure to enroll your child in a gun safety class. Check with the National Rifle Association for the nearest classes in your neighborhood.

4. **Understand Islam, and show Muslims the love of Christ.** Battling Islam for most of us is not about any kind of physical clash. But it can be a fruitful clash of ideas. There are many reports around the world that Muslims are changing faiths and coming to Jesus in numbers never before seen. You can be part of that. Pray

for the Muslim world. Reach out to the Muslims in your community. As Christians we are people who love others. Love is by far
the strongest force on the planet and can change the entire direction of a family—even eternally.

5. **Pray for the persecuted church in the Middle East.** And speak
   up for those believers. The atrocities there are almost too evil to
   believe. We must not stand by and let our society remain ignorant
   or uncaring while this intentional holocaust of Christians is carried
   out in Iraq, Syria, and elsewhere. Bring it up in conversation. Ask
   your pastor to mention it from the pulpit and make time in the
   service to pray for the victims and their families, and the surviving
   believers.

6. **Support politicians who recognize the threat of Islamic jihadists.** This starts at the hyper-local level. City council members
   become state legislators, then members of Congress, then senators,
   and so on. Let's make sure their views on this threat to America
   are known early in their political careers so we don't inadvertently
   elevate the wrong people to higher office.

It's not too dramatic to say we need thousands of Paul Reveres around this
country to sound the alarm that this threat is on our front doorstep. Forewarned
is forearmed, in more ways than one. And while we reach out with love to all
our neighbors and peace-loving citizens, we also know that peace is worth
fighting for.

In 2003 then Commanding General Mattis wrote these words to the 1st
Marine Division:

> You are part of the world's most feared and trusted force. Engage your
> brain before you engage your weapon…For the mission's sake, our
> country's sake, and the sake of the men who carried the Division's colors
> in past battles—*who fought for life and never lost their nerve*—carry
> out your mission and *keep your honor clean.* Demonstrate to the world
> there is "No Better Friend, No Worse Enemy" than a U.S. Marine.[35]

Rest well, Deplorables. Rest well.

Chapter 9

A CHICKEN SANDWICH FOR THE SOUL

I BELIEVE CHICK-FIL-A IS the official chicken of Jesus. I think it ought to be the official poultry of every Deplorable too.

So you can imagine my delight when I learned the famed Southern chicken restaurant would be opening outposts in New York City. And when I discovered they'd be buttering those buns just a block from Fox News—well, I almost started speaking in tongues (which is unusual for a Baptist).

But militant LGBT activists and liberal lawmakers were in a state of rage. They vowed to protest and urged people to abstain from poultry.

New York City Mayor Bill de Blasio, who eats pizza with a fork, called for a citywide boycott. One council member accused Chick-fil-A of spreading a message of hate.[1]

But that's not true. Chick-fil-A is a business serving chicken and waffle fries and deliciously refreshing lemonade. They are also in the business of providing jobs—good jobs. But that doesn't matter to people like Mayor de Blasio. Full and complete compliance with the LGBTQIA (lesbian, gay, bisexual, transsexual, queer, intersex, asexual) agenda is the only thing that matters, even if it means hundreds of New Yorkers lose their jobs.

Fortunately New Yorkers ignored their antipoultry lawmakers and turned out in record numbers to feast upon the hot, juicy chicken breast tucked between warm, buttered buns.[2]

Chick-Fil-A's success has everything to do with its corporate values, which are deeply rooted in the Christian faith of founder S. Truett Cathy.

That faith was on full display in the aftermath of a criminal incident at his Atlanta-area home. The vandals caused $30,000 in damage in 2008, but of all the damage done, what bothered him most was the filthy language the preteen girls scribbled on the walls.[3]

Yet Mr. Cathy asked police not to prosecute the young vandals. He feared a criminal record might tarnish their lives. So instead of jail, Mr. Cathy worked out a deal with their parents.[4] The girls were banned from watching television and playing video games. They had to write a thousand times, "I will not vandalize other people's property."[5]

He wanted to show the girls there was a better way in life.

When Mr. Cathy died in 2014, the nation remembered him as the man who founded Chick-fil-A. But he was much more than that. Beyond the waffle fries and grammatically challenged bovines, Mr. Cathy was a man whose deep and abiding faith in our Lord affected the way he lived.[6]

He was a devout Southern Baptist, who taught Sunday school to thirteen-year-old boys for more than fifty years.[7] Beyond closing his business on Sundays, he launched foster homes, summer camps, and scholarships for young people. And when employees needed help, Mr. Cathy was there.[8] Since 1973 Chick-fil-A has given more than $32 million in financial assistance to workers.[9]

Notice that word *given*. Put principles and people ahead of profits—that's what Mr. Cathy believed.[10] "I'd like to be remembered as one who kept my priorities in the right order," he was known to say. "We live in a changing world, but we need to be reminded that the important things have not changed. I have always encouraged my restaurant operators and team members to give back to the local community. We should be about more than just selling chicken; we should be a part of our customers' lives and the communities in which we serve."[11]

The values that made Chick-fil-A one of the most successful and one of the most popular restaurant chains in the nation also made it a target. In 2012 Chick-fil-A's president, Dan Cathy, told a reporter that the "biblical definition of the family unit" did not include same-sex marriage.[12]

A national firestorm ensued, stoked by militant LGBT activists and liberal lawmakers. It was a jihad against this poultry-powered chain.

Boston and Chicago lawmakers tried unsuccessfully to block new Chick-fil-A locations.[13] Protestors swarmed restaurants; they bullied and harassed workers.[14]

In 2015 LGBT lawmakers in Denver debated whether to allow Chick-fil-A to open a restaurant at Denver International Airport. One gay council member said she was worried about Chick-fil-A using their profits "to fund and fuel discrimination."[15]

"We really want to look into the policies and practices of these companies, and just make sure that they conform to ours in the city, the State of Colorado," council member Robin Kniech said in remarks reported by the *Denver Post*.

"We have a marriage decision nationally. This is really about policies and it's about practices."[16]

No, ma'am. It's about anti-Christian bigotry. Aside from the absurdity of the lawmaker's statement, imagine the nerve of elected officials who think they have the power to decide how a privately owned company spends its money.

The battle over Chick-fil-A then moved to university campuses, with collegiate poultry jihadists declaring that waffle fries make them feel unsafe. Such was the case at Johns Hopkins University, where students approved a resolution that called for blocking a Chick-fil-A in their dining hall.[17] The student government association alleged the restaurant would be a campus "microaggression."[18]

Johns Hopkins student Andrew Guernsey was one of the few brave souls to stand up to the cultural jihadists. His remarks to the student government association were published by the *National Review*. "Whatever your opinion on same-sex marriage, the JHU student government's idea that the mere presence of Chick-fil-A on campus would promote 'homophobia' and amount to discrimination against the LGBT community is absurd," he wrote. "This view is premised, first of all, on the assumption that advocates of traditional marriage are devoid of rational argument and inspired only by hatred, and second, on the notion that allowing a company owned by someone who supports traditional marriage to operate on campus is equivalent to endorsing that support."[19]

The debate that raged at Johns Hopkins University was not so much about waffle fries or chicken nuggets as much as it was about free speech and religious liberty. Now that's actually something I cherish more than Chick-fil-A Sauce.

CHICK-FIL-A AND THE REAL SNOWFLAKES

Despite attacks, Chick-fil-A has remained focused on its mission and its ministry. The Cathy family and their many employees have set a wonderful example of serving others—of going the extra mile and in doing so, demonstrating the love of Christ. And I can't think of a better demonstration of that love than what happened a few winters ago at a Chick-fil-A near Birmingham, Alabama.

A snowstorm in the South is about as rare as a glass of unsweetened tea at a church supper. Folks around Birmingham weren't all that worried though. The storm was only supposed to dust the city, not even enough powder for a Southern snowman.

So when the first snowflakes began to fall, no one paid all that much attention. But then the flakes kept falling. Before too long folks in places such as Hoover and Inverness realized it was much more than a dusting. By that point it was too late for anyone to do anything.

Icy interstates and highways soon became clogged with cars and trucks.

Thousands of motorists found themselves stranded with nowhere to go, including many stuck on Highway 280.

But a good number of those stranded motorists were able to find shelter in the storm thanks to the kindness and generosity of Chick-fil-A restaurant employees and the restaurant's owner, Mark Meadows.[20]

Once the snow started accumulating, Meadows closed the restaurant and sent his staff home. But a few hours later many of them returned, unable to get to their homes. "Our store is about a mile and a half from the interstate, and it took me two hours to get there," manager Audrey Pitt told me. "It was a parking lot as far as I could see."[21]

So Pitt left her car on the side of the interstate and joined a flock of bundled-up drivers trudging through the snow. "At one point there were more people walking than driving," she said.[22]

Some of the drivers had been stuck in their cars for nearly seven hours without any food or water. So the staff of the Chick-fil-A decided to lend a helping hand. "We cooked several hundred sandwiches and stood out on both sides of 280 and handed out the sandwiches to anyone we could get to, as long as we had food to give out," Pitt said.[23]

The staffers braved the falling snow and ice, slipping and sliding, as they offered hot, juicy sandwiches. And Chick-fil-A refused to take a single penny for the food. The meal was a gift, no strings attached.

For the frozen drivers, it was manna from heaven. "They were very excited and extremely thankful," she said. "People were thankful to get something to put in their stomachs."[24]

Pitt said they were especially surprised that the sandwiches were free. Why not make some extra money during the storm? It's not like anyone could go to another restaurant. Chick-fil-A had a captive crowd of hungry customers. So why did they give away their food?

"This company is based on taking care of people and loving people before you're worried about money or profit," Pitt told me. "We were just trying to follow the model that we've all worked under for so long and the model that we've come to love. There was really nothing else we could have done but try to help people any way we could."[25]

Before Pitt and the other employees started handing out sandwiches, Mark Meadows found himself giving away a catering order he couldn't deliver because of the storm. Rather than letting the good food go to waste, he gave it to drivers who had been stranded on the road for hours.

Lauren Dango was one of those stranded motorists. She's known Meadows for years, and she was stunned when she saw him walking from car to car with

Chick-fil-A sandwiches. "I looked up, and I'm like, 'What is he doing'," Dango told me. "He had a catering order and it got canceled, so he pulled over and started giving away food."[26]

And if that wasn't enough, Meadows helped a driver maneuver along the icy road by pushing a car up an incline.

Dango was so touched by Meadows's kindness, she sent a letter to Chick-fil-A's corporate headquarters. "Kudos to Mark Meadows for not only preaching the 'second mile' concept, but actually living by it," she wrote.[27]

"We just wanted to be able to help," Pitt said. "[It] was such a hopeless situation. We wanted to do something to make people feel a little bit better. We were here. We had food and there were people outside who needed food. So it just made sense to do something for them."[28]

But Chick-fil-A's generosity didn't stop there. "We opened up our dining room to anyone who wanted to sleep on a bench or a booth," Pitt told me.[29]

And the following morning the weary staff members fired up their ovens and began preparing chicken biscuits. The only thing that was closed was Chick-fil-A's cash register. "We're not open for business," she said. "We're just feeding people who are hungry.... It's a blessing to us to be able to help people. It really is."[30]

I'm reminded of the words of Jesus when He said, "For I was hungry and you gave Me food. I was thirsty and you gave Me drink, I was a stranger and you took Me in" (Matt. 25:35, MEV). It was a Sunday school lesson illustrated on a snowy winter day along Highway 280 in Alabama with a chicken sandwich and a side of waffle fries.

The following winter that same Chick-fil-A was the scene of another act of kindness. One of the diners who came in that day was a bit unkempt. He was wearing jeans and a hoodie—hardly the kind of clothing for a day like that. Most folks just figured he was a homeless fellow. The man first made eye contact with Meadows, the owner of the Chick-fil-A.[31]

"I was about to leave when this gentleman walked in the door," Meadows told me. "I could tell he needed some help. We have people come in from time to time, so you kind of know."[32]

And sure enough Meadows's instinct was correct. "He asked if there was some work he could do so that he could get something to eat," Meadows said.[33]

Instead of ordering the indigent man to leave, Meadows invited him to have a meal. As the man waited for his chicken sandwich and waffle fries, Meadows could not help but notice the man was rubbing his hands together. "There's a look about somebody's hands that's been out in the cold," Meadows said. "It's got that cold look about them."[34]

The man did not have a pair of gloves. So Meadows gave him his. "I went back and got his food, and he put on the gloves and then he left," Meadows said.[35]

The entire encounter lasted just a few minutes, and that was that. But in this day and age of social networking and smartphones, that was not that.

Andrea Stoker happened to be eating lunch in the restaurant that day with her little boy. And she could not help but notice the interaction between the store owner and the disheveled man. She took a photograph and posted a message on Chick-fil-A's Facebook page—a message that has since gone viral. Here's what she wrote:

> My son and I were at the location on Highway 280 in Birmingham, AL when a man came in to escape the 35 degree temps and strong winds with all of his earthly possessions strapped to his back....I watched as the manager walked up to him and asked if he could do anything for him. Before the man could even answer, the manager asked if he had a pair of gloves and walked to the table at which he'd been sitting and picked up his own. As he handed the man his gloves, he asked another employee to get him something to eat. It was wonderful to see your employees being the hands and feet of Jesus, and that my son was able to witness it all. Thank you for putting your money where your mouth is.[36]

Meadows said he had no idea that anyone was watching or that anyone took a photograph. "She was in tears," he said. "She was very appreciative for what I had done—and she said she used it as a teaching moment for her son."[37]

So why is Chick-fil-A so generous? Well, Mark told me it's the same reason they gave away all those chicken sandwiches during the previous year's blizzard. "It all comes from Truett Cathy and the Cathy family and the principles Chick-fil-A has been established on," he said.[38]

And those principles are "to glorify God by being a faithful steward of all that is entrusted to us and to have a positive influence on all who come into contact with Chick-fil-A."[39]

Chick-fil-A is definitely not your average fast-food restaurant. "It's a different culture than most places," Pitt said. "Within Chick-fil-A you have the freedom to be that kind of person."[40]

No one quite knows for sure what happened to the young man who walked into the Chick-fil-A on that bitterly cold day. His whereabouts are something of a mystery.

Meadows said he'd never seen the man before then and has not seen him since, leading some to wonder just who it was that came by 4620 Highway 280.

"Do not forget to entertain strangers," the book of Hebrews reminds us. "For by so doing some have unwittingly entertained angels" (Heb. 13:2, NKJV). And some might have served them a chicken sandwich and waffle fries.

THE GLORY OF BUSINESS

I believe we Deplorables are a generous people by nature. How can a God-blessed people not be generous? Part of living a Christ-centered life is being there to lend a helping hand.

Awhile back one of my readers in the Midwest sent me a tender story about a farmer who died just before the harvest. Bill Hofmann worked the land in Sutton, Nebraska, for years. He was the kind of guy who would give you the shirt off his back. The townsfolk were shaken to their core when Bill was killed in a farming accident—at just 60 years old.

They buried Bill in the cemetery behind the Reformed Church. He left behind his wife, Pat, two kids, and a grandbaby. He also left behind crops that had to be harvested. While the family mourned, a group of about fifty friends and neighbors and church folks set about to finish what Bill had started. They toiled the better part of a day, and by sunset they had completed the task. They were covered in dirt and sweat—and bone tired. But they had harvested more than five hundred acres of crops across three fields. [41]

The good Samaritans in Sutton, Nebraska, demonstrated not just love for their fellow man, but they also demonstrated the concept of an honest day's work.

We Deplorables are hard workers who understand the value of a day's work. We're not out there looking for a handout or a hand up. It's that "early to bed, early to rise" mentality. It's a value taught to children at a young age—whether it's making up the bed or taking out the trash.

It's that well-worn philosophy—give a man a fish and you feed him for a day; teach a man to fish and he'll invite you over for a fish fry. But if a fellow is short the fixin's, well, you can be sure somebody will bring a mess of hush puppies.

John D. Rockefeller, one of the wealthiest men in American history, demonstrated that philosophy in his business and spiritual life. Rockefeller was a devout Baptist—a man who came to know Christ as a youngster and in adulthood would read the Bible daily, attend prayer meetings, and even lead a Bible study.

In his fascinating biography of Rockefeller, author Ron Chernow said the titan "possessed a form of calling in both religion and business, with Christianity and capitalism forming the twin pillars of his life."[42]

Rockefeller considered making money to be a gift from God.[43] "It has seemed as if I was favored and got increase because the Lord knew that I was going to turn around and give it back," Rockefeller once said.[44]

Every aspect of business is meant to ennoble all people—owners, employees, and customers alike. Creativity and innovation make us feel alive and draw us closer to God, who is the ultimate Creator.

Productive work builds strength and stability into people's lives, and gives a satisfaction no welfare check can deliver. Workplaces become important communities where people flourish as team members and friends. Customers benefit from our products, especially if our focus is on excellence and fair pricing. We support other industries and businesses by buying their equipment, hiring consultants, and all the other things it takes to stay current in the marketplace. And we set an example for our kids and communities of the value of work. Now you're probably thinking, "Todd's cheese has done slid off the cracker." But just think about it. Productive work builds strength and stability into people's lives. A hard day's work gives a man the kind of satisfaction that a welfare check can't deliver.

God is no stranger to the principles of business. He created and invested in each one of us. He built a world and infused it with incredible value and worth. And He desires to see a return from His investment—relationship, love, worship, and honor flowing back to Him.

Take a look at how many of Jesus's parables involved business. He told stories about:

- Venture capitalists (Matt. 25:14–30)
- Field bosses (Matt. 20:1–16)
- Gem merchants (Matt. 13:45–46)
- Small-business people (Matt. 13:47–50)
- Day laborers (Matt. 20:1–16)
- Wealthy entrepreneurs (Luke 12:16–21)
- Widows living on small amounts of money (Luke 21:1–4)
- Farmers (Matt. 13:24–30)
- Middle managers (Luke 16:1–13)
- CEOs (Matt. 24:45–51)
- Regular employees (Matt. 18:31)
- Hirings (Matt. 20:1–16)
- Firings (Matt. 21:33–44; Matt. 25:24–30)
- Dishonest employees (Luke 16:1–13)

+ Risk-averse money managers (Matt. 25:14–30)

+ Career advancement (Luke 19:12–27)

+ Debt forgiveness (Matt. 18:21–35)

He even said, "Where your treasure is, there will your heart be also" (Matt. 6:21, MEV).

Why does business matter to God? Because business displays some of His glory through humanity. And when business is done right, it also brings glory to a country.

Consider this: Solomon wrote that, "When righteous men rejoice, there is great glory; but when the wicked rise, a man hides himself" (Prov. 28:12, MEV). This applies directly to business. When righteous laws govern the land—such as a fair amount of taxation and regulation—businesses flourish. The "glory" of the economy rises as people create jobs, earn more, innovate more, and are rewarded for their labor. There's enough glory to go around!

People within those businesses, like at Chick-fil-A, also rise to a greater level of productivity, earning, satisfaction, generosity, and innovation. Righteous business practices unleash the glory of individuals and nations in a way nothing else is designed to do.

The flip side is that when the wicked rise, "[people] hide [themselves]." Does this mean they hide under rocks or tables or beds? No. It means the glory God intended for them to display is never realized. They are afraid to shine, afraid to flourish, afraid to succeed.

I'd say that's exactly what happened under eight years of liberal tyranny. Because of burdensome tax and regulation, not to mention moral terrorism, people hid their gifts, their talents, their thoughts and ideas.

How many flower shops and small businesses were not started because a potential entrepreneur feared being driven out of business for having politically incorrect beliefs? The glory of our nation has dimmed, just as the Bible said would happen to any nation that allowed wickedness to prevail.

THE MOM-AND-POP BAKERS

The owners of a certain mom-and-pop bakery learned there is a significant price to pay for following their religious beliefs. Aaron and Melissa Klein, the owners of Sweet Cakes by Melissa, were ordered to pay $135,000 in damages to a lesbian couple after they refused to bake them a wedding cake in 2013.[45]

The Oregon Bureau of Labor and Industry (BOLI) awarded $60,000 to Laurel Bowman-Cryer and $75,000 in damages to Rachel Bowman-Cryer.[46] "This case is not about a wedding cake or a marriage," the final order read. "It is about a business's refusal to serve someone because of their sexual orientation. Under Oregon law, that is illegal."[47]

According to the BOLI, the lesbian couple suffered great angst. One of the women "felt depressed and questioned whether there was something inherently wrong with the sexual orientation she was born with." They said she had "difficulty controlling her emotions and cried a lot."[48]

The other woman "experienced extreme anger, outrage, embarrassment, exhaustion, frustration, intense sorrow and shame" simply because the Kleins refused to provide them with a wedding cake.[49]

Wow. That must have been one heck of a cake. I've never heard of anyone being traumatized by frosting.

The state of Oregon seemed to be sending a stern warning to Christian business owners like the Kleins. "Within Oregon's public accommodations law is the basic principle of human decency that every person, regardless of their sexual orientation, has the freedom to fully participate in society," the ruling stated. "The ability to enter public places, to shop, to dine, to move about unfettered by bigotry."[50]

Labor Commissioner Brad Avakian was responsible for leading this government-sponsored political jihad against the Kleins—with the sole intent of forcing them to change their religious beliefs. "The goal is never to shut down a business. The goal is to rehabilitate," he said in 2013.[51]

Does the Bureau of Labor and Industry truly believe that Christians who want to follow the teachings of their faith are bigots? It certainly seems to me the only entity guilty of unfettered bigotry is the Oregon Bureau of Labor and Industry.

Since the day they turned away the lesbian couple's business, the Kleins have suffered greatly. Their business was subjected to boycotts and pickets. LGBT activists and their supporters threatened any wedding vendor that did business with Sweet Cakes by Melissa.

Mrs. Klein told me her five children were subjected to death threats—*death threats*—simply because their parents refused to participate in a same-sex wedding. That doesn't sound very tolerant to me.[52]

Eventually the bullying became so severe the family had to shut down their retail store, and Mr. Klein had to take a job picking up garbage. Today Mrs. Klein continues to make cakes in her home. "We were just running our business the best we could, following the Lord's example," she said. "I'm just blown away by the ruling. They are punishing us for not participating in the wedding."[53]

Mr. Klein said he plans on appealing the ruling and had harsh words for BOLI Commissioner Brad Avakian. "This man has no power over me," Klein said. "He seems to think he can tell me to be quiet. That doesn't sit well with me, and I refuse to comply."[54]

The Kleins were also slapped with a gag order, banning them from speaking publicly about their refusal to participate in or bake wedding cakes for same-sex marriages. They were ordered to "cease and desist from publishing, circulating, issuing or displaying, or causing to be published, circulated, issued or displayed, any communication, notice, advertisement or sign of any kind to the effect that any of the accommodations, advantages, facilities, services or privileges of a place of public accommodation will be refused, withheld from or denied to, or that any discrimination will be made against, any person on account of sexual orientation."[55]

On a side note here, I predicted that once gay marriage was legalized, LGBTQIA supporters would attempt to silence all dissent. The Klein case has demonstrated once again that the Left would let gay rights trump religious liberty. Other Christian business owners should pay close attention.

The Kleins had a choice—to obey the government or to obey God. They chose God—and now they must pay the price.

One final note. In 2016 Commissioner Avakian was defeated in his bid to be Oregon's Secretary of State. It was the first time a Republican had been elected to a statewide office since 2002.[56] Voters saw Avakian for who he really was—an anti-Christian bully with no regard for the US Constitution. Nobody likes a bully, especially a liberal bully.

Deplorables, we cannot allow the Left to tyrannize American businesses anymore. I hope you will take these next ideas to heart and do everything you can as a business owner, employee, or consumer to reward businesses that bring glory to this country and stand with those facing persecution and shaming for their beliefs.

MARCHING ORDERS

1. **"Eat Mor Chikin"!** It's more than a slogan. Let's frequent businesses and establishments that share our values. Be sure to tell them how much you appreciate the way they run their businesses. Be intentional. Companies such as Brim's Snack Foods, In-N-Out Burger, and Hobby Lobby publicly proclaim their faith in Christ. It may cost a few extra dollars, but it's worth it to shop at a place where we know the profits are going to a good cause and good people.

2. **Get organized.** When faith-based companies come under attack from activists, organize a resistance team. Remember what

happened during the great Chick-fil-A war a few years back?
Customers staged Chick-fil-A days and overwhelmed restaurants
with food orders and cheerful hearts. It also sent a message to
future activists that there are more of us than there are of them. If
they want to try to flex their muscle and put a place out of business
for honoring Christ, we'll flex our muscle right back.

3. **Boycott.** Speaking of flexing our muscles, boycotts work. When
Target announced that it would allow men who "identify" as women
to use the bathrooms and changing rooms of their choice, the
American Family Association launched a massive boycott. Hundreds
of thousands signed on. And the result smacked Target's bottom line.
Its stock price cratered.[57] Likewise, when the NFL refused to crack
down on players disrespecting the national anthem, people changed
the channel. To this day the NFL refuses to admit the near-historic
ratings drop in 2016 was because of the national anthem issue.[58]
Target is trying to claw back without admitting their mistake.[59]

Chapter 10

YOU WILL BE FORCED TO COMPLY

ONE OF THE nation's most prominent evangelical leaders issued a dire warning for the nation in the aftermath of the Supreme Court's 5–4 ruling on homosexual marriage.

"I believe God could bring judgment upon America," Franklin Graham told me. "You better be ready, and you better be prepared because it's coming. There will be persecution of Christians for our stand."[1]

What was a warning in 2015 is now a statement of fact. Welcome to the age of pitchforks and torches, America.

Just so we're clear, the Supreme Court may have redefined marriage, but God hasn't redefined anything. I know that may be a politically incorrect thing to say, but then again, this book is not for the politically correct.

Whether it was intentional or not, the Supreme Court ruling declared open season on people of faith. Christian business owners have been targeted. So have Christian students and members of the clergy. And this is no surprise. Read the chilling words from the dissent of Justice John G. Roberts Jr.:

> Hard questions arise when people of faith exercise religion in ways that may be seen to conflict with the new right to same-sex marriage—when, for example, a religious college provides married student housing only to opposite-sex married couples, or a religious adoption agency declines to place children with same-sex married couples....Unfortunately, people of faith can take no comfort in the treatment they receive from the majority today.[2]

Supreme Court Justice Samuel Alito also warned in his dissent that the ruling could lead to a conflict between religious liberty and those on the Left.

"By imposing its own views on the entire country, the majority facilitates the marginalization of the many Americans who have traditional ideas," he wrote. "Recalling the harsh treatment of gays and lesbians in the past, some may think that turn-about is fair play. But if that sentiment prevails, the Nation will experience bitter and lasting wounds."[3]

That sentiment has indeed prevailed. Churches and faith-based businesses are facing lawsuits and government investigations. But it won't stop there. Pastors who refuse to perform gay marriages and who preach from the Bible should prepare for hate-crime charges. Eventually all dissent will be silenced by the government and LGBT activists.

Senator Tammy Baldwin, a Democrat from Wisconsin, told MSNBC that Americans do not have an individual right to religious liberty. Newsbusters transcribed her remarks.

> Certainly the first amendment [sic] says that in institutions of faith that there is absolute power to, you know, to observe deeply held religious beliefs. But I don't think it extends far beyond that. We've seen the set of arguments play out in issues such as access to contraception. Should it be the individual pharmacist whose religious beliefs guides whether a prescription is filled, or in this context, they're talking about expanding this far beyond our churches and synagogues to businesses and individuals across this country. I think there are clear limits that have been set in other contexts and we ought to abide by those in this new context across America.[4]

Baldwin is not alone in her thinking. Even before the same-sex marriage ruling, a message from a government official's Twitter account called defenders of religious freedom "Nazis."[5] And Wyoming Equality argued that churches that do not support same-sex marriage should lose their tax-exempt status.[6]

Broadway stars too have faced militant attacks. John Carroll, a self-described Broadway performer, penned an open letter to Broadway actress Bailey Hanks, publicly shaming her for—brace yourself—eating a Chick-fil-A sandwich. "Just a reminder: You were plucked out of obscurity by a team of gay men, gay men who not only believed in you and gave you the chance of a lifetime but treated you with loving kindness and respect—the same gay men you discriminated against by publicly supporting Chick-fil-A," he wrote.[7]

Oh, for the love of Bob Fosse. Get a hold of yourself, man. It's a chicken sandwich.

But that's the world we live in. You will be made to care. Thought crimes will be punished. Tolerance is not allowed. Consider these examples:

+ A small-town Indiana pizza joint was forced to temporarily close its doors after they announced they would not cater a gay wedding. The owners of Memories Pizza were deluged with horrific threats and messages that were too inappropriate to write in this book.[8] A high school softball coach suggested burning down the restaurant.[9] How's that for tolerance?

+ A former Ford Motor Company engineer claimed in a lawsuit he was fired for posting an antigay comment on the company's website, the *Huffington Post* reported. Thomas Banks, the former employee, wrote that Ford should be "thoroughly ashamed" for promoting a program for LGBT workers.[10]

If only this was the worst of it. Similar incidents are being reported all across this nation.

PRISON CHAPLAINS BANNED

It wasn't so much a choice as it was a demand. Chaplain David Wells was told he could either sign a state-mandated document promising to never tell inmates that homosexuality is "sinful" or else the Kentucky Department of Juvenile Justice would terminate his involvement as a religious volunteer.[11]

"We could not sign that paper," Chaplain Wells told me in a telephone call from his home in Kentucky. "It broke my heart."[12]

The Kentucky Department of Juvenile Justice did terminate his volunteer involvement as a chaplain, ending thirteen years of ministry to underage inmates at the Warren County Regional Juvenile Detention Center.

"We sincerely appreciate your years of service and dedication to the youth served by this facility," wrote Superintendent Gene Wade in a letter to Wells. "However, due to your decision, based on your religious convictions, that you cannot comply with the requirements outlined in DJJ Policy 912, Section IV, Paragraph H, regarding the treatment of LGBTQI youth, I must terminate your involvement as a religious volunteer."[13]

Wells said that every volunteer in his church received the letter, as did a Baptist church in a nearby community. The Kentucky regulation states that volunteers working with juveniles "shall not refer to juveniles by using derogatory language in a manner that conveys bias towards or hatred of the LGBTQI community. DJJ staff, volunteers, interns, and contractors shall not imply or tell LGBTQI juveniles that they are abnormal, deviant, sinful, or that they can or should change their sexual orientation or gender identity."[14]

For years Wells and his team conducted volunteer worship services and counseling to troubled young people, many of whom had been abused. "I sat across the table from a sixteen-year-old boy who was weeping and broken over the life he was in," Wells said. "He had been abused as a child and had turned to alcohol and drugs to cope. He wanted to know if there was any hope for him."[15]

Wells said he had been abused as a young child, so he knew he could answer this young man's question. "I was able to look at him and tell him the saving power of Jesus Christ that delivered me could deliver him," he said.[16]

But under the state's 2014 antidiscrimination policy Wells would not be allowed to have such a discussion should it delve into LGBT issues. "They told us we could not preach that homosexuality is a sin—period," Wells told me. "We would not have even been able to read Bible verses that dealt with LGBT issues."[17]

For the record, Wells said they've never used hateful or derogatory comments when dealing with the young inmates. "They are defining hateful or derogatory as meaning what the Bible says about homosexuality," he told me.[18]

Mat Staver, founder of the legal firm Liberty Counsel, is representing Wells. He said the state's ban on biblical counseling is unconstitutional religious discrimination. "There is no question there is a purging under way," Staver told me. "The dissenters in the recent Supreme Court decision on gay marriage warned us this would happen."[19]

Staver is demanding the state immediately reinstate Wells as well as the other volunteer ministers. "By restricting speech which volunteers are allowed to use while ministering to youth detainees, the State of Kentucky and the Kentucky Department of Juvenile Justice have violated the protections given to private speech through the First Amendment and the Kentucky Constitution," Liberty Counsel stated in a letter to state officials. The policy "requires affirmation of homosexuality as a precondition for ministers providing spiritual guidance to troubled youth, and singles out a particular theological viewpoint as expressly disfavored by the State of Kentucky."[20]

In other words, Kentucky has a religious litmus test when it comes to homosexuality—and according to a letter sent to Liberty Counsel, they aren't going to back down. The DJJ said the regulation "is neutral as to religion and requires respectful language toward youth by all staff, contractors and volunteers."[21]

State senator Gerald Neal, a Democrat, dared Christians to challenge the law in court. "I'm just disappointed that the agendas by some are so narrow that they disregard the rights of others," he told the newspaper. "Let them sue and let the courts settle it."[22]

Among those backing Wells was the American Pastors Network (APN). "Pastors and all Americans must wake up to the reality of expanding efforts to 'cleanse' our nation of all moral truth," APN President Sam Rohrer said in a statement. "When pastors and all Christians...are forced by government agents to renounce sharing the very reality of 'sin,' they are in fact being prohibited from sharing the healing and life-changing potential of redemption."[23]

Folks, I warned you this would happen. The Christian purge has begun, and it's only a matter of time before all of us will be forced to make the same decision Chaplain Wells had to make. Will you follow God or the government?

Sadly there's more.

GOVERNMENT UNION ATTEMPTS TO FIRE DUCK DYNASTY FANS

A union representing federal employees at Eglin Air Force base in Florida demanded that two senior management officials be removed from their posts after someone complained because they put decals on their personal trucks supporting *Duck Dynasty* star Phil Robertson.

Alan Cooper, the executive vice president of the local chapter of the American Federation of Government Employees, said one of the officials also displayed the "I Support Phil" decals in his office and offered them to subordinates. "The BUE (bargaining union employee) was clearly offended and disgusted that a senior management official would display the decal on their pod," read an e-mail Cooper wrote.[24]

"We took offense," Cooper told me. "These two particular individuals have a great amount of influence over individuals who may be gay, who may be African-American, and we have a concern they should not be in a position to exert that influence when it comes to promotions."[25]

In an e-mail that was sent to union members, Cooper said the *Duck Dynasty* decal may be a violation of the Civil Rights Act of 1964. "Phil Robertson has made disparaging remarks against a vast array of people, which created a firestorm in the media in the recent past," Cooper wrote.[26]

He was referring to comments Robertson made in *GQ* magazine about homosexuality and his personal observations about the pre-Civil Rights era.[27] A&E briefly suspended Robertson from his popular reality television show. But the network reversed its decision after they were overwhelmed by supporters of the program.[28]

Cooper told me he wanted the two civilian managers at the Air Force base removed from their positions. "I don't know how long these individuals harbored these views. Could they have impacted employment opportunities for folks that have been disparaged by the likes of a Phil Robertson?" he said.[29]

Regardless, he wants the *Duck Dynasty* fans dealt with, noting "it's definitely

100 percent inappropriate for an organization that espouses a zero tolerance policy" to condone such activity. "If it's zero tolerance, it's zero tolerance for everybody," he said, referring to the military's antidiscrimination policies.[30]

I spoke with one of the individuals being targeted by the government union. He asked that I not disclose his name. He rejected the accusations that he was a racist or homophobe because he supports *Duck Dynasty*. "My intent was not to offend anybody," the individual told me. "My intent was to support the show and to show support for [Robertson's] Christian values."[31]

The individual told me he was especially upset after union workers took photographs of his truck and his license plate and e-mailed the images to other union members. That e-mail was reportedly sent to hundreds and hundreds of personnel. "I see the e-mail that went out accusing me and my boss of being racist," he said. "That couldn't be farther from the truth. I'm pro-family. I'm pro-life. I don't have a problem with anybody who doesn't agree with me."[32]

When we spoke, he said he had absolutely no plans to remove the decal from his truck. "I'm not taking it off," he said. "If they want to make me retire early, that's what I'll do. But I'm not backing down."[33]

The civilian worker told me it's a First Amendment issue. He said there are plenty of vehicles on the military base that are plastered with all sorts of stickers. He said he disagreed with 90 percent of what President Obama believes in, but he never asked anyone to remove an Obama decal from their vehicle. For him, "It's a freedom of speech issue," he said.[34]

And that's exactly what the Air Force believes it is. They investigated the claims the union made and determined that the two civilian workers were well within their rights to support *Duck Dynasty*. "Brigadier General Dave Harris is not taking any action against the individual as the display of such a bumper sticker is considered legally protected speech under the First Amendment," said Andy Bourland, director of public affairs at the military base.[35]

Bourland also told me they looked into the incident involving the decals in the worker's office. They also decided not to take action in that incident.

Eli Craft is a member of the union, and he told me he is furious at how union leadership handled the incident. "It was extremely, extremely upsetting," he said. "The community we live in is a very faith-based community. For someone to say this individual was offensive and if you support him you can't manage or lead a diverse workplace, it blew my mind."[36]

Craft had nothing but praise for the two managers. He said they are longtime veterans of the military and volunteer in the community. "They are Christians. That's how they live their lives," he said.[37]

And Craft said there are plenty of *Duck Dynasty* fans around the Florida

Panhandle. "The *Duck Dynasty* folks represent a lot of the folks who hunt and fish and who are Christians in the Panhandle," he said. "That family and that program represent a way of life we see here."[38]

Tony Perkins, president of the Family Research Council, said the government union wants to shut down free speech. "Could you imagine if someone demanded someone take an Obama bumper sticker off because President Obama is intolerant to orthodox Christian views?" Perkins asked. "Where does this stop?"[39]

He said their attack on the two *Duck Dynasty* fans is an example of the Left's intimidation and intolerance. "They do not want anyone to have a choice to express themselves in a way that counters their own viewpoint, and that's very dangerous to our republic," Perkins said. "This goes back to the underlying emphasis and goal—not to debate the merits of whether someone is right or not; it's to shut down the debate. End of story. No discussion."[40]

CHRISTIAN BUSINESS OWNERS TOLD TO LEAVE RELIGION AT HOME

The same intolerance was on full display in Kentucky. The Human Rights Commission in Lexington had a clear message for Christian business owners who object to providing goods or services to LGBT organizations: leave your religion at home.

"It would be safe to do so, yes," executive director Raymond Sexton told me. "Or in this case you can find yourself two years down the road and you're still involved in a legal battle because you did not do so."[41]

In October 2014 a Lexington Human Rights Commission hearing examiner issued a recommended ruling that the owner of a T-shirt company violated a local ordinance against sexual-orientation discrimination.[42] "It was a landmark decision," Sexton said. "This is a very important ruling for us."[43]

The examiner concluded that Blaine Adamson of Hands On Originals broke the law in 2012 by declining to print shirts promoting the Lexington Pride Festival. The festival organizers, the Gay and Lesbian Services Organization, subsequently filed a complaint.[44]

Alliance Defending Freedom (ADF), a law firm that specializes in religious liberty cases, represented Adamson, a devout Christian. "No one should be forced by the government or by another citizen to endorse or promote ideas with which they disagree," said ADF attorney Jim Campbell. "Blaine declined the request to print the shirts not because of any characteristic of the people who asked for them, but because of the message that the shirts would communicate."[45]

ADF also pointed out that Hands On Originals has a history of doing business with the LGBT community as well has hiring LGBT workers. But Sexton told me the law is the law. And in Lexington it's against the law to discriminate against the LGBT community, regardless of religious beliefs. "We're not telling someone how to feel with respect to religion, but the law is pretty clear that if you operate a business to the public, you need to provide your services to people regardless of race, color, sex, and in this case sexual orientation,"[46] Sexton said.

The hearing examiner recommended the following punishment: First, Hands On Originals cannot discriminate against individuals because of their sexual orientation or gender identity. In other words, the T-shirt company must service LGBT customers—no questions asked. The examiner also ordered Adamson to attend "diversity training" conducted by—wait for it—the Lexington Human Rights Commission.[47]

Take just a moment and let that sink in. A Christian business owner is being ordered to attend diversity training because of his religious beliefs. That's a pretty frightening concept and a mighty dangerous precedent.

"That is certainly one of the dangers of an order like that, for the government to step in and order [what is essentially] a reeducation of its citizens," Campbell told me. "That's a dangerous precedent for the government to engage in."[48]

In essence, the Human Rights Commission is telling Christian business owners they have to change their religious beliefs. It's the idea that the government knows best and Christians must reorient their beliefs.

Sexton, who said he is a Christian, said he's just upholding the law. "The law in Lexington is pretty clear," he said. "You cannot discriminate against people on the basis of sexual orientation or gender identity. Regardless of what your religious beliefs are, if you have a public business, then that's how you have to operate."[49]

It seems to me if a Christian business owner does not want to do business with an LGBT organization, that should be his or her right. And should an LGBT business choose not to do business with a church, that should be their right as well.

There's no denying there's a conflict. Even Sexton admits that. "Our local law has exemptions for religious organizations," he said. "However, religious organizations are narrowly defined. You actually have to be some sort of religious institution to get the exemption."[50]

Meanwhile, a growing number of hardworking Christian business owners are getting caught in the crosshairs of the culture war. "There does tend to be a trend toward that," attorney Campbell told me. "Business owners are being targeted for simply trying to operate their business consistent with their beliefs."[51]

STUDENTS OPPOSED TO LGBT AGENDA
SHAMED IN CLASSROOM

Teenagers at a California high school were publicly shamed for disagreeing with speakers allowed to push an LGBT agenda during an English class, according to several upset parents. The Queer Straight Alliance (QSA) at Acalanes High School in Lafayette lectured students in several ninth-grade English classes about LGBT issues, according to Brad Dacus, president of the Pacific Justice Institute (PJI), which is representing the parents.[52]

During the class the students, ages fourteen and fifteen, were instructed to stand in a circle. Then they were grilled about their personal beliefs and their parents' beliefs on homosexuality, PJI alleges. "The QSA had students step forward to demonstrate whether they believed that being gay was a choice and whether their parents would be accepting if they came out as gay," PJI stated. "Students who did not step forward were ridiculed and humiliated."[53]

PJI is a law firm that specializes in religious liberty cases. They are representing several of the freshman students' families, some of whom were angry because there was no parental notification of the LGBT lecture. "Singling out students for ridicule based on their moral or political beliefs is a Marxist tactic that should have no place in the United States of America," Dacus said.[54]

During the lecture the Queer Student Alliance had students line up to demonstrate where they fell on the "gender spectrum."[55]

"It was an exercise in gender fluidity," the parent of one child told me. "They told the students that one day they could come to school feeling like a boy and the next day they could come to school feeling like a girl."[56]

Students were given a handout with LGBT terminology, including terms such as *pan-sexual*, *demi-boy*, and *gray gender*.[57] *Demi-boy/girl* is defined as "someone who only partially identifies as a man or woman." *Gray gender* defines "those who feel as though they sort of fit inside the gender binary but that their gender is more hazy and undefined."[58]

"Acalanes High School and the district have defied common sense, ignored the law and broken parents' trust," PJI attorney Matthew McReynolds said in a prepared statement. "These administrators are acting like schoolyard bullies. If they think intimidation is going to work on us or these parents, they are greatly mistaken."[59]

"It was a public outing," one parent told me. "My child is being raised in a family with conservative values. We are a Christian family. What bothers me the most is the school is being dishonest and secretive about what's happening.

My son's value system and our belief system are not being respected on many levels."[60]

And on a very practical note, she wants to know why the Queer Student Alliance was allowed to take over an English class. "There's no other club at the high school that gets face time in front of freshman English classes for an entire period," the parent said.[61]

So why did Acalanes High School out students who may not agree with every facet of the LGBT agenda? Superintendent John Nickerson said it's all about tolerance. "The classroom instruction in question was part of a tolerance workshop led by peer educators under the supervision of teachers," Nickerson wrote to me in an e-mail.[62]

That's all well and good, but were the teenagers academically qualified to teach a class on issues like "gender fluidity"? Why weren't the teachers teaching the class? And what about the allegations that students were bullied by the Queer Student Alliance?

"We are aware of the concerns and allegations raised by two parents and the Pacific Justice Institute," he wrote. "We are investigating the situation, learning activities, and classroom environment."[63]

This happens to be the same high school that invited a "pleasure activist" from Planned Parenthood to teach sex education to the freshman class. Students were encouraged to ask each other questions such as, "Is it okay if I take my pants off?"[64]

The parent I spoke to bristled at the notion the LGBT class was about tolerance. "They are tolerant of everyone except people who have Christian values," she told me.[65]

PJI sent a letter to the school district demanding an explanation of what happened. They believe the classroom lecture violated the students' privacy rights. "It should be self-evident that, as a fundamental privacy right, students cannot be 'outed' during class time by being made to declare their beliefs and feelings about sensitive sexual matters, any more than a student could be required to announce their sexual orientation," PJI wrote in their letter to the school district.[66]

Has it really come to this, America—forcing students to declare their allegiance to the LGBT agenda? Maybe schools should just stick to teaching English in English class.

COUNTY CLERK RESIGNS RATHER THAN ISSUE GAY MARRIAGE LICENSES

Linda Barnette issued marriage licenses in Grenada County, Mississippi, for twenty-four years. But after the Supreme Court's ruling on same-sex marriage, she was a clerk no more.

"The Supreme Court's decision violates my core values as a Christian," she wrote. "My final authority is the Bible. I cannot in all good conscience issue marriage licenses to same-sex couples under my name because the Bible clearly teaches that homosexuality is contrary to God's plan and purpose for marriage and family. I choose to obey God rather than man."[67]

Another worker was appointed to replace Barnette.[68] "I told my supervisors awhile back if it happened [if the Supreme Court legalized same-sex marriage], I would tender my resignation," Barnette told me. "I had already decided in my heart that I could not issue marriage licenses to same-sex couples. It's my Christian belief. As a follower of Christ, I could not do it. The Bible teaches it is contrary to His plan."[69]

Barnette is a Southern Baptist, and her husband once helped Franklin Graham with his national festivals.[70] So when it came to choosing between her job and her faith, there never was any real debate.

FLORIDA CITY WAGES SOVIET-STYLE CRACKDOWN ON CHURCHES

A government crackdown on churches had Christians in Lake Worth, Florida, wondering if they live in the United States or the former Soviet Union.

Churches in Lake Worth, population 36,000, were ordered to acquire a business license.[71] As if the church has to get the government's permission to preach and pray.

But wait. It gets worse, folks.

City officials were so concerned about one congregation that they dispatched a code enforcement officer cloaked in a hoodie to spy on a church that was meeting in a coffeehouse.[72]

Folks, it's like the plot of a Cold War spy novel.

"Government employees are public servants and prohibited by the Constitution from inhibiting religious freedom," said Mat Staver of Liberty Counsel. "That is a far cry from sneaking around and into a church and acting like KGB agents."[73]

Staver called on city leaders to immediately rescind the business license mandate on churches. He is also representing Common Ground Church, the congregation the city's investigator targeted.[74]

The church owned and operated a coffeehouse in downtown Lake Worth. For several months it used the coffeehouse for a weekly worship service. Prior to that the congregation rented space in other buildings in the community.[75]

Pastor Mike Olive told me there had not been any problems until he had an encounter with Andy Amoroso, a city commissioner. "After we opened up the coffee bar and started doing services, I heard that he told people we were anti-gay," Olive said. "So I went to his shop to ask him about that."[76]

I reached out to Amoroso, but he did not return my telephone calls.

Pastor Olive told me he tried to convey to Amoroso that the church's message is to love God and love people. "Our message to the gay community is the same as it is to the straight community," he said.[77]

The commissioner, Olive said, did not seem to appreciate his message. "He pointed at me and said, 'Listen, you better not have a church down there," Olive told me.[78]

By the strangest of coincidences, a code enforcement officer showed up for a Sunday service not long after the meeting with Amoroso. He was wearing a hoodie and had a concealed video camera, according to the letter Liberty Counsel sent to the city.[79]

The code enforcement officer's notes read like something out of a KGB report, according to Liberty Counsel. He "walked back to the Coffee Bar and was able to visualize...what appeared to be a ministry in progress," his report said. He documented how he observed "people holding what appeared to be bibles or religious books as one had a cross on it" and "what appeared to be a ministry in progress."[80]

I'm surprised the code enforcement officer didn't call up the National Guard for reinforcements.

The officer wrote that he was "able to capture on [his] city phone a video which will be attached to this case file for future court presentation."[81]

It's pretty shocking stuff for a city that prides itself on being a tolerant, multicultural city. But as we all know, tolerance and diversity do not extend to Christians. "It was pretty shocking," Pastor Olive said. "We had no prior warning."[82]

The following Sunday a city employee showed up again and told the church it had one week to vacate the building. They were accused of operating a church in a business rental property without a Lake Worth business license.[83]

For the record, the church was licensed only to sell java, not preach Jesus.

William Waters, the city's community sustainability director, told me they have nothing against the church. They were simply responding to a complaint. "We had a complaint that a gathering of people was taking place there in the form of a church," he said. "We investigated that and determined that, yes, there were people gathered there."[84]

So if 115 people gather for coffee, that's OK. But if they gather for worship, it's against the law?

"We have to treat everybody the same," Waters said. "We couldn't give preferential treatment to churches versus other businesses."[85]

And in the city's opinion, a church is, in fact, a business—just like a grocery store, a Waffle House, or an adult novelty shop. So why all the super-secret spy stuff? Why send an investigator to infiltrate a worship service? Why not just call the pastor and explain the rules and regulations?

If the case were to go to the special magistrate, Waters told me, evidence would have to be documented to show what the city worker found when he visited that Sunday. Waters said every business in the community received letters about the permits and fees, including churches.[86]

Joan Abell, pastor of the First Presbyterian Church, told the *Lake Worth Tribune* she was troubled by the city regulations.[87] First Presbyterian has existed for ninety-nine years and they've never needed a license, she told the newspaper. "Where do you all of a sudden say the church has to have a license to gather and pray?" she asked.[88]

Waters could not tell me how many churches had complied with the city's demands.[89] Local news accounts indicate the First Baptist Church paid nearly five hundred dollars in fees to the city.[90]

Staver said the city's actions violate the First Amendment to the US Constitution, the Florida Constitution, the Florida Religious Freedom Restoration Act, and the federal Religious Land Uses and Institutionalized Persons Act. "Churches are not businesses and need not obtain such licenses," Staver wrote in a letter to the city.[91]

Waters said any church that refuses to comply could be shut down by the fire department. "There's a variety of things that could happen if you don't comply with the use and occupancy requirement," he said.[92]

As for Pastor Olive, he had one message for the city leaders. "We just want to urge the city—don't allow God and our faith to be zoned out of downtown."[93]

It appears to me that this is a standoff that could use a healthy dose of all that multicultural tolerance and diversity that Lake Worth takes pride in.

THEY SPIT ON A PRIEST!

There were G-strings galore at gay pride celebrations across the fruited plain as scantily clad celebrants took to the streets to herald the Supreme Court's decision to redefine marriage.

Supporters of LGBTQIA marriages waved rainbow-colored flags from San Francisco to New York City. Unfortunately the festivities in the Big Apple turned ugly.

Father Jonathan Morris was walking near Broadway, wearing his cleric's collar, when he stumbled upon the gay pride parade. Father Jonathan, who is also a Fox News contributor, tweeted what happened: "Two men walked by and spat on me," he wrote.[94]

They spit on a priest!

What kind of a person hurls their sputum at a priest? What kind of a human being does that?

But instead of responding with anger, Father Jonathan responded with grace. "The two men who spat on me are probably very good [men] caught up in excitement and past resentment," he wrote. "Most in that parade would not do that."[95]

He dismissed their act of ugliness as simply being caught up in the moment. "Oh well…I deserve worse," he wrote.[96]

In a way, it's a modern-day parable. Those who preach tolerance are the least tolerant of all. But Father Jonathan demonstrated that he not only preaches tolerance, but he also practices it.

The writer John Zmirak wondered in 2015 where the attacks on Christians would eventually lead. "History teaches that mass vilification rarely stops short of spilling blood," he wrote in an essay that appeared on the Stream. "If the media, the law and our elite institutions succeed in lumping Christian sexual morals in *with white racism*, how long will it be before believing Catholics, Protestants, Orthodox (and many religious minorities) find themselves labelled as members of 'extremist sects,' no more to be trusted with the care of their own children than the Branch Davidians were?"[97]

I don't expect you to approve of everything I do. I don't expect you to believe everything I believe. I don't even expect you to enjoy Southern delicacies like sweet potato pie or hush puppies. I don't expect you to listen to Hank or Reba or Dolly or Charlie.

How I choose to live my life is my business, and how you choose to live your life is your business. And that's pretty much what President Obama told us back when the Supreme Court legalized same-sex marriage. "I know that Americans of good will continue to hold a wide range of views on this issue," he said. "Opposition, in some cases, has been based on sincere and deeply held beliefs.

All of us who welcome today's news should be mindful of that fact and recognize different viewpoints, revere our deep commitment to religious freedom."[98]

As the folks over at Breitbart so eloquently summed up, the president was essentially saying, "If you like your religion, you can keep your religion."[99]

It turns out I could've planted a crop of butter beans with all that fertilizer.

I am reminded of something the late Charles Colson wrote: "If we're not willing to fight this, even to the point of breaking the law, or refusing to recognize the law, then we will lose everything."[100]

Given the choice of obeying God or the government, I believe Christians will obey God—even if it costs them.

"The Supreme Court of the United States is not the final authority, nor is the culture itself," declared Dr. Ronnie Floyd, president of the Southern Baptist Convention, the nation's largest Protestant denomination. "The Bible is God's final authority about marriage, and on this book we stand."[101]

Dr. Floyd's powerful and provocative comments were met with thunderous applause and standing ovations from thousands of Southern Baptist messengers who met in Columbus, Ohio, the summer before the Supreme Court ruling.[102]

"While some evangelicals may be bowing down to the deception of the inclusiveness of same-sex marriage, we will not bow down nor will we be silent," Dr. Floyd declared.[103] "We do not need to redefine what God Himself has defined already."[104]

And from there Dr. Floyd went where few prominent pastors have gone before—a Supreme Court showdown. "America: We stand believing that marriage is the uniting of one man and one woman in covenant commitment for a lifetime," he said.[105] "We have believed this and do believe this and will continue to believe this as a convention of churches. We stand for biblical and traditional marriage."[106]

And that is what we must do.

MARCHING ORDERS

1. **Take inventory.** Have a lawyer review your church's bylaws and constitution regarding marriage policies and facility usage. Alliance Defending Freedom, First Liberty Institute, or Liberty Counsel would be great starting points.

2. **Confront the issue.** Encourage your pastor and church staff to address these issues from the pulpit and Sunday school classes or growth groups. Not every LGBT person is going to target you, your business, or your church. The activists are a small but

organized and well-financed group. They will be relentless. We must respond firmly but in a spirit of love.

3. **Be prepared to face persecution** if you stand up to the LGBT movement, especially in public schools. Just remember, you have rights too. You have a right to exclude your child from indoctrination. But there's a right way to approach the issue. First, go to your child's teacher, then the head of the teacher's department. If you still aren't satisfied, take the matter to the assistant principal and then the principal. At that point you have established that you follow protocol and have a legitimate concern. If that doesn't resolve the issue, call your school board office and ask to be placed on the agenda.

4. **Get involved.** It's very important for parents to be involved in the process. Much of the radical LGBT agenda is subtly inserted into the public school curriculum. Ask to see textbooks and training material. Don't take no for an answer. If they won't let you take the books home, schedule an appointment so you can read them in the classroom.

5. **Utilize social networking.** If you have a legitimate concern, post it on Facebook with the photographic evidence. Use Twitter, Pinterest, Instagram—get the word out! But be factual. Don't exaggerate. And don't be nasty. Just present the facts.

Chapter 11

BOYS AND GIRLS
AND ZI AND ZIR

I READILY ADMIT THAT I'm old school. When I was a child, God made only two genders: male and female. But this is the twenty-first century, and according to Facebook, there are now fifty-eight gender options—from cisgender to gender fluid.[1] But the biggest fight being waged is on the issue of transgenderism, and the LGBTQIA activists are pulling out all the stops.

I received a note one day from a reader who asked not to be identified. He told me he was an executive for a publishing company that provided storybooks to grade schools. He was alarmed at the number of books being produced for children under the age of seven that had to do with the LGBTQIA agenda.

At Mitchell Primary School in Kittery, Maine, teachers recently read a story about transgenderism to a bunch of five-year-olds. And the parents were never told about the nature of the story.[2] Talk about an example of a school district circumventing the rights and preferences of moms and dads. In what world do people think it's OK for teachers to discuss transgenderism with a bunch of children? Maybe they should stick to teaching kids how to read and write instead of deconstructing their God-given gender identity.

Back when I was a first-grader at Hope P. Sullivan Elementary School in Southaven, Mississippi, we read nursery rhymes about Jack and Jill going up a hill to fetch a pail of water and the rub-a-dub-dub story. But today, when Jack comes down, he's wearing Jill's dress and going by the name Jackie. And Lord only knows what the three men are doing in the tub.

Last year the Obama administration decided to drop a cultural atomic bomb by declaring that forcing people to use bathroom facilities based on their God-given plumbing was state-sponsored discrimination.[3] Four days later they dropped an even bigger one. The administration issued a directive requiring every public school in the nation to accommodate transgender students under Title IX guidelines.[4]

Boys who identify as girls and vice versa must be allowed to use the bathrooms, locker rooms, and shower stalls of their choosing. They must also be allowed to play on the sports teams of their choosing.

This is complete insanity.

School districts that dare defy the administration's directives could face lawsuits and lose millions of dollars in federal funding. Resistance, in other words, is futile.

"There is no room in our schools for discrimination of any kind, including discrimination against transgender students on the basis of their sex," former Attorney General Loretta Lynch said.[5]

I warned you in my book *God Less America* that the fight over transgenderism would be the next battleground. And here we are—a nation where boys who identify as girls have more rights than girls who were born biological girls.

"It's an outrageous attack on our Creator Himself, upon human sexuality and morality, and a further advancement of the flagrant attack on religious freedom in our culture," Southern Baptist Convention President Ronnie Floyd told me. "Sooner or later we have to determine that enough is enough. It's not going to change until Christians get involved in this battle."[6]

Donald Trump was asked to weigh in on *Fox & Friends*—should boys use the boys' room? "Right now I just don't have an opinion," he told the morning show hosts. "I would like the states to make that decision."[7]

Let's just hope President Trump has greater moral clarity than Candidate Trump.

Texas governor Greg Abbott vowed to fight the Obama administration's decree, telling a gathering of Republicans, "Obama is turning bathrooms into courtroom issues."[8] He added, "Our country is in crisis and Texas must lead the way forward."[9]

Abbott said he would work alongside the embattled governor of North Carolina, "and we are going to fight back."[10]

One of the most forceful rebukes came from Tennessee congresswoman Diane Black. "I believe the Obama administration is now directly responsible for endangering our students," she said. "It is worth noting that this directive does not carry the force of law and I would encourage Tennessee school officials to continue following their consciences."[11]

Family Research Council President Tony Perkins told me the decree should be "resisted with every legal and moral instrument we have available to us in this country."[12]

"Every parent, every school board in America should absolutely refuse to sacrifice the safety of their children for the threat of taking away nine federal pennies that make up every educational dollar," he said.[13]

That's the message from Penny Young Nance, president of Concerned Women for America. "The left always uses children to accomplish its goals of social reengineering," she said. "The adults closest to these children should decide what's best for all the children in the school. Safety and kindness should be the guiding principles, not threats from the bullies in Washington."[14]

The time has come for all Americans to stand up and defy this immoral agenda. If losing federal funding is the price we must pay to protect women and children, then so be it. We will not betray what we know to be true for the government's thirty pieces of silver.

As I mentioned before, not to speak is to speak; not to act is to act.

For far too long American pulpits have remained silent on controversial cultural issues. Preachers don't want to rock the boat. Parishioners don't want to cause trouble. They want to keep their good reputation in the community.

But now the country stands at the edge of a great moral abyss. And we must ask ourselves: Do we defy our leaders and save the nation, or do we keep the peace and sacrifice our children? Consider these stories from the front lines of America's sexual revolution.

A GENDER-NEUTRAL DAY ON ROCKY TOP

You'll like this story—because we win. Educators in the Volunteer State were concerned that students might be offended by the usage of traditional pronouns like she, he, him, and hers, according to a document from the University of Tennessee—Knoxville's Office of Diversity and Inclusion.

"With the new semester beginning and an influx of new students on campus, it is important to participate in making our campus welcoming and inclusive for all," wrote Donna Braquet in a posting on the university's website. "One way to do that is to use a student's chosen name and their correct pronouns."[15]

Braquet, who is director of the university's Pride Center, suggested using a variety of gender-neutral pronouns instead of traditional pronouns. "There are dozens of gender-neutral pronouns," she declared.[16]

For all you folks who went to school back when there were only him and her, here's a primer: some of the new gender-neutral pronouns are ze, hir, hirs, xe, xem, and xyr.[17] "These may sound a little funny at first, but only because they are new," Braquet explained. "The she and he pronouns would sound strange too if we had been taught ze when growing up."[18]

Somehow I sincerely doubt that, but we have to believe anything for the sake of inclusivity, right?

"Instead of calling roll, ask everyone to provide their name and pronouns," she wrote. "This ensures you are not singling out transgender or non-binary students."[19]

For example, the birth certificate might say that Big Earl is a male. But what if Big Earl identifies as a lady who wants to be called Lawanda? According to the procedures outlined by the folks at the Office of Diversity and Inclusion, the professor is obligated to call Big Earl, "Lawanda," or whatever name makes Big Earl feel more included.

"We should not assume someone's gender by their appearance, nor by what is listed on a roster or in student information systems," Braquet wrote. "Transgender people and people who do not identify within the gender binary may use a different name than their legal name and pronouns of their gender identity, rather than the pronouns of the sex they were assigned at birth."[20]

Confusing, right? So thankfully the Office for Diversity and Inclusion has devised a way to prevent students and professors from calling "sir" a "ma'am."

"You can always politely ask," she wrote. "'Oh, nice to meet you, [insert name]. What pronouns should I use?' is a perfectly fine question to ask."[21]

But not everyone was on board with the gender-neutral pronouns. Lots of folks in Big Orange Country turned bloodred when this thing went public.

"It's the most ridiculous thing I've ever heard," Mae Beavers, Republican Tennessee state senator, told me. "If you must interview a student before you greet the student, that's not acceptance—that's just absurd."[22]

Beavers represents a "very conservative" district, and she said her constituents are enraged over how their tax money is being spent by the university. "The idea a child would want to be called by a gender-neutral term is absolutely ridiculous," she said. "It's getting so crazy in this country."[23]

Julie West has two children at the university, not to mention a family dog named after the Volunteer's revered coach, General Neyland. "This isn't inclusion," she said. "This is the radical transformation of our lives and language."[24]

Something rather unusual happened after I reported on the University of Tennessee's gender inclusivity. Taxpayers became enraged. Pastors spoke from the pulpits to urge their parishioners to call their lawmakers. And that's exactly what happened. They called Nashville by the hundreds, demanding to know why their tax money was being used to fund such nonsense.

Not only did the university back down from their "recommendations," but they also changed their policies.[25] You see, when patriots stand up and speak out, they can save the day.

Let's celebrate our victories!

TARGET-ING A LIFEGUARD

Captain Butch Arbin, a forty-year veteran of the beach patrol in Ocean City, Maryland, faced the wrath of City Hall and militant LGBT activists over his handling of a bathroom controversy involving male and female lifeguards.[26]

Here was the problem: female lifeguards had complained that male lifeguards were using their dressing rooms. The male lifeguards are not transgender. But some of the guys were apparently using the ladies room out of convenience, seeing how there are more male lifeguards than female.[27]

So Arbin fired off an e-mail to set things straight. "WE are NOT Target," he wrote to the lifeguards. "USE the locker room that corresponds to your DNA....If you're NOT SURE go to Target."[28]

Now, that right there is funny, folks. It's just too bad that the LGBT activists in Maryland don't share our sense of humor.

Someone leaked the captain's e-mail to the news media, and, well, let's just say the veteran lifeguard landed in some mighty hot water.

"It's nothing short of making fun of transgender people, and it's absolutely unacceptable for a city employee or a public employee to make fun of transgender people at all," FreeState Legal Executive Director Patrick Paschall told *The Washington Post*.[29]

Paschall accused the beach patrol captain of demeaning transgender people and suggested the e-mail might result in physical harm to the LGBTQ community. "No one should be surprised when the increased drumbeat of harassment increases to discrimination and even violence against LGBTQ people," he said.[30]

Oh, please.

Arbin said the e-mail had nothing to do with transgender people. "I used humor to make the point," he said. "I was ONLY looking out for the women of the patrol and was not attempting to put down any group or individual, only maintain a nice facility for the women who choose to use a gender specific facility."[31]

He told the *Baltimore Sun* that the guys were leaving the toilet seats up—and that was an issue for the ladies. "I don't care about being politically correct," he told the newspaper. "That's one of the problems in the country right now."[32]

So the LGBT activists and left-wingers are trying to politically waterboard this poor guy simply because he was looking out for the female lifeguards.

Facing a tsunami of illegitimate outrage, Arbin issued a public "heartfelt" apology.[33] Still, City Hall threw him under the cabana.

Ocean City spokesperson Jessica Waters called his actions "completely inappropriate."[34]

"He just stepped way out of line," she told the *Post*. "It's not a reflection of Ocean City in any way, and we welcome all types of people."[35]

That's a lovely sentiment, dear. But does that mean it's city policy to let men who identify as men leave the seat up in the ladies room?

Ocean City Today, the official newspaper in those parts, issued a brilliant defense of Arbin. They suggested that he should tell his critics to pound sand, writing in a stinging editorial about having to "take special care that we don't put a toe over the line of hurting anyone's feelings."[36]

"Butch Arbin ought to tell those who would see him disciplined for a recent e-mail to take Ocean City's 10 miles of sand and pound it."[37]

They sound like my kind of people. I hope they get a Pulitzer for editorial writing.

PARENTS SUE FEDS AFTER TRANSGENDER STUDENT ALLOWED IN GIRLS LOCKER ROOM

In Illinois, courts are actually going to answer the question: Do the rights of boys who identify as girls trump the rights of girls who are born girls?

Dozens of Illinois parents filed a lawsuit after the Obama administration's Department of Education (DOE) strong-armed their school district into allowing a transgender student the right to use all girls' locker rooms.[38] "The girls are mortified," said Jeremy Tedesco, an attorney with Alliance Defending Freedom (ADF), a religious liberty law firm representing some fifty families. "They are in a constant state of fear that their bodies are going to be exposed to a male in these settings. It's a constant state of stress and anxiety for them."[39]

At least one of the plaintiffs, a female student at the high school, was harassed and bullied because she was uncomfortable changing in the same locker room with a biological boy. "While she was in the changing stall, other girls who were in the locker room began calling her names, including 'transphobic' and 'homophobic,'" the lawsuit states.[40]

At the time of this writing, the DOE had yet to respond to the lawsuit.

In a statement to the *Chicago Tribune*, the American Civil Liberties Union of Illinois said the lawsuit is a "sad development by groups opposed to fair and humane treatment of all students, including those who are transgender."[41]

In 2015 the DOE warned the Township High School District 211 in Palatine that unless they gave a biologically male student unfettered access to the girls' locker rooms, they would revoke $6 million in federal funding.[42]

In other words, the Obama administration committed a de facto act of extortion.

"Every school district in America has gotten the message," Tedesco told me. "The DOE is starting to enforce it through threats of revoking funding. We get calls every week from parents and school administrators asking, what can we do? They are caving because they know the federal government is going to come after them."[43]

Alliance Defending Freedom alleges the Department of Education has been using Title IX to bully and intimidate school districts across the country by redefining what the term *sex* means.[44]

Title IX is a federal statute created in 1972 and amended in 2015 that reads: "No person in the United States shall, on the basis of sex, be excluded from participation in, be denied the benefits of, or be subjected to discrimination under any education program or activity receiving Federal financial assistance."[45]

Tedesco told me that what the DOE is doing is "completely unlawful."[46]

"They are effectively redefining a clear and unambiguous term in a federal statute," he said. "The term is *sex*. For the forty years of that statute's history, sex has always meant male and female. But they redefined the term to include gender identity."[47]

The lawsuit filed in federal court alleges the DOE's actions have (among other things) violated the girls' right of privacy. "Every day these girls go to school, they experience embarrassment, humiliation, anxiety, fear, apprehension, stress, degradation, and loss of dignity because they will have to use the locker room and restroom with a biological male," the lawsuit states.[48]

Alliance Defending Freedom says the district's new policy has already had a "profoundly negative effect" among female students.[49]

- "One girl has started wearing her gym clothes underneath her regular clothes all day, so she only has to peel off a layer instead of exposing her unclothed body in the presence of a biological male in the locker room."
- "Some girls actively avoid the locker rooms all day."
- "Some girls are avoiding the restroom altogether, and others are waiting as long as possible to use the restroom, so they won't have to share it with a biological male."[50]

The ACLU of Illinois was especially offended that Alliance Defending Freedom referred to the transgender student as "he" in the lawsuit.[51] "It's pretty offensive that they don't even fundamentally acknowledge that our client is a girl," ACLU spokesman Ed Yohnka told the *Tribune*. "If you don't understand enough about what it means to be transgender to get that, I don't know how you even begin to opine on this."[52]

In other words, in today's America, your gender identity is based on "feelings" rather than your God-given parts.

Fox Business anchor Trish Regan asked a profound question on her show regarding the transgender bathroom controversy that has gripped the nation: "What about the civil rights of women who don't want men in their bathroom?" she asked. "Do their rights matter at all?"[53]

I'm afraid the answer to that question is no; the rights of women do not matter. And any woman or young girl who complains about sharing locker rooms or shower stalls or bathrooms with a biological male risks being labeled a transphobic bigot.

Sorry, ladies; your civil rights just got double-flushed.

GIRLS EXPOSED TO TRANSGENDER TWERKING IN LOCKER ROOM

In another case a public school district opened its showers and locker rooms to the opposite sex—and turned a blind eye to the stomach-churning behavior that was allowed.

Under the school district's policy the transgender student (identified as Student X) was allowed to use the bathrooms and locker rooms of his choice. The child was also allowed to participate on girls' athletic teams.

Alliance Defending Freedom alleges Student X engaged in inappropriate and sexually suggestive behavior, leaving some girls in tears.[54] Among the allegations:

- "Student X commented on girls' bodies while in the girls locker room, including asking Girl Plaintiff F her bra size and asking her to 'trade body parts' with him."[55]
- "Student X dances to loud music with sexually explicit lyrics in the locker room while 'twerking,' 'grinding,' and lifting up his skirt to reveal his underwear."[56]
- "Student X would dance in a sexually explicit manner— 'twerking,' 'grinding,' or dancing like he was on a 'stripper pole' to songs with explicit lyrics, including 'Milkshake' by Kelis."[57]

The school told girls who felt uncomfortable they should consider using a secondary locker room in the basement of the elementary school.[58] "Plaintiff B and nearly half the junior varsity basketball team changed in the secondary locker room in hope that their privacy would not be violated," the lawsuit states.[59]

Midway through the season Plaintiff A was told she could use a vacant boys' basketball locker room—for privacy. But it wasn't long before the transgender student showed up in that locker room.[60]

"On one such occasion, Student X walked into the boys' basketball locker room while Girl Plaintiff A was in her underwear and removed his pants while he was near her and other girls who were also changing," the lawsuit states. "This incident deeply upset Girl Plaintiff A. It signaled to her that there was no place in the school where she could preserve her privacy under the new Policy."[61]

ADF attorney Matt Sharp told me the school district turned a blind eye to complaints raised by the girls and their parents. "The school was very unsympathetic," Sharp said. "This is showing what we have been warning for months now. When you strip away student privacy, there's going to be consequences for that."[62]

CURT SCHILLING VS. ESPN

Former All-Star pitcher Curt Schilling has offered a good number of politically incorrect statements during his career at ESPN. But it was something he shared on social media about transgender bathrooms that turned out to be the last straw for ESPN.

Schilling was unceremoniously fired because he has a problem with men using the ladies' room.

He shared a photo of a portly man dressed in women's clothing, with the man wearing a wig and holding a purse. His ample bosom protruded from two strategically placed holes. Alongside the eyebrow-raising photo was a message:

"LET HIM IN! to the restroom with your daughter or else you're a narrow-minded, judgmental, unloving racist bigot who needs to die."[63]

Schilling followed up with a statement of his own: "A man is a man no matter what they call themselves," he said. "I don't care what they are, who they sleep with, men's room was designed for [men], women's not so much. Now you need laws telling us differently? Pathetic."[64]

Schilling's commonsense post sent liberals scampering for safe spaces.

The Left-leaning sports network swiftly gave Schilling the heave-ho—much to the delight of LGBT activists and their cronies in sports journalism. "ESPN is an inclusive company," they wrote in a statement to the *New York Times*. "Curt Schilling has been advised that his conduct was unacceptable and his employment with ESPN has been terminated."[65]

In other words, conform to ESPN's radical cultural agenda, or you're off the team.

I suspect that an overwhelming majority of Americans agree with Schilling's perspective on transgender bathrooms. Many moms and dads of any political stripe sincerely do not want their young daughters sharing a bathroom or a locker room with boys or men.

My friend Jeff Katz, a talk-radio host in Richmond, Virginia, told me what his response would be if he saw a grown man using the same bathroom as his young daughter. "I would be absolutely horrified," he told me. "I don't think I'm a bad guy because I think my thirteen-year-old daughter ought to be able to be in a girls' locker room and be among other people. I don't think that makes me a bad person."[66] But many on the Left would say Mr. Katz is a very bad person.

In any case, Curt Schilling joined a growing list of Americans who have been punished for rejecting the basic tenets of the gender revolution. Will ESPN now publicly advocate for professional sports to transform stadium bathrooms into gender-neutral facilities—to accommodate the cultural whims of every ze, zir, and them?

Maybe ESPN's radical agenda is why the network is in a death spiral, having lost four million subscribers in a single year.[67] That's the price you pay for endangering women in America.

So what do we as Deplorables do in the face of this madness? We fight! In the words of Winston Churchill: "Never give in, never give in, never, never, never—in nothing, great or small, large or petty—never give in except to convictions of honour and good sense. Never yield to force; never yield to the apparently overwhelming might of the enemy."[68]

If this isn't a bridge too far for the Left's agenda, I don't know what is. I never thought I would see a day when so-called progressives sold out women for the sake of bizarre new theories about gender identity.

In other words, I think they overplayed their hand. We have a real opening here, America. People of good conscience intrinsically get this one without much explaining, which is why ESPN and Target are hemorrhaging financially for their costly agendas.

MARCHING ORDERS

1. **In short, fight hard.** Don't let your kids' schools or clubs or anyplace endanger your youngsters. If they do, prepare to back up and bring it. Get loud, get noisy, and don't let anyone sell our kids' privacy and sexual safety for some crazy notion. No organization,

public or private, at any level should be allowed to get away with opening a door to abuse and harassment.

2. **Support God-honoring businesses.** Tell ESPN, Target, and other similar businesses and organizations that because of this issue, you will no longer partake of their services.

3. **Use humor to mock these policies.** The Left, as humorless a bunch as ever walked God's green earth, cannot stand to be mocked. So go for it. They deserve it. We're told that God sits in the heavens and laughs and scoffs at man's futile efforts (Ps. 2:4), and that He is scornful toward the scorners but gives grace to the humble (Prov. 3:34). There's your green light. Mock away.

4. **Go back to the Bible.** Explain to your family God's original purpose for making humans male and female. There are deep and beautiful reasons He created two separate genders, and the Bible has much to say about it. Let this be a learning experience and an opportunity for us as Christians to return to the basics of our beliefs.

Chapter 12

I WANNA DECK
SOMEBODY'S HALLS

★ ★ ★ ★

I F YOU'RE AN atheist, this might curdle your eggnog: I believe that Jesus is the reason for the Christmas season. That makes me about as politically incorrect as they come.

I've often wondered why folks like the Freedom From Religion Foundation (FFRF) get their Christmas stockings in a twist at the mere mention of the baby wrapped in swaddling clothes. Maybe all they got for Christmas one year was a package of underwear and a can of Aunt Edna's fruitcake?

Even more bizarre is how they get so worked up over something they don't even believe is real. I'm no psychologist, but I'm sure there's a clinical term for such a condition.

Nevertheless, the atheists have sworn some sort of oath to push Christmas celebrations underground. "Away With the Manger" seems to be their battle cry. Their modus operandi has traditionally been to target small towns and bully city hall and the public school system. They mail nasty letters and threaten them with lawsuits.

And unfortunately many municipalities and schools let the atheists win. "Today, unfortunately, they feel they have to be so politically correct that the joy of Christmas is diminishing," my friend Sarah Palin said.[1]

Palin is correct. Many communities have thrown in the towel. The excuses vary from town to town, but most folks worry about spending tax dollars on lengthy court battles. So instead of standing up for their constitutional rights, they shove the Baby Jesus into storage and take down their "Merry Christmas" signs.

It's been enough to give anyone the Christmas blues.

The atheists have been allowed to wage their Yuletide warfare for the most part without so much as a fight. But that's not the case lately. Lately the town folks are fighting back and are ready to deck somebody's halls and jingle somebody's bells.

MANGER DANGER

One of my new heroes is Terry Calhoun. He's the mayor of Rainbow City, Alabama. The FFRF sent him a terse letter demanding that the town remove its nativity scene.[2]

Mayor Calhoun told the Wisconsin atheists to go back to Wisconsin and eat cheese curds. "As long as I am mayor, I'm going to do what I think is right, and I'm not moving that manger scene," he told television station KTRK.[3]

Bravo, Mayor Calhoun! Somebody send that man a whole shipment of candy canes.

The FFRF also tried to bully a fire station in Utica, New York. It was a strategic error.

The firefighters had posted a holiday sign outside Firehouse No. 4 declaring "Happy Birthday Jesus. We Love You."[4] An FFRF lawyer fired off a letter complaining about how it's "bad policy" for a government agency to celebrate the birth of Jesus. The FFRF fretted that the message excluded, among other people, Muslims.[5]

Well, there's a good reason for that. We aren't celebrating the birthday of Muhammad on December 25.

Fire Chief Russell Brooks decided to stand his ground. He told television station WKTV that the firefighters erected the sign after the terrorist attacks of September 11, 2001. "9/11 brought a lot of the guys closer to God, and they just wanted to show their faith in Jesus," Brooks said. "They had no idea a controversy would arise."[6]

Chalk up another win for the Baby in the manger! Maybe the tide is turning.

Speaking of tide—red tide, in this case—the scrooges at FFRF nearly scored a hit in Piedmont, Alabama, after they demanded the town drop the "Keep Christ in Christmas" theme for the annual holiday parade.

The town complied, but with a slight caveat. They allowed all the parade entrants to post the theme on their floats and trucks and tractors. On the night of the parade virtually every parade float was promoting the reason for the season: "Keep Christ in Christmas."[7]

How's that for winning within the rules?

The FFRF should know better than to mess with folks in Alabama. Out-of-state meddlers are liable to get their tide rolled.

UNIVERSITY CALLS FOR "INCLUSIVE HOLIDAY PRACTICES"

But the battle never ends, does it? At the University of Tennessee, Christmas party planners were told to leave the Baby Jesus and Santa Claus at home.

The taxpayer-funded university's Office for Diversity and Inclusion (ugh!) released an "unofficial" edict calling for the campus to host holiday parties that do not emphasize religion or culture. "Ensure your holiday party is not a Christmas party in disguise," the organization warned in an online document titled "Best Practices for Inclusive Holiday Celebrations in the Workplace."[8]

Ah, yes, Christmas-neutral. It's all the rage on college campuses these days. "Celebrate your religious and cultural holidays in ways that are respectful and inclusive of our students, your colleagues, and our university," the Office for Diversity and Inclusion stated.[9]

Let me pause for just a moment to share a rather frosty note I received from the university's media relations department. They said the "Best Practices for Inclusive Holiday Celebrations in the Workplace" is not an official policy. "It is a list of suggestions for inclusive celebrations," they stated. "We recognize that our campus community is diverse and its members observe various religions and faiths."[10]

The statement went on to point out that they "honor Christmas as one of the celebrations of the season, and the birth of Jesus and the corresponding Christmas observance is one of the Christian holidays on our cultural and religious holidays calendar."[11]

I wonder if the Office for Diversity and Inclusion is aware that such noninclusive and nondiverse activities are occurring on campus. I see an internecine battle brewing.

"I am hoping that you will be fair and objective in your reporting and the inferences you make about the piece," the statement went on to read.[12] Well, I'm not inferring anything. It's written in black and white and Tennessee orange on the university's official website.

Here's some of the nonsense they suggested on Rocky Top:

- Holiday cards should be nondenominational.
- Decorations should not be specific to any religion or culture.
- Refreshment selection should also be general and not specific to any religion or culture.[13]

And my personal favorite:

◆ Holiday parties should not play games with religious or cultural themes.

They singled out Dreidel and Secret Santa as no-nos.[14]

The recommendations drew the ire of alumni, including Rep. John Duncan, a Republican from Tennessee. "The people I represent are disgusted by this," he told me. "People from all over the country are sick and tired of all this political correctness."[15]

Lieutenant governor Ron Ramsey echoed the congressman's concerns about political correctness. "While the advisory makes clear it is not university policy, these 'suggestions' call into question what purpose university offices of diversity serve," he said. Students don't attend college "to have their values and traditions sidelined and undermined," Ramsey went on.[16]

Amen to that!

Sometimes it takes the threat of losing Christmas for people to have any backbone. But we'll take joy to the world wherever we can find it.

PUBLIC SCHOOL KISSES "DOMINANT HOLIDAYS" GOOD-BYE

Believe it or not, all of America's favorite holidays were all given the heave-ho at one Minnesota elementary school.

Bruce Vento Elementary School in St. Paul decided to stop celebrating "dominant holidays" such as Christmas, Thanksgiving, and Valentine's Day. "My personal feeling is we need to find a way to honor and engage in holidays that are inclusive of our student population," Principal Scott Masini wrote in a letter to parents.[17]

The *Star-Tribune* said the letter surfaced on a private Facebook page titled "Supporting St. Paul Students and Teachers." The principal noted, "I have come to the difficult decision to discontinue the celebration of the dominant holidays until we can come to a better understanding of how the dominant view will suppress someone else's view."[18]

The *Star-Tribune* reported that Masini made the decision to can the holidays in consultation with his staff. "One of the concerns that I have," he wrote, "…is whether or not this practice is encroaching on the educational opportunities of others and threatening the culture of tolerance and respect for all."[19]

The principal told me via e-mail that it was "truly not a story," and then referred me to the district for further clarification.[20]

St. Paul Public Schools released a statement to the *Star-Tribune* that certainly seemed to defend the principal's ban on holidays. "Because Saint Paul Public

Schools is a diverse district that is filled with families from around the world we strive to respect all cultures and all students," they wrote. "We recognize that not every student celebrates or participates in some or all holidays. We have a board policy that discourages programs and festivities that celebrate observances unless they are required by law."[21]

It sounds to me like the St. Paul area is infected with a case of ethnic sensitivity—a diagnosis confirmed by the district spokesperson. She explained to me that their schools include many, many cultures—students from around the world, including a very large Somali population.[22]

That's all well and good, but the children live in America now. They are presumably Americans. As such, they and their families should be acclimating to the American way of life.

Am I right? Or have I just had too much eggnog?

INCLUSIVE COMMUNITY BANS SANTA FROM CONCERT

A Massachusetts school that advertises itself as an "inclusive community"[23] banned Santa Claus from its annual Christmas concert in the hometown of Harvard University, all because someone complained.

"I am writing to you today to inform you of a change in our concert series this winter," wrote principal Jennifer Ford in a letter to parents of the Andrew Peabody School in Cambridge. "Our First through Fourth grade concert as well as our Kindergarten concert will not include a visit from Santa Claus this year."[24]

Moms and dads around Cambridge said the principal's ban was naughty, not nice. "I come from a city that celebrates diversity and tolerance," parent Robert Thompson told *Fox & Friends*. "At its base this decision reeks of intolerance."[25]

Jolly Old Saint Nick was relegated to a family sing-along on the day before Christmas Eve. Thompson said it's as if they were saying Santa is not "good enough for the main show."[26] But the school was afraid that even that appearance of Old St. Nick would offend overly sensitive residents.

"I am sensitive to the fact that you may not want your child involved in this event," Ford wrote in a letter obtained by the *Boston Globe*. "If you prefer that your child spend time with me that afternoon, please let me know. I will be in the library, playing games and reading books with the children."[27]

How's that for a dose of holiday Grinchiness? Forget Santa—join me in the library.

Jeffrey Young was the superintendent of this calamitous mess of public education at the time. He told the *Globe* he didn't understand why Santa needed to visit the Peabody School. "There's no anti-Santa sentiment," he told the newspaper. "It's just that there's no pro-Santa sentiment, either." He also said, "Santa's not on the top of my list."[28]

Of course, this is the hometown of Harvard University and the same town that in 2007 stopped a Boy Scout troop from collecting care packages for American soldiers. The Scouts were accused of making a political statement.[29]

And how can we forget about the city's war on carbonation? The mayor wanted to ban any bottled soft drinks larger than sixteen ounces.[30] They also wanted to decide how much popcorn citizens could pop and how many milk-shakes they could slurp.

And if you need further proof that Cambridge is to the left of Vladimir Putin, consider this item from the 2006 edition of the *Harvard Crimson*. A member of the Cambridge Public Schools Committee compared a law mandating the recitation of the Pledge of Allegiance to a "post-9/11 ultra-patriotism push."[31]

Committee member Luc Schuster told the newspaper that "pledging blind allegiance" to the United States stifles the intellectual capacity of children.[32]

You just can't argue with that kind of ignorance, folks. Sounds to me like they've been smoking too much mistletoe, or the spiced cider went hard. As they say back home in Tennessee, the cheese has done slid off the cracker.

VETERANS AFFAIRS CHRISTIAN TREE BAN CAUSES YULETIDE UPRISING

Folks around Salem, Virginia, went holiday red when Salem Veterans Affairs Medical Center implemented a ban on Christmas trees and religious Christmas carols in the public spaces of their hospital. Workers received an e-mail stating, "Trees (regardless of the types of ornaments used) have been deemed to promote the Christian religion and will not be permitted in any public areas this year."[33]

How's that for coal in your stocking?

The VA also warned employees that "public areas may only be decorated in a manner that is celebratory of the winter season."[34]

In other words, candy canes, yes; the Baby Jesus, no. "Displays must not pro-mote any religion," they noted.[35]

The VA went so far as to tell workers what kind of "holiday" music was permissible according to government standards. "Music travels and should be secular (non-religious) and appropriate to the work environment," the e-mail stated.[36]

The VA went into full killjoy mode and banned visiting entertainers from warbling any Christmas carol in which the words *Christ* or *Christmas* were included. "They told me I could sing 'Rudolph the Red-Nosed Reindeer,' but I couldn't sing about Christ," Pastor John Sines Jr. told me. "I couldn't sing about anything that had the word *Christmas* in it. I could sing what they referred to as 'holiday' songs."[37]

Sines, the pastor at Rock Pike Baptist Church in Forest, Virginia, was a bit flustered by the rules. All he wanted to do was entertain the veterans. "My agenda wasn't so I could push Jesus on the veterans," he said. "I just wanted to honor the veterans and to say thank you."[38]

So the good reverend politely told the VA Hospital that he was not going to abide by the rules. "I let those folks know I wasn't going to be bullied into their way of thinking," he said. "We're rednecks. We don't have no problem standing our ground."[39]

Pastor Sines said he wasn't trying to cause any trouble. He just wanted to do what the Constitution allowed him to do. "I have a Constitution that protects my freedom, and I have God who said He would protect me from everything else," the pastor told me.[40]

In addition to Pastor Sines, the VA had to contend with outraged employees, veterans, and local townsfolk. So they reached a compromise. Pastor Sines said he was re-invited to perform,[41] and Christmas trees would once again be allowed in the public spaces, so long as other faiths were also represented.[42]

Officials cited VA Directive 0022, titled "Religious Symbols in Holiday Displays in VA Facilities." The directive states, "Religious symbols may be included in a holiday display in a public area of a VA facility if the display does not favor one religion over another, and conveys a primarily secular message."[43]

So the only way folks can celebrate Christmas is if they also celebrate Kwanzaa and Hanukkah. "This compromise allows for the Salem VAMC to be in full compliance with Federal mandates that prohibit U.S. Government facilities, including the U.S. Department of Veterans Affairs, from 'favoring one religion over another' while providing the diversity and flexibility for employees and Veterans to celebrate the holidays according to their individual faith structure," the VA stated.[44]

The federal government may cite VA directive 0022 for its definition of Christmas, but I prefer to cite the Holy Bible. And the Good Book declares that Jesus is the reason for the season. Period.

MAYHEM AND MISTLETOE

Tell that to the folks at Cornell University who worried about "inclusive seasonal displays."[45] That's academic code for Christmas decorations.

Cornell warned students that some "winter holiday displays" are not consistent with the university's "commitment to diversity and inclusiveness." Among the items on their naughty list: nativity scenes, angels, crosses, and mistletoe.[46]

I'm not quite sure why they frown upon the mistletoe, unless they want to discourage young fraternity men from spreading Christmas cheer among the sorority girls. But for the sake of inclusion, Cornell University recommended ditching the Baby Jesus and hemiparasitic plants (that's mistletoe, for you nonbotanists).

"University members are reminded to be respectful of the religious diversity of our students and colleagues and are encouraged to use an *inclusive* approach in celebrating the holiday season," read a statement on the university's website.[47]

They suggested "focusing on the winter season rather than a particular holiday."[48] Specifically they recommended decorating with snowflakes and "trees decorated with snowflakes and other non-religious symbols."[49]

If Cornell is so concerned about making everybody happy, I wonder if they plan on serving pulled pork during Ramadan—for the sake of inclusivity, of course.

Meanwhile, farther south, MRC-TV's Ashley Rae Goldenberg reported that the student health center at the University of Missouri banned all holiday decorations. "I've decided that holiday decorations will not be displayed this year," Susan Even, the center's executive director, wrote in an e-mail to staff. "Our mission is to provide a safe, comfortable place for all students to receive their health care. Without meaning to, some of the holiday symbols that we may display could contradict that mission."[50]

Who knew that Christmas decorations could cause such consternation?

"I know this decision will be disappointing to some of you, but I can assure you that the kindness, warmth and compassion that you show all students is as important now as any time of the year," Even wrote.[51]

That means no twinkling lights or sugar plum fairies in your safe spaces, kids.

While American universities and government entities try taking the jolly out of our holly, we can fight back and win, like the parade people in Alabama and the Christmas-loving locals in Tennessee. I suggest a two-front war—hit them directly in their so-called guidelines and rules, and then go guerrilla on the bans as well. Let me explain.

MARCHING ORDERS

1. **Resist.** This is where civil disobedience comes in real handy. If your workplace or school puts some limitations on Christmas, test the limits. Force them to draw a line between what is "holiday" and

what is "Christmas." For example, do red-and-green ornaments pass the test? How about star-shaped sugar cookies delivered to your child's class? Gift-wrapped presents? Angel decorations? Three kings? Your ugly Christmas sweater?

What if you offer a "Merry Christmas" in the morning and evening to your coworkers? Or wish them a "blessed and special season"? Or play Handel's *Messiah*?

Small but persistent irritations can wear down bad policy if you're determined to do it. The main idea goes back to Winston Churchill: never give up. Never let them silence you. If they put up a wall, find a way to go around it. Force them to spend time defending their silly rules. Show them that the spirit of Christmas is far more powerful than holiday hypersensitivity. Do it pleasantly, of course, and always offer a "Merry Christmas" and a plate of cookies so they know you're enjoying yourself.

2. **Make a frontal assault on these bogus restrictions as well.** Push back on the idea that your First Amendment rights disappear at the door of the workplace or school campus. Do your research so you know what has worked for others who took a stand. I bet coworkers will rally to your side.

3. **Most of all, keep your Christmas cheer.** The joy of knowing Jesus personally is the most persuasive argument of all, and that light will shine no matter who tries to darken it. Be a happy warrior. After all, Christmas is a joyful holiday!

Chapter 13

THE GENERATION THAT MIGHT SAVE FREEDOM

★ ★ ★ ★

RESIDENT REAGAN ONCE said that freedom is never more than one generation away from extinction.[1] I grew up in the 1980s, and my generation dropped the ball. We became complacent. We gave the nation Madonna and parachute pants, and only slightly redeemed our legacy with *Back to the Future* (totally rad to the max) and the video game Tetris (gnarly, dude).

Since those days of popped collars and pastel colors, traditional American values have been in a downward spiral. But I've noticed something is happening with postmillennials. Maybe you've seen it too. Teenagers are beginning to experience a rebirth of American pride.

Jacob Feazel of Bunker Hill, Indiana, is a classic example of this new kind of American patriot. The seventeen-year-old created a stirring piece of artwork that celebrated our nation. The artwork depicts an American flag made from more than forty-four hundred toy soldiers.[2] The *Kokomo Tribune* reported that it took the teenager more than fifty-six hours of work over eleven days to create the masterpiece.[3]

The artwork was indeed impressive and worthy of the attention it received when his depiction of Old Glory went viral.[4] But I was especially moved by something this young man told the local newspaper. "I did it to honor those who fight so I can make art," Feazel said.[5]

Feazel understands that freedom is never free. He understands the price that must be paid to ensure our freedom. And he understands why we should honor that sacrifice.

Good job, young man! You give us hope.

RALLYING TO THE FLAG

The folks in Richland Township, Pennsylvania, understand the sacrifice too. That's why the local high school launched an investigation after a photograph surfaced of a student desecrating an American flag inside a classroom.[6]

The repulsive photograph showed a young man standing on Old Glory as a female student stands nearby with her middle finger raised.[7] "Seething outrage" would be a good way to describe the reaction in Richland Township, a country town that prides itself on patriotism.

"What a shameful display of ignorance, contempt and utter disregard for the country, flag and veterans' sacrifice," one resident wrote online.[8]

"What a disgrace," wrote another. "Maybe they should be put on the front lines, so they can get a taste of reality."[9]

"This behavior is repulsive," wrote the mother of a Richland High School graduate currently serving in the Armed Forces. "To make matters worse, Richland Township is home to many of the Armed Forces units that also defend that flag."[10]

As detestable as the desecration may have been, the response from the Richland School District was admirable—and downright remarkable. "This photo is not representative of the feelings of the 1,600 students in our district," Superintendent Arnold Nadonley stated. "Out of respect for our veterans— both those who have defended our flag and those still serving in our military— nobody wants to see something like this."[11]

The district posted a message online promising that it would launch a "timely and thorough review of this incident and…implement appropriate legal discipline." They called the photo "unfortunate and unpatriotic."[12]

The students involved in the desecration were not identified. However, the mother of the young man released a statement through the ACLU to apologize. "My son did a stupid and impulsive thing," she said in a statement. "He apologized immediately and regrets what he did. We appreciate the people reaching out with understanding and forgiveness. Our family has the highest respect for our country and military and we would like to issue a sincere apology on behalf of our entire family."[13]

Again, a bit of a pleasant surprise—especially in a day and age when some parents believe their children are incapable of wrongdoing.

Meanwhile the American Civil Liberties Union of Pennsylvania didn't seem to think there was a problem with desecrating Old Glory. "As long as they were trying to send a message of protest, it sounds like they are protected to me," legal director Witold Walczak stated.[14]

Superintendent Nadonley told the local newspaper he understands that "students' rights don't end at the schoolhouse gates."[15] But he said the district would pursue the matter "in whatever legal way we can, with due process and with respect to the flag, our Constitution and our country."[16]

My goodness! I never thought I'd hear a public school administrator stand up to the ACLU and defend American patriotism! But it happened in Richland Township.

We still don't know why the teenagers did what they did, but the school district was planning to use the incident as a teaching tool. Instead of parking the offenders in a holding cell or in-school suspension, maybe they could be dispatched to work at a nearby VA hospital. Perhaps they could do yard work for widows of local war veterans. Or maybe the school could host an assembly featuring graduates currently defending our freedom.

Let's hope those two wayward teenagers have learned their lesson. When you see the Star-Spangled Banner, you stand and salute—you don't stand and stomp.

THE FOOTBALL PLAYER WHO STOOD ALONE

In some cases when you stand up, you stand alone.

Connor Brewer is fiercely loyal to his college football team. But he is also fiercely loyal to the United States of America. So when the Millikin University football team decided to protest the national anthem by remaining inside the locker room instead of on the sidelines, Connor was faced with a decision. Would he join his teammates in their university-approved safe space, or would he stand on the sidelines and honor America?

Connor chose to stand. And he stood alone.[17]

One of my readers sent me a photograph of what transpired at the private Illinois university on a brisk day in October 2016. It was deeply moving.

Here's the back story. In September of that year several football players took a page from disgraced NFL quarterback Colin Kaepernick by taking a knee during the national anthem. The community outrage was apparently so severe the football team decided to "forge a new path."[18]

"Rather than have our message be misunderstood or misconstrued, we are united in our decision to stay in the locker room until kickoff during which time we will engage in a moment of reflection to personally recognize the sacrifice of so many and renew our commitment to living up to those most important words: 'with liberty and justice for all,'" the team wrote in a statement that was published in the *Herald-Review* newspaper.[19]

Instead of standing along the sidelines and showing a little respect for the United States, the football team chose to hunker down in their locker room. "Please let there be no doubt that we have the utmost respect for the sacrifice made by those who served or do serve in our armed forces, including many of our family and friends," the football team wrote. "Therefore, it is our desire to do nothing that could be viewed as disrespectful of their sacrifice."[20]

University president Patrick White offered up a pile of academic gobbledy-gook in defense of the football squad. "We all need to listen to voices and opinions different from our own and listen with our hearts and minds awake to difference," White wrote. "When the issues involve race and justice and differing contentions of what patriotism [means], all of us can stand more education."[21]

Well, I'm fairly certain patriotism does not mean cowering inside a locker room while the "Star-Spangled Banner" is being performed.

I wrote a story about Connor and his courage on that autumn day—and his good deed caused quite a stir among my readers. I was inundated with hundreds of messages from across the fruited plain—all of them affirming Connor.

I was especially touched by a poignant letter I received from a Gold Star mother named Debi Daniels. "Reading your article about Connor broke my heart," she wrote. "It was the loneliness—that he had to be there by himself. Please thank him for me. He has a lot of support."[22]

Daniels said the recent controversy at Millikin University hit close to home for her family. That's because her son Nickolas was a member of the varsity football program at Millikin back in 2004. He played offense and defense and was quite an athlete. In 2010 Nickolas enlisted in the Marines. The following year he was killed in Afghanistan.[23]

Lance Corporal Daniels was a decorated Marine—he had been awarded the Purple Heart, Combat Action Ribbons, a National Defense Service Medal, a Global War on Terrorism Service Medal, and a Sea Service Deployment Ribbon.[24] So you can understand why Daniels has taken an interest in recent developments at the school. "While I have stayed silent about this 'movement,' this struck a tad close to home," she told me.[25]

The Daniels family told me they understand the protests, but they "just think there is another way."[26]

There's a reason we stand for the national anthem and we place our hands over our hearts and pledge allegiance to the flag. It's to honor men and women who shed blood so that we might be free. It's to remember that our freedom comes with a price.

So when athletes take a knee, they don't just disrespect the American flag, they disrespect American heroes like Lance Corporal Nickolas Daniels of Elmwood Park, Illinois.

We salute you, Connor, for standing for guys like that, even though you stood alone that night.

PERSPECTIVE FROM A NEW AMERICAN

Not long after I introduced our readers to Connor, I received a letter from a legal immigrant from India. He posed a very interesting question and offered some intriguing analysis from his perspective as a newcomer to America.

Dear Mr. Starnes,

I am a first-generation naturalized American who was born in India. I am neither white (without white privilege) nor black or Hispanic (not a victim either). I am just a person who came to a land of opportunity with a dream. I have traveled some in this world, and to the best of my knowledge I have not known of any other country where some of the people desecrate their flag, disavow their national anthem, or tear down their own country. If I am wrong, please straighten me out. BUT if I am right, then please address how...we [can] expect any other country to respect ours when we (under the "excuse" of freedom of speech) do not respect it ourselves.

When I became a US citizen, I took an oath denouncing my allegiance to my old country, and even agreed to take up arms against my former country if asked to by the USA. Please check the verbiage of the oath these days, but do oaths mean nothing anymore?

Just like family, we may not always agree with our parents or siblings, but we do not insult or degrade them in public (at least, I don't think [we] should).

I have three comments for your consideration:

1. If they (the desecrators) dislike our country so much, then by the same freedoms that are granted to us through our Constitution and Bill of Rights, they are free to denounce their citizenship and go embrace and live in a country that they think is better than ours. They are free to run and embrace that country's flag and anthem, but I am sorry, I would appreciate them not doing it on our soil. In America, fly the American flag with pride and no other!!!

2. Every immigrant like myself who came here to this wonderful land of opportunity seeking a better future should leave the policies, laws, traditions, and attitudes of their former countries behind and assimilate into our culture, traditions, language, laws, and attitudes. After all, if their old country's ideas, policies, traditions, and laws were so good, then why did they leave and come here in the first place? Go home!

3. I believe immigrants come here either because they admire us and the opportunities we offer or to rape and abuse our country for all that they can pillage. I am sorry, but we must block the latter kind. I

believe that Mr. Trump has the right idea. As for those who were born in this country, wow, what can I say? They were blessed to be born into opportunity, but many unfortunately could not admire the beauty of the forest because they were blinded by the tree in front of them.

I wish to remain anonymous, but I will be glad to answer any questions if needed for clarification.

I am just a man who loves my country and all that it stands for. May God bless the USA.[27]

I get chills just reading it. That's the kind of attitude that makes America great.

A TEENAGE GUN-TOTER

Another great guy is Joshua Bruner, a good ol' boy from north of the Mason-Dixon Line.

The fifteen-year-old country kid from Ringoes, New Jersey, is a lifetime member of the National Rifle Association. He's a member of two state shooting teams, and he serves as a United States Sea Cadet.[28]

The guy likes guns, and he uses them well.

Darcy Meys said her son wants to follow in his great-grandfather's footsteps and enlist in the Marines. "Josh considers himself to be a patriot," she told me. "He loves his country."[29]

Josh had been given an assignment in a photography class at Hunterdon Central Regional High School. He had to take a self-portrait representing self-expression. So Josh and some of his buddies gathered in a field behind his house and set up a tripod, striking their best male model poses.

Josh climbed atop a four-wheeler. He was holding Old Glory in one hand and a shotgun in the other—a Remington pump-action 12-gauge, to be precise. It was, by all accounts, an epic picture that summed up the heart and soul of this teenage patriot.[30]

Now, at Hunterdon Central kids have to upload their assignments to the school's Google site. And that's when Josh learned there was a problem. His self-portrait was rejected because it violated the school's gun policy.[31] "The rules of our school prohibit students from using artwork depicting themselves or another person with any weapon," the teacher wrote to Mrs. Meys.[32]

Mrs. Meys told me she looked at the school policy, and she believes it was referring to actual guns on school property, not a photograph of a gun taken on private property. "Josh was just showing pride for his country and who he is as a shooter and as a kid who wants to be in the Marines and protect his country and follow in his grandfather's footsteps," she told me. "He was not dressed inappropriately. He was not holding the gun incorrectly, and he was respecting the flag."[33]

The school decided to offer Josh a compromise, according to e-mail correspondence between his mother and the teacher. But it's really not much of a compromise. The school agreed to grade Josh's photograph, but they were adamant that it could not be uploaded onto the school's server, nor could it be publicly displayed.

"He will not be able to upload the image to our server, post them to his Google site or display them in his presentation," the teacher wrote. "We would like to recognize his work on the portrait but limit the possibility that the photo can be taken out of context."[35]

Good Lord! It's not pornography, people. It's a kid holding Old Glory and a shotgun.

"They are crushing his spirit," Mrs. Meys told me at the time. "They are stifling his creativity."[36]

And for that matter, they are in effect telling this child that he cannot take pride in who he is, his identity as an American. "If it is OK for people to show pride in their sexuality, why can't my son show pride in his country?" Mrs. Meys asked. "I'm supposed to accept guys going into bathrooms with my daughters and girls going into bathrooms with my boys, but they won't accept my kid for just wanting to be a patriot?"[37]

In this age of tolerance and diversity it's too bad our public school system can't be more tolerant of red-blooded American patriots like Josh Bruner. I feel like posting that epic photo of him on my office wall.

WINNING THE GENDER PRONOUN WARS

When future generations read about the "Great Gender Pronoun Wars" of the early twenty-first century, they will most certainly learn of Grant Strobl, a noble and mighty king.

"His Majesty" is an unlikely title for a twenty-one-year-old political science major from Grosse Pointe, Michigan. "It was definitely activism by accident," he told me.[38]

In less than twenty-four hours the brave conservative single-handedly defeated an army of activists for gender neutrality at the University of Michigan. Think David versus a gender-confused Goliath.

The University of Michigan recently announced a new initiative to allow students to select their preferred gender pronouns through an online service. It was designed as a way to help professors tell the difference between the guys and the gals and the zis and the zirs. "Asking about and correctly using someone's designated pronoun is one of the most basic ways to show your respect for their identity and to cultivate an environment that respects all gender identities," wrote Provost Martha Pollack in an e-mail to students and faculty.[39]

It's all part of the university's effort to foster an "environment of inclusiveness." The university actually created a "pronoun committee" to ensure that faculty members "play a vital role in ensuring all of our community feels valued, respected and included."[40]

It was in that spirit of inclusivity that Grant, a Fox News campus associate, decided to have a bit of fun. He logged into the university's computer system, clicked on the "Gender Identity" tab, and promptly declared his new designated pronoun. "You could put anything you wanted into the system," Grant told me. "So I did."[41]

And so it was that Grant came to be known as "His Majesty"—Noble Ruler of the Wolverines.

Yes, good readers, Grant changed his designated pronoun to "His Majesty."

"'His Majesty' is not a pronoun, but neither is zir or zi," His Majesty told me. "None of them are recognized in the English language. Everything is completely arbitrary now. You can identify as anything you want."[42]

Want to be a shrub? What about a sloth? Well, you can be anything you want to be at the University of Michigan. That's because when you institutionalize stupidity, anything goes.

"I thought it was definitely fitting to point out how absurd this new policy is by choosing 'His Majesty,'" His Majesty said. "It's a recognized honorific, and it is definitely absurd for anybody to be called 'His Majesty' in America."[43]

His Majesty, who is also the founding chairman of the Young Americans for Freedom chapter at the University of Michigan, soon generated a bit of outrage. "Plenty of students have been saying that I'm not supportive of LGBT rights or LGBT students on campus," he said. "They say I'm disrespectful."[44]

But His Majesty said that's just not true. He doesn't even expect his subjects to bow or curtsy.

"As a Christian I believe that all lives are valuable," he told me. "I love all people. And I have no problem with people choosing a designated pronoun."[45]

But the university's young ruler is concerned that professors might be punished if they refuse to identify students by their preferred gender pronoun. "Once we go down that road, it's very dangerous for our society and our democracy," he said.[46]

Quite frankly, I'm taken aback by the lack of tolerance from the university's LGBT community. If His Majesty wants to identify himself as royalty, who are they to object?

"If they want me to be tolerant of their pronouns, they have to be tolerant of my new title," His Majesty said. "Many of the students on campus who call for diversity, they only want diversity for ideas they agree with."[47]

I hope His Majesty King Grant has a long and prosperous reign at the University of Michigan. Let's pray he can fight off the invading horde of left-wing intolerants.

A REAL-LIFE CAPTAIN AMERICA

Alex Dunn, a sixteen-year-old junior at Massey Hill Classical High School in Fayetteville, North Carolina, is a red, white and blue patriot who loves America. And he especially loves the American flag. "I have a father in the military who taught me the way to respect the flag," Alex said.[48]

When he saw that his teacher was desecrating the flag during a classroom discussion, Alex knew he had to do something. And what he did had patriots cheering.[49]

History teacher Lee Francis admitted he desecrated the flag during a lesson on the First Amendment. First, he asked the students for a lighter. Then, he picked up a pair of scissors on his desk and tried to cut the flag. When that did not work, he tossed it on the ground and stomped on Old Glory.[50] "It was such a disgraceful thing for a person to do—especially in front of so many military children who understand the meaning of the flag, apparently unlike him," Alex said.[51]

He was appalled at what his teacher had done. "I didn't want to believe that it was really happening," he said. "But when he stepped on the flag, I just thought about all these men and women who fought for that flag that he just walked on—all these men and women who've come home with that flag draped over their coffin."[52]

So Alex grabbed his phone and snapped a photo—a photo that would eventually go viral on Facebook. Then the teenager rose from his seat, picked up the flag, and took the defiled banner to the principal's office.[53] "We are extremely proud of him," Alex's mother told me. "He did the right thing."[54]

However, doing the right thing could have landed the brave, young patriot in hot water. Mr. Francis told me Dunn "broke the law" and should be punished. "I believe that child does need to be punished in some way—absolutely," the teacher told me. "I can't take a picture of them, and in turn, they cannot do the same of me."[55]

The good news is the school district did not punish Alex—but they did punish the teacher. He was suspended for ten days.[56]

"If it's within Mr. Francis's rights to stomp on it, cut it, and try to burn it, then it is within my child's rights to defend that flag," Mrs. Dunn said.[57]

Sadly, many of the teenager's classmates are siding with the teacher. "There was much more support for what he did than what I did," Alex said, noting that some students even protested by refusing to stand for the Pledge of Allegiance.[58]

The question really isn't about desecrating the flag. The schoolteacher certainly has the right to demonstrate his hatred of America.

"But was it appropriate in a classroom in front of children—in front of military children? No, it was not," Mrs. Dunn told me. "It wasn't the appropriate place to defile an American flag."[59]

If nothing else, the offensive lesson is a reminder of how public schools have become incubators for un-American activities.

Mr. Francis's future in the school district remains a bit cloudy. But should he need to find gainful employment, perhaps he would be more comfortable with a career in the National Football League.

WHEN GRANNY WENT TO THE PROM

I love this real-life evidence that not all Millennials are snowflakes. I want to end with an inspiring story of a kid who made his great-grandmother's day.

You see, Delores Dennison never went to her high school prom. Times were tough. Money was scarce—they had just enough for the necessities.

But if she had gone to the prom, Delores might have imagined wearing a lovely dress and promenading through a sea of balloons and dancing with a handsome young man on a crisp April evening. She might have imagined the band playing the Frank Sinatra song "How I Love the Kisses of Dolores."

But the days of promenades had long passed for Delores, now eighty-nine years old. Youth and vigor had given way to heart trouble and a stroke. And the handsome young man who became the love of her life, the man who used to sing to her that Frank Sinatra song, passed away many years ago.[60]

Some months back Delores received a telephone call from her great-grandson. Austin was nineteen, a senior at Parkway High School in Rockford, Ohio. And he had a very important question for his "Granny DD."

"I asked her if she would be my prom date," Austin told me. "How cool would it be to take my great-grandmother to prom?"[61]

Austin looks like he just stepped out of central casting. He's the sort of kid a dad hopes his daughter will marry. He's an Eagle Scout who plays for the school's football, baseball, and basketball teams. He plays in the school band and faithfully attends church. He's the kind of youngster who says "yes, sir" and "yes, ma'am." He respects his elders.

Still, the proposal took Delores by surprise. It's not every day your great-grandson asks you out to prom. "He was so sweet and adamant about it," Delores told me. "I asked him, 'But are you sure that you wouldn't like to take one of the young ladies who could get out there and do everything with you?' He said no. 'I want you.'"[62]

Before we continue, you might want to grab a box of tissues.

Austin drew his inspiration from his economics teacher. The teacher's older brother had taken his grandmother to prom.[63] Austin remembered that his own Granny DD had never been, so he picked up the phone and made the call. "I couldn't disappoint him, if I had to go on my hands and knees," Delores said.[64]

"At first she was a bit resistant," Austin said. "I assured her I was serious, and she finally said yes. It was my privilege to take her."[65]

But there was much, much work to be done. The first item of business was finding a suitable dress for the big night. "That was an adventure," Delores said. "We were looking at the young girls' dresses. None of those dresses would be OK for me."[66]

Let's just say young ladies don't dress like they did back in the 1930s. "They were either too high or too low, and I didn't want any of that," she said.[67]

Eventually she settled on a pretty blue dress and a clutch purse. "The purse was for my necessities—my nitro and my puffer that I use for breathing," she said.[68]

The night of the prom was magical. Austin serenaded his great-grandmother with a special song and presented her with a pearl necklace.[69] His father chauffeured them to an elegant dinner at the local Bob Evans.[70] "That's one of her favorite places," Austin said.[71]

He ordered the pancakes. She ordered an omelet. "I had to take some of it home," Delores confessed.[72]

Afterward, it was off to the high school where Austin and his lovely date were introduced at the promenade. "We got a standing ovation," he said. "But we had to cut across the dance floor because she didn't have enough energy."[73]

Delores managed to get a few laughs as she hit the balloons with her cane.[74] "It was wonderful, and I just loved all the girls in their fancy gowns and the gentlemen in their tuxedos. It was quite a night," she said. "Everyone there just could not have been more polite. Everyone got an A+."[75]

One of Austin's friends even tried to make a move on his grandmother. "He tried to cut in," Austin said with a good-natured laugh. "He asked for a dance, but she didn't have the energy."[76]

And her date? Well, she declared, "He was a perfect gentleman. He was everything you would expect of a young man."[77]

"I respect my elders greatly," Austin told me. "They have a great influence on my life. To be able to sit down and talk to them and learn from them and their experiences is a great thing."[78]

But Austin had one more surprise waiting for his great-grandmother. As he escorted her onto the dance floor, a tune from another time filled the gymnasium. It was that song, from a long time ago: "How I Love the Kisses of Dolores."

"I chose that song because Grandpa Ed used to sing that song to her," Austin said. "We shared that dance. It was really sweet."[79]

And that's the story of how Delores Dennison went to prom. She wore a lovely dress and promenaded through a sea of balloons and danced with a handsome young man on a crisp April evening. And all the while the band played on, "How I love the kisses of Dolores…"

If that doesn't make your heart swell with hope, I don't know what will.

MARCHING ORDERS

The marching orders this time are simple: Be like these people. Do awesome stuff. Act in ways that deserve to show up in local or national headlines.

- Take a stand, even if it means standing alone.
- Rally to the flag when she's mistreated.
- Show your patriotism proudly.
- Raise great kids who respect their elders.
- Honor the generations that went before.

If each of us does these things consistently, courageously, and humbly, our country can't help but be great again.

Chapter 14

PROFILES IN COURAGE

I've HAD THE honor of interviewing so many brave Christians over the past decade at Fox News Channel—men and women who stepped out in faith to follow the teachings of Christ. They chose to fight the good fight in an era when some pastors were calling for Christians to stand down and retreat from the culture war. Thankfully these patriot saints have chosen to ignore those calls, and in doing so, they've set a tremendous example for all of us.

THE BAPTIST FIREFIGHTER

Kelvin Cochran was five years old when he realized that he wanted to be a firefighter. "My family was very, very poor," Cochran told me. "We were living in a shotgun house in an alley—three big brothers, two little sisters."[1]

One Sunday afternoon the Cochran children heard a fire truck stop across from their neighbor's home. Miss Maddie's house was on fire. "That's the day that God convicted me in my heart that I wanted to be a firefighter when I grew up," Cochran said. "All I thought about growing up in Shreveport was not being poor and being a firefighter."[2] And God granted Kelvin Cochran the desires of his heart. The little boy in the shotgun shack grew up to become the fire chief of Shreveport, Louisiana. He was named the Atlanta fire chief in 2008—a position he served until 2009 when he was called to serve in the Obama administration as the fire administrator. In 2010 he returned to Atlanta, where he was unanimously confirmed to once again be the city's fire chief.[3]

But Chief Cochran's storied career went up in smoke—all because of a book he wrote for a men's Bible study group at his Baptist church.

Atlanta Mayor Kasim Reed fired Chief Cochran. The announcement came on the same day Cochran was supposed to return to work following a thirty-day suspension.[4] "The LGBT members of our community have a right to be able to express their views and convictions about sexuality and deserve to be respected for their position without hate or discrimination," Cochran told me in an exclusive interview. "But Christians also have a right to express our belief regarding our faith and be respected for our position without hate and without discrimination. In the United States no one should be vilified, hated, or discriminated against for expressing their beliefs."[5]

Cochran had been suspended because of a passage he wrote about homosexuality in a book titled *Who Told You That You Were Naked?* The book's theme is biblical morality.[6]

"This is about judgment," Mayor Reed said during a press conference. "This is not about religious freedom. This is not about free speech. Judgment is the basis of the problem."[7]

The mayor even posted a public condemnation of the fire chief on his official Facebook page. "I profoundly disagree with and am deeply disturbed by the sentiments expressed in the paperback regarding the LGBT community," the mayor wrote. "I will not tolerate discrimination of any kind within my administration."[8]

The mayor went on to inform the public that Cochran had been suspended without pay and was ordered to complete a sensitivity training class.[9] "I want to be clear that the material in Chief Cochran's book is not representative of my personal beliefs, and is inconsistent with the Administration's work to make Atlanta a more welcoming city for all of her citizens—regardless of their sexual orientation, gender, race and religious beliefs," Mayor Reed wrote.[10]

So what in the world did Cochran write that was so offensive to the mayor and the LGBT community? According to the *GA Voice*, a publication that covers the LGBT community, there were two items that caused concern:

- "Uncleanness—whatever is opposite of purity; including sodomy, homosexuality, lesbianism, pederasty, bestiality, all other forms of sexual perversion."
- "Naked men refuse to give in, so they pursue sexual fulfillment through multiple partners, with the opposite sex, the same sex and sex outside of marriage and many other vile, vulgar and inappropriate ways which defile their body-temple and dishonor God."[11]

Cochran said he referenced homosexuality on less than half a page in the one-hundred-sixty-page book. "I did not single out homosexuality," he said. "I simply spoke to sex being created by God for procreation and He intended it to

be between a man and a woman in holy matrimony and that any other sex outside of that is sin."[12]

Cochran told me that someone within the department obtained a copy of the
book and took it to openly gay city council member Alex Wan.[13] Wan released
a statement supporting Cochran's termination and said it "sends a strong message to employees about how much we value diversity and how we adhere to a
non-discriminatory environment."[14]

The book caused a firestorm within Atlanta's LGBT community, and there
were many calls for Cochran to be fired—a decision the mayor finally agreed to.

"I guess they got what they asked for," Cochran said.[15]

Georgia Equality Executive Director Jeff Graham told *GA Voice* that Cochran's
"anti-gay" views could result in a hostile work environment.[16] "This is not about his
religious views but...about his ability to lead a diverse work force," he said. "It's
unfortunate that this had to happen. I feel the mayor has done the right thing to
ensure all employees are treated fairly."[17]

The allegations against Cochran amount to a he said-he said between the
fire chief and the mayor. Reed said that he had no knowledge that Cochran was
writing a book. However, Cochran said the director of Atlanta's ethics office
had given him permission to not only write the book, but to also mention in his
biography that he was the city's fire chief.[18]

Cochran said he gave a copy of the book to Mayor Reed in January 2014,
and the mayor told him he planned on reading it during an upcoming trip.[19]
Cochran also said he gave copies of the book to several members of the fire
department, individuals with whom he had personal relationships.[20]

The mayor also took issue with Cochran speaking publicly about his suspension. However, Cochran said he honored the mayor's guidance and did not speak
to the media. He did, however, share his testimony in several churches.[21] "I did
not dishonor him in the process," Cochran told me.[22]

Cochran wants to make clear that he does not hate anyone. "The essence of
the Christian faith is a love without condition, sir," he told me. "I have demonstrated that love in the fire service for thirty-four years. There's not any person
of any people group that has interacted with me for any measure of time that
can say I have hate or disregard or discrimination in my heart for any people
group."[23]

Cochran's plight has drawn condemnation from a number of religious groups
across Georgia, including the influential Georgia Baptist Convention. "This is
appalling," said Robert White, president of the Georgia Baptist Convention.
"This has everything to do with his religious beliefs."[24]

White told me he believes the mayor succumbed to pressure from the city's

LGBT community. "It's a frightening day in the United States when a person cannot express their faith without fears of persecution following," he told me. "It's persecution when a godly fire chief loses his job over expressing his Christian faith."[25]

And the fire chief's firing sparked public protests and demonstrations from the state's Christian community. "We're past the point of taking a public stand," White told me. "Christians must stand up for their rights."[26]

And even though he lost his job, don't go feeling sorry for Chief Cochran. "I'm not discouraged, and I'm not downtrodden," he said. "This is a God thing, and He's going to do great things, and He will vindicate me publicly."[27]

A SAFE HARBOR IN STORMY SEAS

A chaplain who once ministered to Navy SEALs was in danger of being thrown out of the military after he was accused of failing "to show tolerance and respect" in private counseling sessions with regard to issues pertaining to faith, marriage, and sexuality, specifically homosexuality and premarital sex.

Lieutenant Commander Wes Modder, who is endorsed by the Assemblies of God, was accused of being unable to "function in the diverse and pluralistic environment" of the Naval Nuclear Power Training Command in Goose Creek, South Carolina.[28]

"On multiple occasions he discriminated against students who were of different faiths and backgrounds," the chaplain's commanding officer, Capt. Jon R. Fahs, wrote in a memorandum.[29]

Modder is a highly decorated, nineteen-year veteran of the military. Prior to becoming a Navy chaplain, he served in the Marine Corps. His assignments included tours with the 11th Marine Expeditionary Unit and Naval Special Warfare Command, where he served as the Force Chaplain of the Navy SEALs.[30]

His record is brimming with accolades and endorsements—including from Captain Fahs. In Modder's most recent review Fahs declared that the chaplain was "the best of the best" and a "consummate professional leader" worthy of an early promotion.[31]

So how did Chaplain Modder go from being the "best of the best" to being unfit for service in the US military in a span of five months?

The Navy did not return my calls seeking comment, so all we can do is rely on their written accusations and evidence. Michael Berry, a military veteran and attorney with the religious liberty law firm First Liberty Institute, is representing Modder. In a letter to the Navy, Berry accused the military of committing a gross injustice against the chaplain.[32]

He told me they will respond forcefully and resolutely to the allegations—which they categorically deny. "We are starting to see cases where chaplains have targets on their backs," Berry said. "They have to ask themselves, 'Do I stay true to my faith or do I keep my job?'"[33]

He said Modder is being punished because of his Christian faith. "They want chaplains to be glorified summer camp counselors and not speak truth and love into people's lives," Berry told me. "There are some antireligious elements in our military. Anytime somebody wants to live their faith out, there are people who say that is offensive."[34]

Modder told me he was devastated by the accusations. He believes charges have been trumped up. "The military now wants a 2.0 chaplain instead of a legacy chaplain," Modder said. "They want a chaplain to accommodate policy that contradicts Scripture."[35]

Modder's troubles started when an assistant in his office showed up to work with a pair of Equal Opportunity representatives and a five-page complaint documenting grievances against the chaplain. The lieutenant junior grade officer went on to detail concerns about Modder's views on "same-sex relationships/marriages, homosexuality, different standards of respect for men and women, premarital sex and masturbation."[36]

Modder said the young officer had been working with him for only about a month and would constantly pepper him with questions pertaining to homosexuality. He had no idea the officer was in fact gay—and married to another man. "His five-page letter of complaint was unconscionable," Modder said. "He said I had a behavioral pattern of being discriminatory of same-sex orientation."[37]

The chaplain was not even given a chance to defend himself. He was immediately removed from his duties and told to clean out his office. "It was insulting, and it was devastating," Modder said. "I felt discriminated against. How could something like this happen at this stage of my career?"[38]

Zollie Smith, the executive director for the Assemblies of God US Missions, told me his organization stands firmly behind the chaplain "100 percent."[39]

In hindsight Berry believes the officer was setting up his client—and in so doing may have committed a crime. "I believe some of what the lieutenant has alleged could constitute a military crime—false statements, taking what the chaplain said and twisting or misconstruing it—in an attempt to get the chaplain punished," he said. "He abused the position he was placed in as a chaplain's assistant."[40]

Berry believes the officer may have gained access to private counseling files. "To be clear, Chaplain Modder does not dispute that during private, one-on-one pastoral care and counseling sessions he expressed his sincerely held religious belief that sexual acts outside of marriage are contrary to biblical teaching, and homosexual behavior is contrary to biblical teaching, and homosexual orientation or temptation, as distinct from conduct, is not sin," Berry said.[41]

Modder said many Americans may be shocked to discover how much military culture has changed over the past few years. "This new generation is very secular and very open sexually," he said. "The values that the military once held—just like the Boy Scouts of America—are changing. The culture wants this. Culture is colliding with truth. That's at the heart of this."[42]

Modder recalled an incident that occurred when he first arrived on the base. He was about to deliver the invocation at a graduation ceremony when the captain pulled him aside. "He looked at me and said, 'Hey chaplain—do not pray in Jesus's name,'" he recalled.[43]

Modder said he understands the firestorm surrounding his case, but he remains resolute. "I need to stand up for righteousness, and this is something I cannot walk away from," he told me.[44]

The reality is that many other chaplains could find themselves in Chaplain Modder's shoes. The Roman Catholic Church and the Southern Baptist Convention have nearly identical positions on the issues that the Navy found problematic with Modder.

"It's going to be a hard road for me," he said. "But it's what God has called me to do."[45]

Ultimately for Modder the fight was about leaving a legacy and setting an example for his wife and four young children. The day he was relieved of his duties, Chaplain Modder's fourteen-year-old son tagged along to help pack up his dad's office. A few senior enlisted men were there as well.[46]

As they were driving away, the boy told his father that the enlisted men had spoken to him. "They told my son that 'you can be proud of your father because he's keeping the faith,'" Modder said. "'The whole command knows that Chaplain Modder is keeping the faith.'"[47]

And Chaplain Modder did keep the faith—through some very difficult and painful days. Yet in late 2015 the chaplain received some astounding news. He had been exonerated. His good name was cleared.[48]

Let's pray that more cases like this end this way—with righteousness and freedom upheld.

A TALE OF TWO COACHES

Now a tale of two high school football coaches from Washington State. Both took a knee at a football game.

Coach Joe Kennedy of Bremerton High School took a knee to pray to God.

He was fired.[49] Coach Joey Thomas of Garfield High School took a knee to protest America. He was praised.[50]

The men coach in different school districts, so the rules on prayer and protest may vary, but it demonstrates how public schools embrace anti-American sentiment while rejecting freedom of religion.

Coach Thomas made national headlines in mid-September 2016 after he joined the entire high school football team in a protest during the national anthem. "The conversation started two weeks ago, and we were talking about life and some of the things some of the young men have experienced as far as social injustices, and how to deal with certain situations being a man of color," Coach Thomas told the local NBC-affiliate KING 5. "It's very refreshing to see these young men and women stand up for what they believe in."[51]

And by stand up, he meant sit down.

The coach told local news reporters the team planned to thumb its nose at America for the entire season. He went on to say that the idea for the protest came from the players.[52] "I support it 110 percent and that's where my mind and heart was, but this is what they wanted," the coach said. "And I think that's what makes this so special. This is student driven."[53]

Spoken like a true community organizer.

The school district seemed content with the team's behavior. "Students kneeling during the national anthem are expressing their rights protected by the First Amendment," the district wrote in a statement to our Seattle Fox television affiliate. "Seattle Public Schools supports all students' right to free speech."[54]

I feel sorry for the Garfield High School football team. Coaches are supposed to help shape teenage boys into young men—to teach them about duty and honor. Instead, the youngsters at Garfield are being coached by a man who clearly has a beef with the land of the free and the home of the brave.

On a different field, with a different kind of faith, was Coach Kennedy. Since 2008 Kennedy had taken a knee at the fifty-yard line at the conclusion of every football game to offer a brief, quiet prayer of thanksgiving for player safety, sportsmanship, and spirited competition.[55]

The coach's petition to the Almighty usually lasted about thirty seconds. He did not proselytize nor did he compel players or anyone else to participate.[56] In other words, it was a private prayer—not a Billy Graham Crusade.

He was inspired to pray after watching *Facing the Giants*, a faith-based film about a high school football team. "Coach Kennedy made a covenant with God that he would give thanks through prayer, at the end of each game, for what the players had accomplished and for the opportunity to be part of their lives through the game of football," a lawsuit stated.[57]

Lawsuit? That's right. Coach Kennedy, a former Marine Corps gunnery sergeant, filed a federal lawsuit against the Bremerton School District claiming he was let go because of his religious beliefs. At the time of this writing the school district had yet to respond to the lawsuit.[58]

"They fired him for praying," said the coach's attorney, Michael Berry, who is with First Liberty Institute, one of the nation's largest law firms handling religious liberty cases. "If a school can do this to someone like Coach Kennedy, they can do it to anybody."[59]

You see, over time some of the teenage players asked Coach Kennedy if they could join him in prayer and the coach replied, "This is a free country; you can do what you want."[60]

Other coaches engaged in religious expression at the beginning and the end of football games. The lawsuit specifically mentioned David Boynton, an assistant coach who delivered a Buddhist chant near the fifty-yard line. "Coach Boynton has never been suspended, let alone dismissed, on the basis of his religious expression," the lawsuit states.[61]

It's not quite clear what led to the school district's investigation, but on September 17, 2015, Coach Kennedy received a letter informing him that the district was conducting an inquiry into a policy regarding "Religious-Related Activities and Practices."[62]

The district directed the coach to refrain from praying around students—or doing anything that might cause people to think he was praying. He was forbidden from bowing his head or kneeling too.[63]

However, Coach Kennedy chose to defy the district's demands, and on October 23, 2015, he walked out to the fifty-yard line after the football game and prayed. On October 28, 2015, the coach was placed on paid administrative leave and banned from participating in the football program. "The District stated that it had placed Coach Kennedy on administrative leave because he 'engage[d] in overt, public religious displays on the football field while on duty as a coach,'" the lawsuit states.[64]

In November 2015 Coach Kennedy received a poor performance evaluation—after years of receiving stellar performance reviews.[65] The evaluation recommended that the coach not be rehired based on his alleged failure to follow district policy regarding religious expression and his alleged failure to supervise students after games.[66] In January 2016 Coach Kennedy's contract was not renewed.[67]

Attorney Berry said they tried to reach out to the school district on a number of occasions, but the district's attorney declined to meet. So on January 30, 2016, the coach filed a discrimination charge with the Equal Employment Opportunity Commission. In June of that year the Department of Justice issued a right-to-sue letter.[68]

Coach Kennedy told me he has no regrets. "I wouldn't do anything differently," he said. "I've always taught my guys to stand up for what they believe in—even if it's not popular."[69]

Now what he wants most is to get his job back. "All we really want for him is to be back on the sideline coaching those kids, and nothing more," Berry said.[70]

Again it's hard to believe we have come to a place in this country's history where solid, spiritual people like Coach Kennedy are fired for exercising their faith. But I suspect there are lots of folks in Bremerton who would rather stand alongside a Christian Marine Corps veteran than a bunch of godless school district bureaucrats.

THE KIM DAVIS STORY

This profile in courage made national headlines, and for good reason. I spoke with Kim Davis for this book after she had spent time as a federal prisoner in a Kentucky jail cell.

"When I went back into that holding cell, I hit my knees and just prayed, just cried out for God to give me some peace and assurance that all was going to be well, and I prayed and I sang," she said.[71]

It was September 3, 2015—the day Davis became the first Christian jailed as a result of the Supreme Court ruling legalizing gay marriage.[72]

Federal Judge David Bunning ordered her jailed for contempt of court after she defied a federal court order to issue marriage licenses to gay couples. He denied her request to accommodate her religious beliefs by simply removing her name from the marriage form.[73]

"That's all I ever asked for," she said. "I didn't ask for them to jump over the moon and give me the stars and pull the sun down for me. I asked for a very simple and doable accommodation."[74]

Davis, the clerk in Rowan County, was released five days later after she agreed to not interfere with deputies who were issuing licenses to gay couples. Bunning said he was "satisfied that the Rowan County Clerk's Office is fulfilling its obligation to issue marriage licenses to all legally eligible couples."[75]

However, the American Civil Liberties Union, representing four Kentucky couples, contends that Davis altered marriage licenses, making them possibly invalid. And they want her held in contempt—again.[76]

The validity of the licenses is questionable at best, ACLU attorneys told the

Washington Post. The ACLU called the altered marriage licenses "a stamp of animus against the LGBT community, signaling that, in Rowan County, the government's position is that LGBT couples are second-class citizens unworthy of official recognition and authorization of their marriage licenses but for this Court's intervention and Order."[77]

To be clear, the ACLU wanted to set an example with Davis.

"They want her scalp to hang on the wall as a trophy," said Mat Staver, president of Liberty Counsel, the law firm representing Davis.[78]

Davis is a follower of the apostolic Christian faith and a devoutly religious woman. She is uncomfortable in the public spotlight. "I've been called Hitler, a homophobe, a hypocrite—words I didn't even use when I was in the world, words that are very vile and nasty," she said. "I've been called pretty much anything that you can think in your mind."[79]

But the words did not hurt. "It's a righteous thing to defend the Word of God, and I am so much of a nothing. To be used of God is just an honor and a privilege," she said. "I count it all joy."[80]

The mainstream media and the activists have been ruthless. She's been smeared by tabloid-style reports on her checkered past. They've written extensively about her failed marriages.

It's true that she's been married four times.[81] But what's missing in the mainstream media coverage is the context. Her life was radically changed by Jesus Christ in 2011, and since then she has become a different person.

"My God in heaven knows every crack, every crevice, every deep place in my heart," she said. "And He knows the thoughts that are in my mind before I even think them. And He has given me such a beautiful and wonderful grace through all of this."[82]

She once lived for the devil, but now she lives for God. She's a sinner saved by grace. "I had created such a pit of sin for myself with my very own hands," she told me.[83]

So how does she handle the reporters and talking heads who call her a hypocrite? "All I can say to them is if they have a sordid past like what I had, they too can receive the cleansing and renewing, and they can start a fresh life, and they can be different," she said. "They don't have to remain in their sin; there's hope for tomorrow."[84]

Pastor Rick Warren once told me the fight for religious liberty would become the civil rights issue of our generation.[85]

The arrest of Kim Davis fulfilled that prediction.

I truly believe Judge Bunning wanted to intimidate Christians and send a very clear message to the rest of the nation that resistance to same-sex marriage would not be tolerated. Judge Bunning did with the gavel what Bull Connor tried to do with dogs and hoses. He tried to intimidate the people.

Davis did not seek the national spotlight. She had no intention of becoming a spokeswoman for religious liberty, and she bristles at the idea that she is a hero of the faith. "I'm just a vessel God has chosen for this time and this place," she said. "I'm no different than any other Christian. It was my appointed time to stand, and their time will come."[86]

Our conversation was sprinkled with references to Bible passages and worship songs. She frequently became emotional when talking about her relationship with God. She spent most of her time in jail reading her Bible, writing notes, and singing songs such as, "What a Mighty God We Serve."[87]

She especially took comfort in a passage of Scripture from the New Testament. "God did not give us a spirit of fear, but of power and of love and of a sound mind," she said, quoting 2 Timothy 1:7.[88]

But it was the next verse that gave her courage: "Therefore do not be ashamed of the testimony of our Lord, nor of me His prisoner, but share with me in the sufferings for the gospel according to the power of God," she said.[89] (See 2 Timothy 1:8, NKJV.)

"I walked and prayed and sang praises in the jail cell and just really drew comfort from God's Word when I was there," she told me.[90]

Staver said he marveled at his client's composure during their first meeting inside the jailhouse. "We hugged and shed a few tears and the first words out of her mouth were, 'All is well,'" Staver told me. "I went in there to encourage her, but we went away being encouraged ourselves by her."[91]

She was at complete peace, Staver said. "I think it's hard for people to understand that, but there was a definite peace," he said.[92]

Davis told me it was worth every day behind bars. "The Lord died and suffered so terribly for us, and I count it such a privilege and an honor and a joy that I would have to sit a mere five days in jail to uphold His Word," she said. "For me, it's worth it."[93]

Life has returned to normal for Davis. She went back to work at the clerk's office—in early, out late. She dotes on her children and grandson. And she finds time to read her Bible atop a hill on the family's property.[94]

And despite the media firestorm, this nationally known defender of religious liberty even found time to celebrate her birthday on September 17, which just happens to be Constitution Day.

MARCHING ORDERS

1. **Remember the real heroes.** Celebrities and star athletes are not necessarily heroes, but the people in this chapter are. Let's remember what they did and share their stories with those around us—our children, our fellow churchgoers, our friends, and our neighbors. These stories must not fade into the background or get drowned out by those who want to make heroes of immoral, cowardly people.

   Talk about Kim Davis and her bravery. Talk about Coach Kennedy and the knee he took, which cost him his job. Talk about Chief Cochran's resolve. If you're a homeschooling parent or private school teacher, use their examples in your classroom. Make it clear this is modern American persecution meted out to faithful people for following Christ. Shape the current conversation and the next generation.

   A nation is known for who its heroes are. It's time to start praising the right people for doing the right things.

2. **Prepare now.** You might become the next Coach Kennedy, the next Chaplain Modder, the next Kim Davis, the next Chief Cochran. How do you prepare? By putting down deep roots now. By living by your convictions when nobody is looking. They each had spent a life building up to that point of courage.

   What are you doing to strengthen your character and resolve right now? Be prepared. When that unexpected situation arises, you will be ready.

   You may very well be the next hero.

3. **Promote your values.** When persecution breaks out against a coach, civil servant, student, member of the military, pastor, flower shop owner, or whoever, post about it on social media. Don't let it go unnoticed. Use the platform you have to promote the values you hold dear.

We may never meet these people, but we can stand with them like fellow soldiers. That's the deplorable thing to do.

THE SHINING CITY ON A HILL

THERE'S PROBABLY NO better way to conclude this guide than with the words of the Great Communicator, Ronald Reagan. In his farewell address from the Oval Office, he seemed to peer into the future and see our present moment.

"Because we're a great nation," he said, "our challenges seem complex. It will always be this way. But as long as we remember our first principles and believe in ourselves, the future will always be ours. And something else we learned: Once you begin a great movement, there's no telling where it will end."[1]

Reagan went on to say:

> "We the People" tell the government what to do; it doesn't tell us. "We the People" are the driver; the government is the car. And we decide where it should go, and by what route, and how fast. Almost all the world's constitutions are documents in which governments tell the people what their privileges are. Our Constitution is a document in which "We the People" tell the government what it is allowed to do. "We the People" are free.[2]

Has there been a more eloquent, heartfelt affirmation of the American citizen? I like to picture the scene this way...

As the first rays of morning light wash over the Eastern Seaboard, a flag is unfurled with broad stripes and bright stars. A soldier stands guard over sleeping heroes, known only to their Maker.

A resting place for the common man.

A farmer in the Heartland gathers his crop as golden wheat shimmers in the breeze. A rancher gallops along the Texas Hill Country, herding his cattle to the stockyards. A river boat captain pilots his boat down the muddy waters of the Mississippi.

A job for the common man.

In a Kansas church house a candle flickers, a preacher prays on bended knee, asking God to bless our land, to shed on us His grace.

A prayer for the common man.

When the floodwaters rise and the storm clouds billow, we stand ready to help—feeding the hungry, mending the wounded, rebuilding homes and lives.

Goodwill for the common man.

And in some distant land a soldier stands guard defending our nation, tending Lady Liberty's flame. They are young men and young women from our big cities and small towns, willing to sacrifice their lives so that we can be free.

A protector for the common man.

We are the sons and daughters of the common man.

We are noble people forged by freedom's fire.

We are an uncommon nation established by common men.

We are proud Americans, and this is our fanfare.

For the past eight years Americans have been told we are the problem, that we are not a Christian nation, that we are not an exceptional nation. Our traditions and our values have been ridiculed and marginalized.

As I mentioned earlier in this book, nearly half of our fellow countrymen are no longer proud of what our nation has become—this vast wasteland of perpetually offended people, divided by demographics.

But like Reagan and all true patriots, I still have hope for America. I still believe that "We the People" can restore what former president Obama fundamentally transformed. And I believe that together we can forge a new path.

We can do that with people like Vita Tonga, a high school football player in Hurst, Texas. He had torn his ACL and was in a wheelchair on the sidelines. But when the national anthem began, young Vita Tonga lifted himself out of that wheelchair and joined his teammates in honoring our nation. "People gave their lives just so I can stand up over here in the United States," Tonga told *Sports Day*. "So I feel as an American citizen I should stand."[3]

I have hope in our nation because of the young people at Big Rapids Middle School who gather around the flag pole on the first day of every school year. A trumpeter sounds reveille, the military bugle call, and then a huge crowd of students and teachers recites the Pledge of Allegiance. "When you see the flag flying, you think about the sacrifices of those who have gone before to give us the freedom to either say the pledge or not say the pledge," said teacher Mark Brejcha, an Air Force veteran.[4]

And I have hope because of the moms and dads in Weber City, Utah, who raised up a generation of young patriots. When teenagers at the local high school noticed that someone had set an American flag on fire, they extinguished the blaze, disposed of the flag—and then decided to make a public statement.

The following day dozens of students brought their personal American flags and wore patriotic clothing to send a message. "It's not just the material part of the flag. It's the meaning behind it," said teenager Ben Schofield. "We're just showing that we can fly our flags and we always will."[5]

President Reagan said freedom is just one generation away from extinction.[6] In 2016 we came close—too close.

And the time has come for all of us to stand together—Baptist and Wesleyan, Presbyterian and Pentecostal, Catholic and Calvinist—and with one voice declare that we are one nation under God.

There's a scene in that wonderful film *We Were Soldiers* that depicts the Battle of the la Drang Valley. Lieutenant Colonel Hal Moore and his Army rangers were surrounded. The enemy was advancing. All appeared hopeless.

Joe Galloway, a United Press International reporter, was caught in the melee, and when the bullets started flying, the reporter dropped to the ground.

In the middle of the chaos and carnage Sergeant Major Basil Plumley stood resolute. He walked over and delivered a swift kick of his boot and told the terrified journalist, "You can't take no pictures lying down there, sonny."

He tossed the reporter a rifle, but the reporter rejected the weapon with the words, "I'm a noncombatant, sir."

To which the sergeant major replied, "Ain't no such thing today, boy."[7]

My fellow countrymen, we are surrounded. The cultural bullets are flying. The enemy is advancing. And the time has come for all of us to stand resolute.

In November 2016 we halted our nation's slide into almost-certain socialistic oblivion. We stopped just shy of complete moral meltdown, the crumble of our nation's physical (not to mention spiritual) infrastructure. We made a stand that said, "Morality and values and borders and fiscal responsibility all matter."

But we're not out of danger yet. Our nation stands between two fates—the one behind, from which we have been mercifully spared for the moment—and the one ahead, which represents an entirely new—or shall we say, renewed—vision of what our nation can become. Again.

Welcome, America, to your history-making, tide-changing, nation-reclaiming turning point.

Deplorable Americans had their say on Election Day, and we decided to make America great again. That's more than a slogan on a red hat—it's a heart slogan that we deeply, profoundly feel and know.

But it's not about one man in the White House. It's about *us*. Here. Wherever we are across this great country. President Reagan said it well in his 1989 farewell address:

> All great change in America begins at the dinner table. So, tomorrow
> night in the kitchen I hope the talking begins. And children, if your
> parents haven't been teaching you what it means to be an American,
> let 'em know and nail 'em on it. That would be a very American thing
> to do.[8]

The White House is changing hands and—oh, thank the good Lord in heaven!—changing governing philosophies. What will you and I do to make America great again, aside from eating more Chick-fil-A sandwiches and sipping Rush Limbaugh's iced tea? Great changes are afoot in our land. This book has been about how we Deplorables can participate—how normal, middle-of-the-country Americans can get behind and push the great changes that need to happen.

We voted. Now comes the other 99 percent of the work.

Winning America back, making our nation great again, means more than victory parties or celebratory Facebook posts. It means more than watching the progress of the new administration. It means more than enjoying the headlines, which seem to endlessly broadcast liberal terror at what the new administration will do to America—written by your unbiased captains of journalism, of course, as they watch their Marxist fantasies go down the tubes.

It means more than explaining to your misguided friends and bereaved loved ones that their worst fear—a conservative presidency—is actually their greatest hope because *their* income will go up. *They* will have more job choices because there will be more jobs. *Their* freedoms will be restored.

Winning America back means restoring not just our paychecks but our pride and our freedom, and unshackling even the most liberal among us from the fetters of a federal government that just didn't know when to stop growing. Quoting Reagan in that same 1989 address, "Man is not free unless government is limited. There's a clear cause and effect here that is as neat and predictable as a law of physics: As government expands, liberty contracts."[9]

We can make America great again—right where we are—because Reagan was right. America's heroes really aren't in the grand, shiny offices in capitols around our nation. They are in the shops, the workplaces, the fields and factories, the homes, the homeschool meetings, the churches, the parks and playgrounds.

They are living everyday life, the way God intended it to be lived, without fear of a government that is working against our basic beliefs, our faith, our freedom, and our pocketbooks.

Making America great again starts in our houses and communities. It's up to us.

You say, "Todd, I'm not a fighter."

Well, there just ain't no such thing today.

Do not hide liberty's light under a bushel. No! Hold it high!

And if we stay the course, I believe the historians will look back on this age and declare that our exceptional nation became a beacon for hope once more.

Oh, how I long for that day. Let the nations be glad. Let the people rejoice. Let the flame of freedom burn bright so all the world can see that we are once again that shining city on a hill.

Deplorables of America, this is our moment. Let's back up and bring it—and make America great again!

NOTES

Introduction

1. "History of Two If By Tea," RushRevere.com, accessed December 17, 2016, http://www.rushrevere.com/tea/moreinfo/historyoftwoifbytea.html.

2. Seema Mehta, "Transcript: Clinton's Full Remarks as She Called Half of Trump Supporters 'Deplorables,'" *Los Angeles Times*, September 10, 2016, accessed December 17, 2016, http://www.latimes.com/nation/politics/trailguide /la-na-trailguide-updates-transcript-clinton-s-full-remarks-as-1473549076-html story.html.

3. "Franklin Graham: America Is at a Tipping Point," Billy Graham Evangelistic Association, April 7, 2016, accessed December 17, 2016, https://billygraham .org/story/franklin-graham-america-is-at-a-tipping-point/.

4. "Read the Opinion: Supreme Court Rules States Cannot Ban Same-Sex Marriage," Cable News Network, June 26, 2015, accessed December 17, 2016, http://www.cnn.com/2015/06/26/politics/scotus-opinion-document-obergefell -hodges/index.html.

5. "New Details Emerge About Deadliest Mass Shooting In U.S. History," Huffington Post, June 16, 2016, accessed December 17, 2016, http://www .huffingtonpost.com/entry/terror-shooting-at-gay-club_us_575d5938e4b0e39a28 add1b4; "San Bernardino Shooting," Cable News Network, December 7, 2015, accessed December 17, 2016, http://www.cnn.com/specials/san-bernardino -shooting.

6. Dan Evon, "Baby Parts for Sale," Snopes.com, January 15, 2016, accessed December 17, 2016, http://www.snopes.com/pp-baby-parts-sale/.

7. Todd Starnes, "West Point General Says Football Prayer Crossed the Line," FoxNews.com, September 13, 2016, accessed December 17, 2016, http:// www.foxnews.com/opinion/2016/09/13/west-point-general-says-football-prayer -crossed-line.html.

8. Todd Starnes, "Parents Furious Over School's Plan to Teach Gender Spectrum, Fluidity," FoxNews.com, May 15, 2015, accessed December 17, 2016, http://www.foxnews.com/opinion/2015/05/15/call-it-gender-fluidity-schools-to -teach-kids-there-s-no-such-thing-as-boys-or-girls.html; Todd Starnes, "Graphic Middle School Sex Class Outrages Parents," FoxNews.com, accessed December 17, 2016, http://radio.foxnews.com/toddstarnes/top-stories/middle-school-sex-class

-shows-kids-how-to-use-condoms.html; Todd Starnes, "Back to School: Let the Left-Wing Indoctrination Begin," FoxNews.com, September 1, 2015, accessed December 17, 2016, http://www.foxnews.com/opinion/2015/09/01/universities-are-becoming-gender-neutral-zones-where-free-thought-is-outlawed.html.

9.   Kirsten Powers, "Kansas Legislators Tried to Make Discrimination Easy," *USA Today*, February 19, 2014, accessed December 17, 2016, http://www.usatoday.com/story/opinion/2014/02/18/gays-lesbians-kansas-bill-religious-freedom-christians-column/5588643/.

10.   Abraham Lincoln, "Proclamation 97—Appointing a Day of National Humiliation, Fasting, and Prayer," March 30, 1863, online by Gerhard Peters and John T. Woolley, The American Presidency Project, accessed December 17, 2016, http://www.presidency.ucsb.edu/ws/?pid=69891.

11.   Billy Hallowell, "Houston Gov't Subpoenaed Pastors' Sermons. Now, They're Fighting Back.," TheBlaze, Inc., August 3, 2015, accessed December 17, 2016, http://www.theblaze.com/stories/2015/08/03/houston-pastors-hit-back-against-mayor-with-lawsuit-alleging-their-religious-freedoms-were-trampled/.

12.   James C. McKinley Jr., "Houston Is Largest City to Elect Openly Gay Mayor," The New York Times Company, December 12, 2009, accessed December 17, 2016, http://www.nytimes.com/2009/12/13/us/politics/13houston.html.

13.   Ronald Reagan, "Inaugural Address: January 5, 1967," Ronald Reagan Presidential Library and Museum, accessed December 17, 2016, https://reaganlibrary.archives.gov/archives/speeches/govspeech/01051967a.htm.

14.   "Reagan's Farewell Speech," PBS, *American Experience*, accessed December 17, 2016, http://www.pbs.org/wgbh/americanexperience/features/primary-resources/reagan-farewell/.

CHAPTER 1: THE HAPPY WARRIOR

1.   *The Patriot*, directed by Roland Emmerich (Culver City, CA: Sony Pictures Home Entertainment, 2000).

2.   Ibid.

3.   "Oliver Hart Collection: Biography," James B. Duke Library, accessed December 17, 2016, http://library.furman.edu/specialcollections/baptist/hart_biography.htm; Robert Wilson Gibbes, *Documentary History of the American Revolution: Consisting of Letters and Papers Relating to the Contest for Liberty: Chiefly in South Carolina, from Originals in the Possession of the Editor, and Other Sources, 1764–1776* (New York: D. Appleton & Co., 1855), 164.

4.   Thomas S. Kidd, "From Dissenters to Patriots: Baptists and the American Revolution," Georgetown College, accessed December 17, 2016, http://www.georgetowncollege.edu/cdal/files/2011/06/2011-Thomas-Kidd.pdf.

5.   John Stonestreet, "You Really Want Us to Keep Our Faith to Ourselves?," *BreakPoint*, April 8, 2015, accessed December 17, 2016, http://www.breakpoint.org/bpcommentaries/entry/13/27154.

6.   Napp Hazworth, "Christians Who Have Avoided the Culture Wars May No Longer Have a Choice With Religious Freedom in Jeopardy, Legal Scholar Says," *Christian Post*, May 9, 2015, accessed December 17, 2016, http://www

.christianpost.com/news/christians-who-have-avoided-the-culture-wars-may-no
-longer-have-a-choice-with-religious-freedom-in-jeopardy-legal-scholar-says-138897/.

7.   Douglas Laycock et al., "Brief as Amici Curiae in Support of Petitioners,
Supreme Court of the United States, Case Nos. 14-556, 14-562, 14-571, and
14-574," accessed December 20, 2016, https://www.supremecourt.gov
/ObergefellHodges/AmicusBriefs/14-556_Douglas_Laycock.pdf.

8.   *Peaceful Coexistence*, US Commission of Civil Rights, September 2016,
accessed December 17, 2016, http://media.washtimes.com.s3.amazonaws.com
/media/misc/2016/09/09/Peaceful-Coexistence-09-07-16-6.pdf.

9.   Ibid.

10.   Jessica Chasmar, "Pentagon Training Course Says Modern Sexism
Rooted in Bible, Constitution," The Washington Times, LLC, April 14, 2015,
accessed December 20, 2016, http://www.washingtontimes.com/news/2015/apr
/14/pentagon-training-course-says-modern-sexism-rooted/.

11.   Tom Fitton, in communication with the author, August 2013.

12.   "AFSS 0910 Equal Opportunity and Treatment Incidents (EOTI),"
Defense Equal Opportunity Management Institute, January 2013, accessed
December 17, 2016, http://www.judicialwatch.org/wp-content/uploads/2013
/08/2161-docs.pdf.

13.   Fitton, in communication with the author, August 2013.

14.   "AFSS 0910 Equal Opportunity and Treatment Incidents (EOTI),"
Defense Equal Opportunity Management Institute.

15.   Fitton, in communication with the author, August 2013.

16.   "AFSS 0910 Equal Opportunity and Treatment Incidents (EOTI),"
Defense Equal Opportunity Management Institute.

17.   Todd Starnes, "US Army Defines Christian Ministry as 'Domestic Hate
Group,'" FoxNews.com, October 14, 2013, accessed December 20, 2016, http://
www.foxnews.com/opinion/2013/10/14/us-army-defines-christian-ministry-as
-domestic-hate-group.html.

18.   In communication with the author, April 2013.

19.   Ibid.

20.   Susan Berry, "State Representatives Attack Declaration of Independence
on Louisiana House Floor," Breitbart, May 27, 2016, accessed December 17, 2016,
http://www.breitbart.com/big-government/2016/05/27/state-representatives
-attack-declaration-of-independence-on-louisiana-house-floor/.

21.   Valarie Hodges, in communication with the author, May 2016

22.   Ibid.

23.   Ibid.

24.   Berry, "State Representatives Attack Declaration of Independence on
Louisiana House Floor."

25.   Todd Starnes, "Do Louisiana Lawmakers Really Think the Declaration
of Independence Is Racist and Sexist?," FoxNews.com, May 31, 2016, accessed
December 20, 2016, http://www.foxnews.com/opinion/2016/05/31/do-louisiana
-lawmakers-really-think-declaration-independence-is-racist-and-sexist.html

26.   Hodges, in communication with the author, May 2016.

27.   "Franklin Graham: Calling the Nation to Repentance," Billy Graham Evangelistic Association, December 23, 2015, accessed December 17, 2016, https://billygraham.org/decision-magazine/january-2016/franklin-graham-calling -the-nation-to-repentance/.

28.   Franklin Graham, in communication with the author, January 2016.

29.   Ibid.

30.   Ibid.

31.   Ibid.

32.   Ibid.

33.   Ibid.

34.   Alex McFarland, in communication with the author, December 2016. See also Joel D. Vaughan, *The Rise and Fall of the Christian Coalition: The Inside Story* (Eugene, OR: Resource Publications, 2009), 202.

35.   As relayed by Alex McFarland, in communication with the author, December 2016.

36.   Adrian Rogers, "Christian Citizenship" sermon, delivered July 5, 1998, at Bellevue Baptist Church in Memphis, Tennessee. Used with permission.

37.   Ibid.

38.   "The Declaration of Independence: A Transcription," The U.S. National Archives and Records Administration, accessed December 17, 2016, https://www .archives.gov/founding-docs/declaration-transcript.

39.   "The Bill of Rights: A Transcription," The U.S. National Archives and Records Administration, accessed December 17, 2016, https://www.archives.gov /founding-docs/bill-of-rights-transcript.

40.   Rogers, "Christian Citizenship" sermon.

CHAPTER 2: THE GREAT UNRAVELING

1.   Cindy Boren, "'Duck Dynasty' Star Prays at NASCAR Race for a 'Jesus Man' to Be Elected President," *Washington Post*, April 11, 2016, accessed December 17, 2016, https://www.washingtonpost.com/news/early-lead/wp/2016 /04/11/duck-dynasty-star-prays-at-nascar-race-for-a-jesus-man-to-be-elected -president/?utm_term=.fd68fbd56444.

2.   Ibid.

3.   See, for example, Hemant Meht, "*Duck Dynasty* Dad Opens NASCAR Race with Prayer That We 'Put a Jesus Man in the White House,'" April 10, 2016, accessed December 17, 2016, http://www.patheos.com/blogs/friendlyatheist/2016 /04/10/duck-dynasty-dad-opens-nascar-race-with-prayer-that-we-put-a-jesus-man -in-the-white-house/; David Whitley, "NASCAR Doesn't Need Phil Robertson's Prayers," *Orlando Sentinel*, April 11, 2016, accessed December 17, 2016, http:// www.orlandosentinel.com/sports/nascar/os-nascar-prayer-david-whitley-0412-2016 0411-column.html.

4.   Timothy Burke, "NASCAR Invocation Features Prayer to Elect a Republican President," *Deadspin* (blog), April 9, 2016, accessed December 17, 2016, http://screengrabber.deadspin.com/nascar-invocation-features-prayer-to -elect-a-republican-1770094804.

5.   Jenna Fryer, "Column: NASCAR Clouding It's Image With Politics," AP Sports, April 11, 2016, accessed December 17, 2016, http://racing.ap.org/article /column-nascar-clouding-its-image-politics.

6.   Whitley, "NASCAR Doesn't Need Phil Robertson's Prayers."

7.   Christopher Olmstead, "NASCAR: Analyzing Whether or Not Religion Still Belongs in the Sport," FanSided, accessed December 17, 2016, http:// beyondtheflag.com/2016/04/11/nascar-analyzing-whether-or-not-religion-still- belongs-in-the-sport/.

8.   "'Duck Dynasty' Star's Prayer Message Defended by TMS' President," Star-Telegram, April 10, 2016, accessed December 17, 2016, http://www.star -telegram.com/sports/nascar-auto-racing/article71062092.html.

9.   Joel Ebert, "Tennessee Senate Committee Approves Bible Bill," Tennessean, March 29, 2016, accessed December 17, 2016, http://www.tennessean.com /story/news/politics/2016/03/29/senate-committee-approves-bible-bill/82392814/.

10.   David Plazas, "Tennessee Lawmakers Who Back Bible Bill Are Theocrats," Tennessean, March 31, 2016, accessed December 17, 2016, http://www .tennessean.com/story/opinion/editorials/2016/03/31/tennessee-lawmakers-who -back-bible-bill-theocrats/82448516/.

11.   Ibid.

12.   Ibid.

13.   "Professor: Take Our Country Back, From the Constitution," CBS Interactive Inc., January 27, 2013, accessed December 17, 2016, http://www.cbsnews .com/news/professor-take-our-country-back-from-the-constitution/.

14.   Ibid.

15.   Ibid.

16.   Ibid.

17.   Sommer Bauer, in communication with the author, October 2014.

18.   Ibid.

19.   Ibid.

20.   Ibid.

21.   Ed Alexander, in communication with the author, October 2014.

22.   Ibid.

23.   Julie West, in communication with the author, October 2014.

24.   Ibid.

25.   Ibid.

26.   "UCI Student Support Letter," accessed December 17, 2016, https://docs .google.com/forms/d/e/1FAIpQLSerV5dpbbyqzRfPE3tdTu4aoBFBA -Oz4lPAzCcL4IQ-RFKxog/viewform.

27.   Caleb Bonham, "Professors Endorse Flag Ban," Leadership Institute, March 10, 2015, accessed December 17, 2016, http://www.campusreform.org /%5C?ID=6349.

28.   Matthew Guevara, "Flags and Decoration Adjustment for Inclusivity," no. 81, R50-70, March 3, 2015, accessed December 17, 2016, http://www.asuci.uci .edu/legislative/legislations/R50-70.html.

29.   Adelle Nazarian, "UC Irvine Student: US Flag Banned to Avoid 'Triggering' Hurt Feelings Among Illegals," Breitbart, March 8, 2015, accessed

December 17, 2016, http://www.breitbart.com/california/2015/03/08/student-u-s
-flag-banned-to-avoid-triggering-hurt-feelings-among-illegals/.

30. Robin Abcarian, "Here's a Banner Headline: UC Irvine's Flag Flap Has
Gotten Absurd," *Los Angeles Times*, March 12, 2015, accessed December 17,
2016, http://www.latimes.com/local/orangecounty/la-me-0313-abcarian-students
-flags-20150313-column.html.

31. Reza Zomorrodian, in communication with the author, March 2015.

32. "UCI Legislative Council Meeting Scheduled for Tonight Cancelled Due
to Violence Threat," University of California, Irvine, March 12, 2015, accessed
December 17, 2016, http://www.asuci.uci.edu/flag/.

33. Patrick McGreevy, "After UCI Student Effort to Ban Flag, Angry Lawmakers Have a Proposal," *Los Angeles Times*, March 9, 2015, accessed December
17, 2016, http://www.latimes.com/local/political/la-me-pc-lawmakers-would-bar
-california-universities-from-banning-the-us-flag-on-campus--20150309-story.html.

34. Merle Haggard, "The Fightin' Side of Me."

35. Kim Kimzey, "Woodruff High Principal Says Flags on Trucks Violated
School Policy," GateHouse Media, September 12, 2014, accessed December 17,
2016, http://www.goupstate.com/news/20140912/woodruff-high-principal-says
-flags-on-trucks-violated-school-policy.

36. Ibid.

37. Rallie Liston, in communication with the author, September 2014.

38. Ibid.

39. Ibid.

40. Jessica Chasmar, "S.C. High School Confiscates American Flags on Sept.
11," *Washington Times*, September 16, 2014, accessed December 17, 2016, http://
www.washingtontimes.com/news/2014/sep/16/sc-high-school-confiscates-students
-american-flags/.

41. Liston, in communication with the author, September 2014.

42. Ibid.

43. Ibid.

44. Cheryl K. Chumley, "Michigan School Subs Out Betsy Ross, Einstein
for Obama, Oprah," *Washington Times*, September 16, 2014, accessed December
17, 2016, http://www.washingtontimes.com/news/2014/nov/14/michigan-school
-subs-out-betsy-ross-einstein-for-o/.

45. Craig Bergman, in communication with the author, November 2014.

46. Chumley, "Michigan School Subs Out Betsy Ross, Einstein for Obama,
Oprah."

47. Todd Holliday, in communication with the author, November 2014.

48. Bergman, in communication with the author, November 2014.

49. Jennifer Hoff, in communication with the author, November 2014.

50. Bergman, in communication with the author, November 2014.

51. Ibid.

52. Hoff, in communication with the author, November 2014.

53. Ibid.

54. Ibid.

55. Bergman, in communication with the author, November 2014.

56.   Phaedra Trethan, "ACLU: No 'God Bless America' in Haddon Heights School," *Courier-Post*, January 6, 2016, accessed December 17, 2016, http://www.courierpostonline.com/story/news/2016/01/04/aclu-no-god-bless-america-haddon-heights-school/78263384/.

57.   Ibid.

58.   Sam Sassano, in communication with the author, January 2016.

59.   Trethan, "ACLU: No 'God Bless America" in Haddon Heights School."

60.   Sassano, in communication with the author, January 2016.

61.   Ibid.

62.   Ibid.

63.   Debi Krezel, in communication with the author, January 2016.

64.   Ibid.

65.   Sassano, in communication with the author, January 2016.

66.   Hiram Sasser, in communication with the author, January 2016.

67.   Scott Johnson, "'God Bless America' Sparks Controversy at School," Graham Media Group, February 13, 2015, accessed December 17, 2016, http://www.news4jax.com/news/local/god-bless-america-sparks-controversy-at-school.

68.   Sharyl Wood, in communication with the author, February 2015.

69.   Johnson, "'God Bless America' Sparks Controversy at School."

70.   Monica Miller, Appignani Humanist Legal Center, letter sent to Nassau County School District and Yulee High School via e-mail on February 9, 2015, accessed December 17, 2016, http://archive.americanhumanist.org/system/storage/2/45/5/5484/Yulee_HS_FL_Letter_2-9-15_final.pdf.

71.   Ibid.

72.   Horatio G. Mihet, Liberty Counsel, letter sent to Yulee High School via e-mail on February 12, 2015, accessed December 17, 2016, https://www.liberty.edu/media/9980/attachments/2015/021215_Ltr_-_to_Yulee_High_Principal.pdf.

73.   Wood, in communication with the author, February 2015.

74.   Ibid.

75.   Ibid.

76.   Jeremy Dys, in communication with the author, February 2015.

77.   Ibid.

78.   Kristi Palma, "'American Pride' Dance Will Go On at Lexington High," Boston Globe Media Partners, LLC, March 24, 2015, accessed December 17, 2016, http://www.boston.com/news/local-news/2015/03/24/american-pride-dance-will-go-on-at-lexington-high.

79.   Kristi Palma, "Theme of Lexington High's 'American Pride' Dance Changed for Excluding Other Nationalities," Boston Globe Media Partners, LLC, March 23, 2015, accessed December 17, 2016, http://www.boston.com/news/local-news/2015/03/23/theme-of-lexington-highs-american-pride-dance-changed-for-excluding-other-nationalities.

80.   Kelli O'Hara, "American-Themed Dance Causes Controversy in Lexington," WorldNow and WHDH, March 23, 2015, accessed December 17, 2016, https://web.archive.org/web/20150324175636/http://www.whdh.com/story/28577340/american-themed-dance-causes-controversy-in-lexington.

81.   Palma, "'American Pride' Dance Will Go On at Lexington High."

82.   O'Hara, "American-Themed Dance Causes Controversy in Lexington."

83.   Laura Lasa, in communication with the author, March 2015.

CHAPTER 3: PANTSUITS, YUGE HANDS, AND THE 2016 PRESIDENTIAL RACE

1.   Tim Jones, "Dewey Defeats Truman," *Chicago Tribune*, accessed
December 17, 2016, http://www.chicagotribune.com/news/nationworld/politics
/chi-chicagodays-deweydefeats-story-story.html.

2.   Dana Blanton, "Fox News Poll: Fewer Americans Feeling Proud,"
FoxNews.com, June 30, 2016, accessed December 17, 2016, http://www.foxnews
.com/politics/2016/06/30/fox-news-poll-fewer-americans-feeling-proud.html.

3.   "Remarks by President Obama at YSEALI Town Hall," The White
House, September 7, 2016, accessed December 17, 2016, https://www.whitehouse
.gov/the-press-office/2016/09/07/remarks-president-obama-yseali-town-hall.

4.   Ibid.

5.   "Joint Press Availability With President Obama and President Gul of
Turkey," The White House, April 6, 2009, accessed December 17, 2016, https://
www.whitehouse.gov/the-press-office/joint-press-availability-with-president-obama
-and-president-gul-turkey.

6.   "Remarks by the President at National Prayer Breakfast," The White
House, February 5, 2015, accessed December 17, 2016, https://www.whitehouse
.gov/the-press-office/2015/02/05/remarks-president-national-prayer-breakfast.

7.   Ibid.

8.   Family Research Council's Facebook page, May 31, 2015, accessed
December 17, 2016, https://www.facebook.com/familyresearchcouncil/
posts/10153379420267442.

9.   "Person of the Year: Donald Trump—President of the Divided States of
America," *TIME*, December 19, 2016 issue, accessed January 6, 2017, http://time
.com/time-person-of-the-year-2016-donald-trump-choice/.

10.   E. J. Dionne Jr., "Ted Cruz and the Revenge of New York Values," *Washington Post*, April 19, 2016, accessed December 17, 2016, https://www
.washingtonpost.com/blogs/post-partisan/wp/2016/04/19/ted-cruz-and-the
-revenge-of-new-york-values/?utm_term=.54bd2dbbf31f.

11.   Ibid.; Jeremy Diamond, "Trump Hits Cruz Over 'New York Values' on
Long Island," Cable News Network, April 7, 2016, accessed December 17, 2016,
http://www.cnn.com/2016/04/06/politics/donald-trump-new-york-values-ted
-cruz/; Jennifer Hansler, "9/11 Widower Invites Ted Cruz to Learn About 'New
York Values,'" ABC News, January 16, 2016, accessed December 17, 2016, http://
abcnews.go.com/Politics/911-widower-invites-ted-cruz-learn-york-values/story
?id=36321959; Ben Wolfgang, "Clinton Dings Cruz, Touts Her 'New York values'"
Washington Times, April 14, 2016, accessed December 17, 2016, http://www
.washingtontimes.com/news/2016/apr/14/hillary-clinton-dings-ted-cruz-touts-her
-new-york-/.

12.   Mike Waterhouse, "Mayor De Blasio 'Disgusted' Over Ted Cruz's 'New
York Values' Comment, Says Senator Should Apologize," ABC Inc., April 15,
2016, accessed December 17, 2016, http://abc7ny.com/politics/de-blasio-disgusted
-over-cruzs-new-york-values-comment-says-senator-should-apologize/1160363/.

13.   Joseph Spector, "N.Y. Governor on Ted Cruz: 'If He Had Any Class, He Would Apologize," *USA Today*, January 15, 2016, accessed December 17, 2016, http://www.usatoday.com/story/news/politics/onpolitics/2016/01/15/new-york -governor-ted-cruz-apologize/78844538/.

14.   Jessica Chasmar, "Gov. Cuomo: Pro-Life, Pro-Gun Conservatives 'Have No Place' in New York," *Washington Times*, January 19, 2014, accessed December 17, 2016, http://www.washingtontimes.com/news/2014/jan/19/gov-cuomo-pro-life -conservatives-have-no-place-new/.

15.   "Topless Women of Times Square Say They Can't Be Restricted," *Newsday*, October 11, 2015, accessed December 17, 2016, http://www.newsday .com/news/new-york/topless-women-of-times-square-say-they-can-t-be-restricted -1.10948209.

16.   Stephen Stromberg, "Occupy Wall Street vs. Tea Party," *Washington Post*, October 14, 2011, accessed December 17, 2016, https://www.washingtonpost .com/blogs/post-partisan/post/occupy-wall-street-vs-tea-party/2011/10/13 /gIQA3YrViL_blog.html?utm_term=.8784c708dc53; John Nolte, "Occupy Wall Street's Rap Sheet," FoxNews.com, October 30, 2011, accessed December 17, 2016, http://nation.foxnews.com/occupy-wall-street/2011/10/30/occupy-wall -streets-rap-sheet.

17.   Todd Starnes, "Dallas Attack: The 'Pigs in a Blanket' Crowd Got What They Wanted," FoxNews.com, July 8, 2016, accessed December 17, 2016, http:// www.foxnews.com/opinion/2016/07/08/dallas-attack-pigs-in-blanket-crowd-got -what-wanted.html.

18.   Sharon Otterman, "Supreme Court Leaves Intact New York's Ban on Religious Services in Schools," The New York Times Company, March 30, 2015, accessed December 17, 2016, http://www.nytimes.com/2015/03/31/nyregion /supreme-court-leaves-intact-new-yorks-ban-on-religious-services-in-schools.html.

19.   Christian George, "How Would Spurgeon Vote," The Spurgeon Center and Midwestern Baptist Theological Seminary, November 8, 2016, accessed December 17, 2016, http://center.spurgeon.org/2016/11/08/how-would-spurgeon -vote/.

20.   Samuel Rodriguez, in communication with the author, May 2016.

21.   Franklin Graham, in communication with the author, May 2016.

22.   Ibid.

23.   Mike Huckabee, in communication with the author, May 2016.

24.   "Sen. John McCain Attacks Pat Robertson, Jerry Falwell, Republican Establishment as Harming GOP Ideals," Cable News Network, February 28, 2000, accessed December 17, 2016, http://transcripts.cnn.com/TRANSCRIPTS /0002/28/se.01.html.

25.   "About," Decision American Tour, accessed December 17, 2016, https:// decisionamericatour.com/about/.

26.   Graham, in communication with the author, May 2016.

27.   J. C. Derrick, "Evangelical Backlash Against Trump Grows," WORLD News Group, October 13, 2016, accessed December 17, 2016, https://world.wng .org/2016/10/trump_faces_growing_evangelical_backlash; "A Declaration by American Evangelicals Concerning Donald Trump," Change.org, Inc., accessed

December 17, 2016, https://www.change.org/p/donald-trump-a-declaration-by
-american-evangelicals-concerning-donald-trump.

28.   "Police Officer Assaulted, Punches Thrown After San Jose Trump Rally,"
CBS Local Media, June 2, 2016, accessed December 17, 2016, http://sanfrancisco
.cbslocal.com/2016/06/02/protesters-clash-with-trump-supporters-at-san-jose-rally/;
"Violence as Trump Brings Immigration Rhetoric to Border," CBS Interactive Inc.,
May 28, 2016, accessed December 17, 2016, http://www.cbsnews.com/news/donald
-trump-protesters-violent-california-rally-gop-election-2016/; Jennifer Wadsworth,
"Donald Trump Rally Sparks Protests, Violence in San Jose," San Jose Inside, June 3,
2016, accessed December 17, 2016, http://www.sanjoseinside.com/2016/06/03
/donald-trump-rally-sparks-protests-violence-in-san-jose/; Jeremy Diamond and
Theodore Schleifer, "Trump Supporters, Protesters Clash After Chicago Rally Post-
poned," Cable News Network, March 12, 2016, accessed December 17, 2016, http://
www.cnn.com/2016/03/11/politics/donald-trump-chicago-protests/; Jaime Delage
and Will Ashenmacher, "Have You Seen the Video? Trump Supporters Harassed
and Spit On in Minneapolis," Digital First Media, August 22, 2016, accessed
December 17, 2016, http://www.twincities.com/2016/08/20/trump-supporter
-reports-cellphone-robbery-after-minneapolis-event/.

29.   "Police Officer Assaulted, Punches Thrown After San Jose Trump Rally,"
CBS Local Media.

30.   John Santucci, Candace Smith, and David Caplan, "Violence Breaks Out
at Trump Rally in San Jose, Protesters Hurl Eggs, Throw Punches, Intimidate
Supporters," ABC News, June 3, 2016, accessed December 17, 2016, http://
abcnews.go.com/Politics/violence-breaks-trump-rally-san-jose-protesters-hurl
/story?id=39576437.

31.   Eli Watkins, Jeremy Diamond, and Sara Murray, "Protesters Take to
Streets After Trump Rally in San Jose," Cable News Network, June 3, 2016,
accessed December 17, 2016, http://www.cnn.com/2016/06/02/politics/donald
-trump-california-protesters/.

32.   Shadi Rahimi's Twitter account, May 2, 2016, accessed December 17,
2016, https://twitter.com/shadirahimi/media,.

33.   "Judicial Watch Uncovers USDA Records Sponsoring U.S. Food Stamp
Program for Illegal Aliens," Judicial Watch, Inc., April 25, 2013, accessed
December 17, 2016, http://www.judicialwatch.org/press-room/press-releases
/judicial-watch-uncovers-usda-records-sponsoring-u-s-food-stamp-program-for
-illegal-aliens/; Eyder Peralta, "Under Executive Action, Immigrants Are Entitled
to Social Security Benefits," NPR, December 3, 2015, accessed December 17,
2016, http://www.npr.org/sections/thetwo-way/2014/12/03/368216062/under
-executive-action-immigrants-are-entitled-to-social-security-benefits; Stephen
Dinan, "Obama Amnesty Creates Loophole for Illegal Immigrants to Vote in
Elections," *Washington Times*, February 12, 2015, accessed December 17, 2016,
http://www.washingtontimes.com/news/2015/feb/12/obama-amnesty-creates
-loophole-for-illegal-immigra/.

34.   Charles Thomas and Ben Bradley, "Donald Trump Supporters, Protesters Gather at South Bend Rally," ABC Inc., May 2, 2016, accessed December

17, 2016, http://abc7chicago.com/politics/trump-supporters-protesters-gather-at
-south-bend-rally/1319075/.

35.   "Violence as Trump Brings Immigration Rhetoric to Border," CBS Interactive Inc.; Wadsworth, "Donald Trump Rally Sparks Protests, Violence in San
Jose."

CHAPTER 4: PAUL, SILAS, AND SWEET HOME ALABAMA

1.   Michelle Cox, "Music to God's Ears," *Guideposts*, May 25, 2016, accessed
December 18, 2016, https://www.guideposts.org/blog/music-to-god-s-ears.

2.   Denny Burke, "A Florist Loses Religious Freedom, and Much More,"
Cable News Network, February 20, 2015, accessed December 18, 2016, http://
www.cnn.com/2015/02/20/living/stutzman-florist-gay/.

3.   Ibid.

4.   Barronelle Stutzman, in communication with the author, February 2015.

5.   "Judge: Washington Florist Who Refused Gay Wedding Broke Law,"
The Seattle Times Company, February 18, 2015, accessed December 18, 2016,
http://www.seattletimes.com/seattle-news/judge-washington-florist-who-refused
-gay-wedding-broke-law-1888-2/.

6.   Ibid.

7.   Kristen Waggoner, in communication with the author, February 2015.

8.   Ibid.

9.   "Judge: Washington Florist Who Refused Gay Wedding Broke Law," The
Seattle Times Company.

10.   Waggoner, in communication with the author, February 2015.

11.   Ibid.

12.   "Judge: Washington Florist Who Refused Gay Wedding Broke Law," The
Seattle Times Company.

13.   Stutzman, in communication with the author, February 2015.

14.   Ibid.

15.   Ibid.

16.   Waggoner, in communication with the author, February 2015.

17.   Ibid.

18.   Stutzman, in communication with the author, February 2015.

19.   "Florist Who Refused to Serve Gay Couple Rejects Settlement," Cox
Media Group, February 20, 2015, accessed December 18, 2016, http://www.kiro7
.com/news/florist-who-refused-serve-gay-couple-rejects-settl/43384613.

20.   Ibid.

21.   Jake Perlman, "HGTV Cancels 'Flip It Forward' Pilot Amid Hosts'
Anti-Gay Controversy," Entertainment Weekly Inc., May 7, 2014, accessed
December 18, 2016, http://www.ew.com/article/2014/05/07/hgtv-cancels-pilot.

22.   Brian Tashman, "HGTV Picks Anti-Gay, Anti-Choice Extremist for
New Reality TV Show," Right Wing Watch, May 6, 2014, accessed December 18,
2016, http://www.rightwingwatch.org/post/hgtv-picks-anti-gay-anti-choice
-extremist-for-new-reality-tv-show/.

23.   Ann Oldenburg, "Benham Brothers: 'If Our Faith Costs Us a Television
Show, Then So Be It.,'" Washington Post, May 8, 2014, accessed December 18,

2016, https://www.washingtonpost.com/national/religion/benham-brothers
-if-our-faith-costs-us-a-television-show-then-so-be-it/2014/05/08/c325e524-d6d3
-11e3-8f7d-7786660fff7c_story.html?utm_term=.a00eceb1db4a.

24.   Lisa Respers France, "Benham Brothers Lose HGTV Show After 'Anti-Gay' Remarks," Cable News Network, May 9, 2014, accessed December 18, 2016, http://www.cnn.com/2014/05/08/showbiz/tv/benham-brothers-hgtv/.

25.   HGTV's Twitter account, May 7, 2014, accessed December 18, 2016, https://twitter.com/hgtv/status/464072338309275648.

26.   Tashman, "HGTV Picks Anti-Gay, Anti-Choice Extremist for New Reality TV Show."

27.   Ibid.

28.   "Same-Sex Marriage Ban Is in the Hands of North Carolina Voters," Cable News Network, May 8, 2012, accessed December 18, 2016, http://www.cnn.com/2012/05/08/politics/primaries/.

29.   France, "Benham Brothers Lose HGTV Show After 'Anti-Gay' Remarks."

30.   Ibid

31.   Janet Mefferd, in communication with the author, May 2014.

32.   Tom Tradup, in communication with the author, May 2014.

33.   Gina Mei, "Chip and Joanna Gaines's Pastor Preaches 'Homosexuality Is a Sin,'" Hearst Communications, Inc., November 20, 2016, accessed December 18, 2016, http://www.cosmopolitan.com/entertainment/tv/a8381774/chip-joanna-gaines-fixer-upper-pastor-jimmy-seibert/.

34.   Kate Aurthur, "Chip and Joanna Gaines' Church Is Firmly Against Same-Sex Marriage," BuzzFeed, Inc., November 29, 2016, accessed December 18, 2016, https://www.buzzfeed.com/kateaurthur/chip-and-joanna-gaines-church-same-sex-marriage?utm_term=.sj6vmxMq8A#.jp730qKa96.

35.   Mei, "Chip and Joanna Gaines's Pastor Preaches 'Homosexuality Is a Sin.'"

36.   Ibid.

37.   Aurthur, "Chip and Joanna Gaines' Church Is Firmly Against Same-Sex Marriage."

38.   Sarah Stites, "Takedown? 'Fixer Upper' Stars Face Media Scrutiny for Pastor's Traditional Marriage Stance," Media Research Center, November 30, 2016, accessed December 18, 2016, http://www.newsbusters.org/blogs/culture/sarah-stites/2016/11/30/takedown-fixer-upper-stars-face-media-scrutiny-pastors; "Chip and Joanna Gaines' Church Is Very Much Against Same-Sex Marriage, " Us Weekly, November 29, 2016, accessed December 18, 2016, http://www.usmagazine.com/celebrity-news/news/chip-joanna-gaines-church-is-against-same-sex-marriage-w452792.

39.   Aurthur, "Chip and Joanna Gaines' Church Is Firmly Against Same-Sex Marriage."

40.   Ibid.

41.   In communication with the author, November 2016.

42.   Mei, "Chip and Joanna Gaines's Pastor Preaches 'Homosexuality Is a Sin.'"

43.   Brian Ross and Rehab El-Buri, "Obama's Pastor: God Damn America, U.S. to Blame for 9/11," ABC News, March 13, 2008, accessed December 18, 2016, http://abcnews.go.com/Blotter/DemocraticDebate/story?id=4443788.

44.   David Benham, in communication with the author, November 2016.

45.   Jason Benham, in communication with the author, November 2016.

46.   David Benham, in communication with the author, November 2016.

47.   Aurthur, "Chip and Joanna Gaines' Church Is Firmly Against Same-Sex Marriage."

48.   Jerry A. Johnson, in communication with the author, November 2016.

49.   Ibid.

50.   Jimmy Seibert, in communication with the author, November 2016.

51.   Ibid.

52.   Ibid.

53.   Ibid.

54.   Ibid.

55.   Ibid.

56.   Ibid.

57.   Ibid.

58.   Chip Gaines's Twitter account, December 3, 2016, accessed December 18, 2016, https://twitter.com/chippergaines/status/804977263297069057.

59.   David and Jason Benham, in communication with the author, November 2016.

60.   Stutzman, in communication with the author, February 2015.

CHAPTER 5: INDOCTRINATION 101

1.   Fred Barbash, "Does America's First Flag Symbolize 'Exclusion and Hate,' As This Mich. School Superintendent Said?," *Washington Post*, September 15, 2016, accessed December 18, 2016, https://www.washingtonpost.com/news/morning-mix/wp/2016/09/15/does-americas-first-flag-symbolize-exclusion-and-hate-like-this-mich-school-superintendent-said/?utm_term=.579810c5e7dc.

2.   Ibid.

3.   Marvin Herring, "Superintendent Apologizes for Display at Football Game," WOOD Television LLC, September 10, 2016, accessed December 18, 2016, http://woodtv.com/2016/09/10/debate-sparks-over-student-display-at-high-school-football-game/

4.   Ibid.

5.   Matthew Patulski's Facebook page, "An Open Letter to the Leadership of Forest Hills Public Schools," September 10, 2016, accessed December 18, 2016, https://www.facebook.com/notes/matthew-patulski/an-open-letter-to-the-leadership-of-forest-hills-public-schools/10155180355084348/.

6.   Jason Halcombe and Rodney Manley, "Lord's Prayer Fills Moment of Silence," *Courier Herald*, August 24, 2015, accessed December 18, 2016, http://matchbin-assets.s3.amazonaws.com/public/sites/654/assets/1DJT_CH_8_24_15_WEBSITE.pdf.

7.   Americans United for Separation of Church and State, in communication with the author, August 2014.

8.   Ibid.
9.   Halcombe and Manley, "Lord's Prayer Fills Moment of Silence."
10.   Juliann Alligood, in communication with the author, August 2015.
11.   Ibid.
12.   Ibid.
13.   Halcombe and Manley, "Lord's Prayer Fills Moment of Silence."
14.   Ibid.
15.   Kate Royals, "Brandon Band Reportedly not Allowed to Perform Christian Hymn," www.clarionledger.com, August 22, 2015, accessed December 18, 2016, http://www.clarionledger.com/story/news/2015/08/21/brandon-high-school-how-great-thou-art/32143307/.
16.   Ibid.
17.   Ibid.
18.   "Brandon High Football Fans Sing 'How Great Thou Art' at Halftime," YouTube video, August 22, 2015, posted by Mississippi PEP, accessed December 18, 2016, https://www.youtube.com/watch?v=PeI6FYIfOSg; Hadas Brown, "Support Grows for Brandon Band Banned Over Song Choice," WAPT News, August 24, 2015, accessed December 18, 2016, http://www.wapt.com/article/support-grows-for-brandon-band-banned-over-song-choice/2095033.
19.   Brittany Mann, in communication with the author, August 2015.
20.   Ibid.
21.   Mandy Miller, in communication with the author, August 2015.
22.   Ibid.
23.   Mike Morris, "Pastor Thought Baptism on Georgia School Field Was by the Book," Cox Media Group, September 4, 2015, accessed December 18, 2016, http://www.ajc.com/news/local/pastor-thought-baptism-georgia-school-field-was-the-book/k0YutgkncxdwvW4tAiQCwK/.
24.   "VR High School Baptisms," YouTube video, September 16, 2016, posted by First Baptist Villa Rica, accessed December 18, 2016, https://www.youtube.com/watch?v=0EAZb2bfzeo.
25.   "Mass Baptism at Georgia High School Spurs Controversy," CBS Interactive Inc., September 3, 2015, accessed December 18, 2016, http://www.cbsnews.com/news/mass-baptism-georgia-public-high-school-football-field-brews-controversy/; "VR High School Baptisms," YouTube.
26.   "VR High School Baptisms," YouTube.
27.   Tyler Estep, "Carroll Schools Investigating 'Mass Baptism' at Football Practice," Cox Media Group, September 2, 2015, accessed December 18, 2016, http://www.ajc.com/news/local/carroll-schools-investigating-mass-baptism-football-practice/8hRg0b3h19eLfjYzp5WeyM/.
28.   Freedom From Religion Foundation, in communication with the author, September 2015.
29.   Ibid.
30.   Kevin Williams, in communication with the author, September 2015.
31.   Morris, "Pastor Thought Baptism on Georgia School Field Was by the Book."
32.   Williams, in communication with the author, September 2015.

33.   Winston Jones, "Parents Seek Training on Teen Suicide Prevention," *Douglas County Sentinel*, March 28, 2015, accessed December 18, 2016, http://www.douglascountysentinel.com/news/parents-seek-training-on-teen-suicide-prevention/article_d4364b9e-d595-11e4-8bb1-bb72acaf909d.html.

34.   Williams, in communication with the author, September 2015.

35.   Ibid.

36.   "VR High School Baptisms," YouTube.

37.   "A Crisis in Civic Education," American Council of Trustees and Alumni, January 2016, accessed December 18, 2016, https://www.goacta.org/images/download/A_Crisis_in_Civic_Education.pdf.

38.   Ibid.

39.   Ibid.

40.   Jacob Poushter, "40% of Millennials OK With Limiting Speech Offensive to Minorities," Pew Research Center, November 20, 2015, accessed December 18, 2016, http://www.pewresearch.org/fact-tank/2015/11/20/40-of-millennials-ok-with-limiting-speech-offensive-to-minorities/.

41.   *Judge Judy*, television show aired on February 9, 2010, accessed December 18, 2016, http://mreplay.com/transcript/judge_judy/510/KPIX/Tuesday_February_09_2010/190661/.

42.   Mary Cooley, "'Drawing the Line': High Mount Parent Upset With Muslim History Unit," *Belleville News-Democrat*, October 16, 2015, accessed December 18, 2016, http://www.bnd.com/news/local/education/article39505947.html.

43.   Ibid.

44.   Ibid.

45.   Ibid.

46.   Ibid.

47.   Renee Eng, "Palmdale Student Ordered to Stop Handing Out Bible Verses," Charter Communications, June 17, 2016, accessed December 18, 2016, http://www.twcnews.com/ca/antelope-valley/news/2016/06/17/palmdale-student-ordered-to-stop-handing-out-bible-verses-.html.

48.   "School Calls Sheriff to Stop 7-Year-Old From Handing Out Bible Verses," Liberty Counsel, June 2, 2016, accessed December 18, 2016, https://www.lc.org/newsroom/details/school-calls-sheriff-to-stopyearold-from-handing-out-bible-verses-1.

49.   "California School Backs Down and Will Allow Elementary Student to Share Bible Verses," Liberty Counsel Action, August 15, 2016, accessed December 18, 2016, http://libertycounsel.com/california-school-backs-down-and-will-allow-elementary-student-to-share-bible-verses/.

50.   Richard L. Mast Jr. and Mary E. McAlister, Liberty Counsel, letter sent to Palmdale School District via e-mail on May 25, 2016, accessed December 18, 2016, https://www.lc.org//PDFs/Attachments2PRsLAs/2016/060216-Ltr-Superintendent-Maldonado-Palmdale-CA.pdf.

51.   Ibid.

52.   Richard Mast, in communication with the author, June 2016.

53.   Horatio Mihet, in communication with the author, June 2016.

54. "School Calls Sheriff to Stop 7-Year-Old From Handing Out Bible Verses," Liberty Counsel.

55. Kendall Forward, "East Liverpool Students Reject Demand to Remove Lord's Prayer From Graduation," Sinclair Broadcast Group, May 22, 2016, accessed December 18, 2016, http://wtov9.com/news/local/east-liverpool-students -reject-demand-to-remove-lords-prayer-from-graduation.

56. Ibid.

57. Lisa Ensinger, in communication with the author, May 2016.

58. Bobby Hill, in communication with the author, May 2016.

59. Ibid.

60. Mr. Hill, in communication with the author, May 2016.

61. Ibid.

62. Ibid.

63. *Andrew Cash v. The Governors of Missouri State University*, United States District Court Western District of Missouri Southern Division, Case No.: 2016-CV-, ThomasMoresociety.org, accessed December 18, 2016, https://www .thomasmoresociety.org/wp-content/uploads/2016/04/CASH-Complaint_As -Filed.pdf.

64. Harrison Keegan, "MSU Sued by Student Who Told Professor He Wouldn't Counsel Gay Couples," *Springfield News-Leader*, April 21, 2016, December 18, 2016, http://www.news-leader.com/story/news/education/2016 /04/21/msu-sued-student-who-told-professor-he-wouldnt-counsel-gay-couples /83352890/.

65. *Andrew Cash v. The Governors of Missouri State University*.

66. Ibid.

67. Ibid.

68. Tom Olp, in communication with the author, May 2016.

69. Ibid.

70. *Andrew Cash v. The Governors of Missouri State University*.

71. Ibid.

72. Ibid.

73. Olp, in communication with the author, May 2016.

74. *Grace Christian Life v. W. Randolph Woodson, Warwick A. Arden, TJ Willis, and Mike Giancola*, In the United States District Court for the Eastern District of North Carolina Western Division, Verified Complaint, accessed December 18, 2016, https://adflegal.blob.core.windows.net/web-content-dev/docs /default-source/documents/case-documents/grace-christian-life-v.-woodson/grace -christian-life-v-woodson---complaint.pdf?sfvrsn=4.

75. Ibid.

76. Ibid.

77. Tyson Langhofer, in communication with the author, April 2016.

78. *Grace Christian Life v. W. Randolph Woodson, Warwick A. Arden, TJ Willis, and Mike Giancola*.

79. Ibid.

80. Hannalee Alrutz, in communication with the author, April 2016.

81.   "Court Quickly Halts NC State Policy That Requires Permits for Any, All Speech," Alliance Defending Freedom, June 6, 2016, accessed December 18, 2016, http://www.adfmedia.org/News/PRDetail/9981.

82.   Ibid.

83.   *Grace Christian Life v. W. Randolph Woodson, Warwick A. Arden, TJ Willis, and Mike Giancola.*

84.   Ibid.

85.   "Student Group Sues NC State for Requiring Permits for Any, All Speech," Alliance Defending Freedom, April 26, 2016, accessed December 18, 2016, https://www.adflegal.org/detailspages/press-release-details/student-group -sues-nc-state-for-requiring-permits-for-any-all-speech.

86.   Alrutz, in communication with the author, April 2016.

87.   Brian Bensimon, "University of Texas Issues 29-Point Checklist on Offensive Halloween Costumes," The College Fix, October 28, 2016, accessed December 18, 2016, http://www.thecollegefix.com/post/29680/.

88.   "Costume & Theme Selection," The University of Texas at Austin: Sorority and Fraternity Life, accessed December 18, 2016, https://drive.google .com/file/d/0B3YCK9fSaQmHVUFfTDRyblZzSnc/view.

89.   Ibid.

90.   Ibid.

91.   "Halloween Costume Choices," University of Florida, October 10, 2016, accessed December 18, 2016, http://gatortimes.ufl.edu/2016/10/10/halloween -costume-choices-4/.

92.   "Yale Uproar Not Really About Halloween," *Hartford Courant*, November 12, 2015, accessed December 18, 2016, http://www.courant.com /opinion/editorials/hc-ed-yale-racial-sensitivity-20151111-story.html.

93.   Tuft University letter to Greek community, accessed December 18, 2016, http://media.wix.com/ugd/54d45b_9f5a1fffbccb49519ea6bdb049edeffa.pdf.

94.   Ibid.

95.   David Wilson, "Tipton Rally in Support of Prayers Draws Crowd," Central Missouri Newspapers Inc., September 15, 2016, accessed December 18, 2016, http://www.californiademocrat.com/news/local/story/2016/sep/15/tipton-rally -support-prayers-draws-crowd/640180/.

96.   Ibid.

97.   John Fawcett, "Blest Be the Tie That Binds," public domain.

98.   "Missouri School District Drops Prayer, Religious Hymn After Complaint," CBN News, September 12, 2016, http://www1.cbn.com/cbnnews/us/2016 /september/missouri-school-district-drops-prayer-religious-hymn-after-complaint.

99.   Ibid.

100.   Daniel Williams, in communication with the author, September 2016.

101.   Ibid.

102.   Don Hinkle, in communication with the author, September 2016.

CHAPTER 6: SAFE SPACES, MICROAGGRESSIONS, AND SNOWFLAKES

1.   Collins Dictionary, s.v. "snowflake generation," accessed December 18, 2016, https://www.collinsdictionary.com/dictionary/english/snowflake-generation;

Claire Fox, "Generation Snowflake: How We Train Our Kids to Be Censorious Cry-Babies," The Spectator (1828) Ltd, June 4, 2016, accessed December 19, 2016, http://www.spectator.co.uk/2016/06/generation-snowflake-how-we-train-our-kids-to-be-censorious-cry-babies/.

2.   "Diversity in the Classroom," UCLA Diversity & Faculty Development, accessed December 18, 2016, https://equity.ucla.edu/wp-content/uploads/2016/06/DiversityintheClassroom2014Web.pdf.

3.   Eugene Volokh, "University of California Considering Recognizing a 'Right' to Be 'Free From…Expressions of Intolerance,'" *Washington Post*, September 11, 2015, accessed December 18, 2016, https://www.washingtonpost.com/news/volokh-conspiracy/wp/2015/09/11/university-of-california-considering-recognizing-a-right-to-be-free-from-expressions-of-intolerance/?utm_term=.b7e09753249b.

4.   Ibid.

5.   Ibid.

6.   Ibid.

7.   Tara Dorill, "University of Michigan 'Inclusive Language Campaign' Banned Words List Sparks Free Speech Debate," The Inquisitr News, February 11, 2015, accessed December 18, 2016, http://www.inquisitr.com/1832592/university-of-michigan-inclusive-language-campaign-banned-words-list-sparks-free-speech-debate/; Briana Lung, "The Inclusive Language Campaign and the War Over Words," Alumni Association of the University of Michigan, accessed December 19, 2016, http://alumni.umich.edu/newsletter/the-inclusive-language-campaign-and-the-war-over-words/.

8.   Emily Newton, "University Responds to Controversial 'Hotty Toddy Holiday' Name Change," HottyToddy.com, December 9, 2015, accessed December 19, 2016, http://hottytoddy.com/2015/12/09/university-responds-to-controversial-hotty-toddy-holiday-name-change/.

9.   Isabel Rosales, Pete DeLea, and Devin Turk, "JMU Student Leaders Prohibit Religious Songs From Tree-Lighting Event," Gray Digital Media, December 4, 2015, accessed December 19, 2016, http://www.whsv.com/content/news/360603901.html.

10.   "Inclusive Holiday Practices," The Ohio State University—Office of Diversity and Inclusion, accessed December 19, 2016, https://web-beta.archive.org/web/20150922174018/https://odi.osu.edu/about/ohio-state-diversity-officers/inclusive-holiday-practices.html.

11.   "Editorial on Diversity," *University of Tennessee Daily Beacon*, December 8, 2015, accessed December 19, 2016, http://www.utdailybeacon.com/opinion/editorial-on-diversity/article_84f61596-9db8-11e5-9773-3bdb8bbc890f.html.

12.   Poushter, "40% of Millennials OK With Limiting Speech Offensive to Minorities," Pew Research Center.

13.   Holden Kurwicki, "Greater Clark Could Scrap Valedictorian System," WHAS-TV, August 30, 2016, accessed December 19, 2016, http://www.whas11.com/news/education/greater-clark-could-scrap-valedictorian-system/311429761.

14.   For more on how we helped create the snowflake generation, see Claire Fox's article, "Generation Snowflake: How We Train Our Kids to Be Censorious Cry-Babies."

15.   Bradford Richardson, "Berkeley Protesters Form Human Chain to Stop White Students From Getting to Class," The Washington Times, LLC, October 24, 2016, accessed December 19, 2016, http://www.washingtontimes.com/news/2016/oct/24/berkeley-protesters-form-human-chain-stop-white-st/.

16.   Spencer Irvine, "University of Michigan Adds Required Diversity Course in Their Business School," Accuracy In Academia, November 23, 2015, accessed December 19, 2016, http://www.academia.org/university-of-michigan-adds-required-diversity-course-in-their-business-school/.

17.   In communication with the author, October 2016, name withheld.

18.   "How Privileged Are You?," Arizona Board of Regents, accessed December 19, 2016, https://humanities.asu.edu/how-privileged-are-you.

19.   In communication with the author, October 2016, name withheld.

20.   "How Privileged Are You?," Arizona Board of Regents.

21.   In communication with the author, October 2016, name withheld.

22.   Ibid.

23.   Ibid.

24.   Ibid.

25.   Ibid.

26.   Avery Coffman, "Tampa Teacher Quits Over 'Privilege' Form," April 4, 2016, accessed December 19, 2016, http://www.wtsp.com/news/education/tampa-teacher-quits-over-privilege-form/121622647.

27.   Kellan Howell, "U.S. Army Lectured Soldiers on Dangers of 'White Privilege,'" The Washington Times, LLC, March 10, 2016, accessed December 19, 2016, http://www.washingtontimes.com/news/2016/mar/10/us-army-lectured-soldiers-on-dangers-of-white-priv/.

28.   Coffman, "Tampa Teacher Quits Over 'Privilege' Form."

29.   Ibid.

30.   Todd Starnes, "Hey Kids, How Much Privilege Do You Have? Quiz Riles Florida Parents," FoxNews.com, April 6, 2016, accessed December 19, 2016, http://www.foxnews.com/opinion/2016/04/06/hey-kids-how-much-privilege-do-have-quiz-riles-florida-parents.html.

31.   Coffman, "Tampa Teacher Quits Over 'Privilege' Form."

32.   Ibid.

33.   Tanya Arja, in communication with the author, April 2016.

34.   Ibid.

35.   "Suspend Professor Carol Swain," Change.org, Inc., accessed December 19, 2016, https://www.change.org/p/vanderbilt-university-suspend-professor-carol-swain; Adam Tamburin, "Vanderbilt Chief Responds to Call to Suspend Carol Swain," Tennessean, accessed December 19, 2016, http://www.tennessean.com/story/news/education/2015/11/11/vanderbilt-chancellor-responds-call-suspend-swain/75607986/.

36.   Zach Young, "YOUNG: Free Speech, not Disruption," *Yale Daily News*, November 9, 2015, accessed December 19, 2016, http://yaledailynews.com/blog /2015/11/09/young-free-speech-not-disruption/.

37.   "Eyes Wide Open at the Protest," *Dartmouth Review*, November 14, 2015, accessed December 19, 2016, http://www.dartreview.com/eyes-wide-open -at-the-protest/.

38.   Evan Lips, "University of Vermont to Hold Another 'White Privilege' Student Retreat," Boston Media Networks, September 1, 2016, accessed December 19, 2016, http://newbostonpost.com/2016/09/01/university-of-vermont -to-hold-another-white-privilege-student-retreat/; "University of Vermont Statement on Examining White Privilege Retreat," University of Vermont, November 11, 2015, accessed December 19, 2016, http://www.uvm.edu/~uvmpr/?Page=news &&storyID=21882&category=ucomm&utm_source=Facebook.com&utm _medium=social&utm_campaign=UVM_FB_general.

39.   "Christian Fraternity Loses Recognition at CSU Stanislaus Over Leadership Rules," CBS Local Media, March 20, 2015, accessed December 19, 2016, http://sacramento.cbslocal.com/2015/03/20/christian-fraternity-loses-recognition -at-csu-stanislaus-over-leadership-rules/.

40.   Ibid.

41.   Ibid.

CHAPTER 7: MEET THE DEPLORABLES

1.   Amy Chozick, "Hillary Clinton Calls Many Trump Backers 'Deplorables,' and G.O.P. Pounces," The New York Times Company, September 10, 2016, accessed December 18, 2016, http://www.nytimes.com/2016/09/11/us/politics /hillary-clinton-basket-of-deplorables.html?_r=0.

2.   Marc A. Thiessen, "Obama Finally Meets Those 'Bitter' Americans Who 'Cling to Guns,'" *Washington Post*, January 11, 2016, accessed December 18, 2016, https://www.washingtonpost.com/opinions/obama-finally-meets-those-bitter -americans-who-cling-to-guns/2016/01/11/91462812-b86c-11e5-829c -26ffb874a18d_story.html?utm_term=.81900b7b4e2e.

3.   David Brody, "Obama to CBN News: We're No Longer Just a Christian Nation," CBN News, July 30, 2007, accessed December 18, 2016, http://www.cbn .com/cbnnews/politics/2007/july-/obama-to-cbn-news-were-no-longer-just-a -christian-nation-/?mobile=false.

4.   Chozick, "Hillary Clinton Calls Many Trump Backers 'Deplorables,' and G.O.P. Pounces."

5.   Ibid.

6.   Kelly Riddell, "Hillary Clinton Calls the Entire Nation Racist," The Washington Times, LLC, September 26, 2016, accessed December 18, 2016, http://www.washingtontimes.com/news/2016/sep/26/hillary-clinton-calls-us -racist-debate/.

7.   Pam Key, "Clinton Campaign Manager Mook Doubles Down: 'A Lot' of Trump Supporters Are 'Deplorable,'" Breitbart, October 2, 2016, accessed December 18, 2016, http://www.breitbart.com/video/2016/10/02/clinton -campaign-manager-doubles-lot-trump-supporters-deplorable/.

8.　Addie Mena, "Leaked Emails Show Clinton's Team Should Read a Catechism," CAN, October 11, 2016, accessed December 18, 2016, http://www .catholicnewsagency.com/blog/leaked-emails-show-clintons-team-should-read-a -catechism/.

9.　"Conservative Catholicism," WikiLeaks, accessed December 18, 2016, https://wikileaks.org/podesta-emails/emailid/4364.

10.　Ibid.

11.　Ibid.

12.　Ibid.

13.　Ibid.

14.　Ibid.

15.　"Clinton Must Sanction Her Bigoted Chiefs," The Catholic League, October 11, 2016, accessed December 18, 2016, http://www.catholicleague.org /clinton-must-sanction-her-bigoted-chiefs/.

16.　Tony Perkins, in communication with the author, October 2016.

17.　Susan Jones, "Clinton: 'Deep-Seated Cultural Codes, Religious Beliefs… Have to Be Changed,'" CNSNews.com, April 27, 2015, accessed December 18, 2016, http://www.cnsnews.com/news/article/susan-jones/clinton-deep-seated -cultural-codes-religious-beliefshave-be-changed.

18.　Morgan Winsor and David Caplan, "Clinton's 'Deplorables' Comment Show Disdain for Working People, Trump Camp Says," ABC News, September 10, 2016, accessed December 18, 2016, http://abcnews.go.com/Politics/hillary -clinton-half-donald-trumps-supporters-basket-deplorables/story?id=41993204.

19.　Katie Reilly, "Hillary Clinton Says She Regrets Part of Her 'Deplorables' Comment," TIME, September 10, 2016, accessed December 18, 2016, http://time .com/4486601/hillary-clinton-donald-trump-basket-of-deplorables-half/.

20.　Winsor and Caplan, "Clinton's 'Deplorables' Comment Show Disdain for Working People, Trump Camp Says."

21.　Jennifer Palmieri, "Our Campaign Lost the Election. But Trump's Team Must Own Up to How He Won," Washington Post, December 7, 2016, accessed December 18, 2016, https://www.washingtonpost.com/opinions/our-campaign -lost-the-election-but-trumps-team-must-own-up-to-how-he-won/2016/12/07 /4a6a4c24-bcbd-11e6-94ac-3d324840106c_story.html?utm_term=.cb7b97afd985.

22.　Daniel Halper, "Hillary Losing White Male Vote Because of Guns, Gays, and God: Pelosi," NYP Holdings, Inc., July 28, 2016, accessed December 18, 2016, http://nypost.com/2016/07/28/hillary-losing-white-male-vote-because-of -guns-gays-and-god-pelosi/.

23.　Dana Blanton, "Fox News Poll: Fewer Americans Feeling Proud," FoxNews.com, June 20, 2016, accessed December 18, 2016, http://www.foxnews .com/politics/2016/06/30/fox-news-poll-fewer-americans-feeling-proud.html.

24.　Wyatt Massey, "NAACP: Banish Confederate Symbols From Stone Mountain in Georgia," Cable News Network, July 14, 2014, accessed December 18, 2016, http://www.cnn.com/2015/07/14/living/feat-stone-mountain-georgia -naacp-confederate-symbol/.

25.　Bianca Phillips, "Council Committee Agrees On Relocating Forrest Statue and Remains," Contemporary Media, July 7, 2015, accessed December 18,

2016, http://www.memphisflyer.com/NewsBlog/archives/2015/07/07/council
-committee-agrees-on-relocating-forrest-statue-and-remains.

26.   Eliott C. McLaughlin, "Ole Miss Removes State Flag From Campus,"
Cable News Network, October 26, 2015, accessed December 18, 2016, http://
www.cnn.com/2015/10/26/us/ole-miss-confederate-state-flag-removed-campus/.

27.   "National Lab Faces Backlash After Offering 'Southern Accent Reduction' Class," Lab Manager, August 13, 2014, accessed December 18, 2016, http://
www.labmanager.com/news/2014/08/national-lab-faces-backlash-after-offering
-southern-accent-reduction-class?fw1pk=2#.WFQYKPArLcs.

28.   Alan Greenblatt, "Y'all Keep Talking: Lab Scratches 'Southern Accent
Reduction' Course," NPR, July 29, 2014, accessed December 18, 2016, http://
www.npr.org/sections/thetwo-way/2014/07/29/336364371/yall-keep-talking-lab
-scratches-southern-accent-reduction-course.

29.   Ibid.

30.   Ibid.

31.   Ibid.

32.   Ibid.

33.   Todd Starnes, "Hey Y'all, What's Wrong With a Drawl?," FoxNews.com,
August 1, 2014, accessed December 18, 2016, http://www.foxnews.com/opinion
/2014/08/01/hey-yall-whats-wrong-with-drawl.html.

34.   Ibid.

35.   Gordon Dickson, "Cross-Dressing Cowboy Not Welcome in Ladies'
Room at North Texas Barbecue Joint," *Star-Telegram*, June 7, 2016, accessed
December 18, 2016, http://www.star-telegram.com/news/state/texas
/article82279607.html.

36.   John Sanford, in communication with the author, June 2016.

37.   Ibid.

38.   Ibid.

39.   Dickson, "Cross-Dressing Cowboy Not Welcome in Ladies' Room at
North Texas Barbecue Joint."

40.   Sanford, in communication with the author, June 2016.

41.   Michael Gartland, "New City Ad Blitz Tells People to Use Bathroom
'Consistent With Who You Are,'" NYP Holdings, June 6, 2016, accessed January
6, 2017, http://nypost.com/2016/06/06/new-city-ad-blitz-tells-people-to-use
-bathroom-consistent-with-who-you-are/.

42.   Dickson, "Cross-Dressing Cowboy Not Welcome in Ladies' Room at
North Texas Barbecue Joint."

43.   Sanford, in communication with the author, June 2016.

44.   Julia Moskin, "Southern Farmers Vanquish the Clichés," The New York
Times Company, December 27, 2011, accessed December 18, 2016, http://www
.nytimes.com/2011/12/28/dining/southern-farmers-vanquish-the-cliches.html?
_r=1&ref=dining.

45.   Ibid.

46.   Ibid.

47.   Ibid.

48.   Ibid.

49.   Urbandictionary.com, s.v. "Old Gray Lady," accessed December 18, 2016, http://www.urbandictionary.com/define.php?term=Old%20Gray%20Lady.

50.   Daniel Kreps, "Warner Bros. Bans 'Dukes of Hazzard' Car With Confederate Flag," *Rolling Stone*, June 24, 2015, accessed December 18, 2016, http://www.rollingstone.com/tv/news/warner-bros-bans-dukes-of-hazzard-car-with-confederate-flag-20150624.

51.   Deborah Barfield Berry, "Confederate Emblem Removed at U.S. Capitol," *USA Today*, April 21, 2016, accessed December 18, 2016, http://www.usatoday.com/story/news/politics/2016/04/21/confederate-flag-removed-us-capitol-tunnel/83337106/.

52.   Nora Kelly, "Mitch McConnell to Kentucky Capitol: Lose the Jefferson Davis Statue," The Atlantic Monthly Group, June 23, 2015, accessed December 18, 2016, http://www.theatlantic.com/politics/archive/2015/06/mitch-mcconnell-to-kentucky-capitol-lose-the-jefferson-davis-statue/448515/.

53.   Riley Snyder, "Harry Reid Calls on UNLV to Consider Changing 'Rebel' Mascot," *Las Vegas Sun*, June 23, 2015, accessed December 18, 2016, http://lasvegassun.com/news/2015/jun/23/harry-reid-calls-unlv-consider-changing-rebel-masc/.

CHAPTER 8: THE RISE OF RADICAL ISLAM

1.   Paul Szoldra, "19 Unforgettable Quotes From Legendary Marine Gen. James 'Mad Dog' Mattis," Business Insider Inc., December 1, 2016, accessed December 18, 2016, http://www.businessinsider.com/general-mattiss-best-quotes-2016-11.

2.   Ibid.

3.   Ibid.

4.   Ibid.

5.   Ali Arouzi, "Iran Marks Revolution With 'Death to America' Chants," NBCNEWS.com, February 11, 2016, accessed December 18, 2016, http://www.nbcnews.com/news/world/iran-marks-revolution-death-america-chants-n516406.

6.   Ben Shapiro, "White House on Ayatollah's 'Death to America': 'Intended for Domestic Political Audience,'" Breitbart, March 24, 2015, accessed December 18, 2016, http://www.breitbart.com/national-security/2015/03/24/white-house-on-ayatollahs-death-to-america-intended-for-domestic-political-audience/.

7.   Daniella Diaz, "Obama: Why I Won't Say 'Islamic Terrorism,'" Cable News Network, September 29, 2016, accessed December 18, 2016, http://www.cnn.com/2016/09/28/politics/obama-radical-islamic-terrorism-cnn-town-hall/.

8.   Mike Levine, "DHS Secretary Won't Describe ISIS As 'Islamic' Terrorists," ABC News, July 23, 2015, accessed December 18, 2016, http://abcnews.go.com/International/dhs-secretary-describe-isis-islamic-terrorists/story?id=32641415.

9.   Cheryl Chumley, "Homeland Chief Likens Quran to 'American Values,'" WND.com, March 26, 2015, accessed December 18, 2016, http://www.wnd.com/2015/03/homeland-chief-likens-quran-to-american-values/.

10.   "Purported ISIS Warning Claims Terror Cells in Place in 15 States," FoxNews.com, May 6, 2015, accessed December 18, 2016, http://www.foxnews.com/us/2015/05/06/purported-isis-warning-claims-terror-cells-in-place-in-15-states.html.

11.   Joel Rosenberg, in communication with the author, January 2016.

12.   Ibid.

13.   Ibid.

14.   Ibid.

15.   Ibid.

16.   Ibid.

17.   Ibid. Ashley Fantz and Ben Brumfield, "More Than Half the Nation's Governors Say Syrian Refugees Not Welcome," November 19, 2015, accessed December 18, 2016, http://www.cnn.com/2015/11/16/world/paris-attacks-syrian-refugees
-backlash/.

18.   "Paris Attacks: What Happened on the Night," BBC, December 9, 2015, accessed December 18, 2016, http://www.bbc.com/news/world-europe-34818994.

19.   Julian Robinson, "English-Speaking ISIS Jihadi Warns America They Will Be Attacked 'Very Soon' and 'By Allah's Permission Do to Your Country What We Did To Paris,'" Associated Newspapers Ltd, March 9, 2016, accessed December 18, 2016, http://www.dailymail.co.uk/news/article-3483857/English
-speaking-ISIS-jihadi-warns-America-attacked-soon-Allah-s-permission-country
-did-Paris.html.

20.   Franklin Graham's Facebook page, November 16, 2015, accessed December 18, 2016, https://www.facebook.com/FranklinGraham/posts
/1043775762345271.

21.   Juliet Eilperin, "Obama Calls Idea of Screening Syrian Refugees Based on Religion 'Shameful,' Defends White House Strategy," *Washington Post*, November 16, 2015, accessed December 18, 2016, https://www.washingtonpost
.com/news/post-politics/wp/2015/11/16/obama-calls-idea-of-screening-syrian
-refugees-based-on-religion-shameful-defends-white-house-strategy/?utm_term
=.69a3ed68ad54.

22.   David Francis, "Here Are the Growing Number of U.S. Governors Saying No to Syrian Refugees," *Foreign Policy*, November 16, 2015, http://
foreignpolicy.com/2015/11/16/here-are-the-nine-u-s-states-saying-no-to-syrian
-refugees/.

23.   Todd Starnes, "We're Not Islamophobic, Mr. Obama, We Just Don't Want to Get Blown Up," FoxNews.com, November 17, 2015, accessed December 19, 2016, http://www.foxnews.com/opinion/2015/11/17/were-not-islamophobic
-mr-obama-just-dont-want-to-get-blown-up.print.html.

24.   "Press Conference by President Obama—Antalya, Turkey," The White House, November 16, 2015, accessed December 18, 2016, https://www
.whitehouse.gov/the-press-office/2015/11/16/press-conference-president-obama
-antalya-turkey.

25.   Todd Starnes, *God Less America* (Lake Mary, FL: FrontLine, 2014), 168–173.

26.   Danielle Staub, "UPDATE: Marietta Bible College Reaccreditation Official," The News Center, January 13, 2015, accessed December 18, 2016, http://
www.thenewscenter.tv/home/headlines/Marietta-Bible-College-Students-Facing
-Deportation--283285821.html.

27.   Tatiana Sanchez, "Iraqi Detainees to Be Deported, Some Charged With Fraud," *San Diego Union-Tribune*, September 9, 2015, accessed December 18, 2016, http://www.sandiegouniontribune.com/news/immigration/sdut-Iraqi-detainees-chaldeans-deported-2015sep09-story.html.

28.   "Press Conference by President Obama—Antalya, Turkey," The White House.

29.   Sarah Pulliam Bailey, "Jerry Falwell Jr.: 'If More Good People Had Con-cealed-Carry Permits, Then We Could End Those' Islamist Terrorists," *Washington Post*, December 5, 2015, accessed December 18, 2016, https://www.washingtonpost.com/news/acts-of-faith/wp/2015/12/05/liberty-university-president-if-more-good-people-had-concealed-guns-we-could-end-those-muslims/?utm_term=.361ddcfce826.

30.   Ibid.

31.   Ibid.

32.   Liz Kreutz, "Hillary Clinton Says 'We're Not Winning' Fight Against ISIS," ABC News, December 6, 2015, accessed December 18, 2016, http://abcnews.go.com/Politics/hillary-clinton-winning-fight-isis/story?id=35585947.

33.   Bailey, "Jerry Falwell Jr.: 'If More Good People Had Concealed-Carry Permits, Then We Could End Those' Islamist Terrorists."

34.   James Mattis's letter to 1st Marine Division, Wikimedia, March 2003, accessed December 18, 2016, https://upload.wikimedia.org/wikipedia/commons/4/4b/Genmattisltr.jpg.

Chapter 9: A Chicken Sandwich for the Soul

1.   Carly Hoilman, "De Blasio Urges New Yorkers to Boycott Chick-fil-A Over Company's Stance on Marriage," TheBlaze, Inc., May 4, 2016, accessed December 18, 2016, http://www.theblaze.com/stories/2016/05/04/de-blasio-urges-new-yorkers-to-boycott-chick-fil-a-over-companys-stance-on-marriage/.

2.   Kerry Picket, "Chick-fil-A Succeeds in New York City Despite De Blasio Boycott," The Daily Caller, May 12, 2016, accessed December 18, 2016, http://dailycaller.com/2016/05/12/chick-fil-a-dominates-in-new-york-city-despite-de-blasio-boycott/.

3.   Mark I. Johnson, "Restaurant Founder Dishes Out Punishment to Van-dals," GateHouse Media, August 1, 2008, accessed December 18, 2016, http://www.news-journalonline.com/news/20080801/restaurant-founder-dishes-out-punishment-to-vandals.

4.   Ibid.

5.   Ibid.

6.   "Controversial Chick-fil-A Founder Dies at 93," Catholic Online, Sep-tember 8, 2014, accessed December 18, 2016, http://www.catholic.org/news/hf/faith/story.php?id=56826.

7.   Ibid.

8.   Ibid.

9.   Ibid.

10.   Ibid.

11.   Ibid.

12.   Jena McGregor, "Chick-fil-A CEO Dan Cathy Steps Into Gay-Marriage Debate," *Washington Post*, July 19, 2012, accessed December 18, 2016, https://www.washingtonpost.com/blogs/post-leadership/post/chick-fil-a-president-dan-cathy-bites-into-gay-marriage-debate/2012/07/19/gJQACrvzvW_blog.html?utm_term=.2acd97c40b59.

13.   Michael Scherer, "Chick-fil-A Meets a First Amendment Buzzsaw in Chicago," *TIME*, July 26, 2012, accessed December 18, 2016, http://swampland.time.com/2012/07/26/chick-fil-a-meets-a-first-amendment-buzzsaw-in-chicago/.

14.   James Nye, "'I Feel Sorry for Him and His Family': Chick-fil-A Worker Bullied by Executive Says She Wants to Meet Him," Associated Newspapers Ltd., August 7, 2012, accessed December 18, 2016, http://www.dailymail.co.uk/news/article-2185218/Chick-fil-A-worker-Rachel-Elizabeth-bullied-customer-anti-gay-stance-says-feels-sorry-him.htm; "Former CFO Now Unemployed, on Food Stamps After Viral Video," YouTube video, March 28, 2015, posted by ABC News, accessed December 18, 2016, https://www.youtube.com/watch?v=8LqoLBQ68Uw.

15.   Jon Murray, "Chick-fil-A Location at DIA Paused After Denver Council Cites Chain's LGBT Stances," Digital First Media, August 19, 2015, accessed December 18, 2016, http://www.denverpost.com/2015/08/19/chick-fil-a-location-at-dia-paused-after-denver-council-cites-chains-lgbt-stances/.

16.   "Denver City Council Pauses Chick-fil-A Location at DIA," Southflorida gaynews.com, August 21, 2015, accessed December 18, 2016, http://southfloridagaynews.com/National/denver-city-council-pauses-chick-fil-a-location-at-dia.html.

17.   Richard Gorelick, "Johns Hopkins Students Oppose 'Hypothetical' Chick-fil-A," *Baltimore Sun*, April 24, 2015, accessed December 18, 2016, http://www.baltimoresun.com/entertainment/dining/baltimore-diner-blog/bal-johns-hopkins-oppose-chick-fil-a-20150424-story.html.

18.   Samantha Audia, "Chick-fil-A Rejected for Johns Hopkins Univ., Eatery Called 'Microaggression,'" The College Fix, April 23, 2015, accessed December 18, 2016, http://www.thecollegefix.com/post/22170/.

19.   Andrew Guernsey, "The Johns Hopkins Chick-fil-A Ban and the Coming Gay-Marriage Witch Hunt," *National Review*, April 22, 2015, accessed December 18, 2016, http://www.nationalreview.com/article/417305/johns-hopkins-chick-fil-ban-and-coming-gay-marriage-witch-hunt-andrew-guernsey.

20.   Jesse Chambers, "Highway 280 Chick-fil-A Took 'Opportunity to Help,' Gave Food to Drivers, Others Stranded in Snow," Alabama Media Group, January 29, 2015, accessed December 18, 2016, http://blog.al.com/spotnews/2014/01/highway_280_chick-fil-a_took_o.html.

21.   Audrey Pitt, in communication with the author, January 2014.

22.   Ibid.

23.   Ibid.

24.   Ibid.

25.   Ibid.

26.   Lauren Dango, in communication with the author, January 2014.

27.   Ibid.

28.   Pitt, in communication with the author, January 2014.

29.   Ibid.

30.   Ibid.

31.   Suzan Clarke, "Chick-fil-A Franchisee Gives Needy Man Free Meal, His Own Gloves," ABC News, January 13, 2015, accessed December 18, 2016, http://abcnews.go.com/US/chick-fil-franchisee-needy-man-free-meal-gloves/story?id=28182111.

32.   Mark Meadows, in communication with the author, January 2015.

33.   Ibid.

34.   Ibid.

35.   Ibid.

36.   Andrea Stoker's Facebook page, accessed December 18, 2016, https://www.facebook.com/photo.php?fbid=919102291443013&set=o.21543405100&type=1&theater.

37.   Meadows, in communication with the author, January 2015.

38.   Ibid.

39.   Chick-fil-A Corporate Purpose, accessed December 18, 2016, https://www.chick-fil-a.com/About/Who-We-Are.

40.   Pitt, in communication with the author, January 2014.

41.   Jessica Stevenson, "Volunteers Lend a Hand for Hofmann's Harvest," Sinclair Broadcast Group, November 16, 2016, accessed December 18, 2016, http://nebraska.tv/features/good-morning-nebraska/volunteering-for-hofmanns-harvest.

42.   Ron Chernow, *Titan: The Life of John D. Rockefeller, Sr.* (New York: Vintage Books, 1998), 51.

43.   "John D. Rockefeller," Wikipedia, accessed December 20, 2016, https://en.wikipedia.org/wiki/John_D._Rockefeller#Religious_views.

44.   Chernow, *Titan: The Life of John D. Rockefeller, Sr.*, 55.

45.   Casey Parks, "Oregon Lawyers: Sweet Cakes by Melissa $135,000 Damage Award Was Justified," Oregon Live LLC, August 25, 2016, accessed December 18, 2016, http://www.oregonlive.com/portland/index.ssf/2016/08/oregon_lawyers_sweet_cakes_by.html.

46.   Casey Parks, "The Hate Keeps Coming: Pain Lingers for Lesbian Couple Denied in Sweet Cakes Case," Oregon Live LLC, August 24, 2016, accessed December 18, 2016, http://www.oregonlive.com/pacific-northwest-news/index.ssf/2016/07/sweet_cakes_lesbians.html.

47.   George Rede, "Sweet Cakes Final Order: Gresham Bakery Must Pay $135,000 for Denying Service to Same-Sex Couple," Oregon Live LLC, July 2, 2015, accessed December 18, 2016, http://www.oregonlive.com/business/index.ssf/2015/07/sweet_cakes_final_order_gresha.html.

48.   Sylvia Tan, "Anti-Gay Bakers Get Final Order to Pay US$135,000 in Damages," Gay Star News, July 3, 2014, accessed December 18, 2016, http://www.gaystarnews.com/article/anti-gay-bakers-get-final-order-to-pay-us135000-in-damages/#gs.fETQ=Pw.

49.   Ibid.

50.   Rede, "Sweet Cakes Final Order: Gresham Bakery Must Pay $135,000 for Denying Service to Same-Sex Couple."

51.   Maxine Bernstein, "Lesbian Couple Refused Wedding Cake Files State Discrimination Complaint," Oregon Live LLC, January 20, 2014, accessed December 18, 2016, http://www.oregonlive.com/gresham/index.ssf/2013/08/lesbian_couple_refused_wedding.html.

52.   Melissa Klein, in communication with the author, July 2015.

53.   Ibid.

54.   Aaron Klein, in communication with the author, July 2015.

55.   Bureau of Labor and Industries, "In the matter of: Melissa Elaine Klein, dba Sweetcakes by Melissa, and Aaron Wayne Klein, dba Sweetcakes by Melissa," Case nos. 44-14 and 45-14, accessed December 20, 2016, http://www.oregon.gov/boli/SiteAssets/pages/press/Sweet%20Cakes%20FO.pdf.

56.   Todd Starnes, "Oregon Official Who Bullied Christian Bakery Owners Loses Election," FoxNews.com, November 16, 2016, accessed December 18, 2016, http://www.foxnews.com/opinion/2016/11/16/oregon-official-who-bullied-christian-bakery-owners-loses-election.html.

57.   Bradford Richardson, "Target Stock Tumbles as Transgender Bathroom Boycott Reaches 1 Million," The Washington Times, LLC, May 4, 2016, accessed January 6, 2017, http://www.washingtontimes.com/news/2016/may/4/target-stock-tumbles-transgender-bathroom-boycott-/.

58.   Ryan Wilson, "Poll: Main Reason for NFL Ratings Drop Due to Players Kneeling During Anthem," CBS Interactive, October 27, 2016, accessed January 6, 2017, http://www.cbssports.com/nfl/news/poll-main-reason-for-nfl-ratings-drop-due-to-players-kneeling-during-anthem/.

59.   "Did Target's Transgender Bathroom Policy Plunge Its Stock?," The Christian Broadcasting Network, Inc., May 25, 2016, accessed January 6, 2017, http://www1.cbn.com/cbnnews/2016/may/did-targets-transgender-bathroom-policy-plunge-its-stock.

CHAPTER 10: YOU WILL BE FORCED TO COMPLY

1.   Franklin Graham, in communication with the author, June 2015.

2.   Sarah Pulliam Bailey, "Here Are the Key Excerpts on Religious Liberty From the Supreme Court's Decision on Gay Marriage," *Washington Post*, June 26, 2015, accessed December 19, 2016, https://www.washingtonpost.com/news/acts-of-faith/wp/2015/06/26/here-are-the-key-excerpts-on-religious-liberty-from-the-supreme-courts-decision-on-gay-marriage/?utm_term=.8101ed8fdd0e.

3.   Eric Zorn, "Same-Sex Marriage May Still Have Opponents, But 'It Is So Ordered,'" *Chicago Tribune*, June 25, 2015, accessed December 19, 2016, http://www.chicagotribune.com/news/opinion/zorn/ct-oh-we-ll-get-over-it-20150626-story.html.

4.   Tom Blumer, "Sen. Tammy Baldwin: 'Freedom of Religion' Is for 'Institutions of Faith'—Period," Media Research Center, June 30, 2015, accessed December 19, 2016, http://www.newsbusters.org/blogs/tom-blumer/2015/06/30/sen-tammy-baldwin-freedom-religion-institutions-faith-%E2%80%94-period.

5.   Jessica Chasmar, "Labor Dept. Economist Under Review After Tweet Calling Christians Nazis," The Washington Times, LLC, March 30, 2015, accessed December 19, 2016, http://www.washingtontimes.com/news/2015/mar/30/elizabeth-ashack-labor-dept-economist-under-review/.

6.   "Exclusive—LGBT Group: Shut Churches Down!," Conservative Colorado, April 1, 2015, accessed December 19, 2016, http://www.conservativecolorado.com/top-stories/2015/4/1/exclusive-lgbt-group-shut-churches-down/.

7.   John Carroll, "Gays Giveth and Gays Taketh Away: An Open Letter to Bailey Hanks," TheHuffingtonPost.com, Inc., February 2, 2016, accessed December 19, 2016, http://www.huffingtonpost.com/john-carroll/bailey-hanks-chick-fil-a_b_1765077.html.

8.   "Fund Raises $840,000 for Memories Pizza After Attacks Over Gay Marriage Views," NBCNews.com, April 4, 2015, accessed December 19, 2016, http://www.nbcnews.com/news/us-news/fund-site-closes-memories-pizzeria-supported-controversial-indiana-law-n335811.

9.   "Northeast Indiana Coach Invites Twitter to 'Burn Down' RFRA-Supporting Pizzeria," WTHR.com, April 14, 2016, accessed December 19, 2016, http://www.wthr.com/article/northeast-indiana-coach-invites-twitter-to-burn-down-rfra-supporting-pizzeria.

10.   Kate Abbey-Lambertz, "Ford Worker Fired for Anti-Gay Comment Sues for Religious Discrimination," TheHuffingtonPost.com, Inc., July 14, 2015, accessed December 19, 2016, http://www.huffingtonpost.com/entry/thomas-banks-ford-lawsuit_us_55a42530e4b0a47ac15d2669.

11.   Albert Mohler, "State of Kentucky Ejects Chaplains From Juvenile Center for Believing Homosexuality Is Sin," Kentucky Today, accessed December 19, 2016, http://kentuckytoday.com/stories/state-of-kentucky-ejects-chaplains-from-juvenile-center-for-believing-homosexuality-is-sin,1266.

12.   David Wells, in communication with the author, August 2015.

13.   Letter provided by David Wells, in communication with the author, August 2015.

14.   Justice Cabinet Department of Juvenile Justice Policy and Procedures, "Prison Rape Elimination Act of 2003 (PREA), Reference 505 KAR 1:170, accessed December 19, 2016, http://djj.ky.gov/900%20Policy%20Manual/DJJ%20912%20Sex%20Orientation%20and%20Gender%20Identity.pdf.

15.   Wells, in communication with the author, August 2015.

16.   Ibid.

17.   Ibid.

18.   Ibid.

19.   Mat Staver, in communication with the author, August 2015.

20.   Richard L. Mast, Liberty Counsel, letter sent to Kentucky Department of Juvenile Justice via facsimile on July 23, 2015, accessed December 19, 2016, http://www.lc.org/PDFs/072415_Ltr_-_to_KY_Dept_of_Juvenile_Justice.pdf.

21.   John Cheves, "Kentucky Juvenile Justice Department Says It Won't Change Policy Prohibiting Anti-Gay Comments," Lexington Herald Leader, July 31, 2015, accessed December 19, 2016, http://www.kentucky.com/news/state/kentucky/article44613156.html.

22.   Ibid.

23.   American Pastors' Network, "New Kentucky Policy Strips Pastors of Religious Freedom," August 11, 2015, accessed December 19, 2016, https://americanpastorsnetwork.net/2015/08/11/new-kentucky-policy-strips-pastors-of-religious-freedom/.

24.   In communication with the author, June 2014, name withheld.

25.   Alan Cooper, in communication with the author, June 2014.

26.   In communication with the author, June 2014, name withheld.

27.   Drew Magary, "What the Duck?," Condé Nast, December 17, 2013, accessed December 19, 2016, http://www.gq.com/story/duck-dynasty-phil-robertson.

28.   "A&E Lifts Phil Robertson's 'Duck Dynasty' Suspension," CBS Interactive Inc., December 27, 2013, accessed December 19, 2016, http://www.cbsnews.com/news/ae-lifts-phil-robertson-duck-dynasty-suspension/.

29.   Alan Cooper, in communication with the author, June 2014.

30.   Ibid.

31.   In communication with the author, June 2014, name withheld.

32.   Ibid.

33.   Ibid.

34.   Ibid.

35.   Andy Bourland, in communication with the author, June 2014.

36.   Eli Craft, in communication with the author, June 2014.

37.   Ibid.

38.   Ibid.

39.   Tony Perkins, in communication with the author, June 2014.

40.   Ibid.

41.   Raymond Sexton, in communication with the author, October 2014.

42.   *Aaron Baker for Gay and Lesbian Services Organization; Lexington-Fayette County Human Rights Commission vs. Hands On Original, Inc.*, Human Rights Commission HRC No. 03-12-3135, accessed December 20, 2016, http://www.adfmedia.org/files/HOOrecommendation.pdf.

43.   Sexton, in communication with the author, October 2014.

44.   *Aaron Baker for Gay and Lesbian Services Organization; Lexington-Fayette County Human Rights Commission vs. Hands On Original, Inc.*

45.   Jim Campbell, in communication with the author, October 2014.

46.   Sexton, in communication with the author, October 2014.

47.   *Aaron Baker for Gay and Lesbian Services Organization; Lexington-Fayette County Human Rights Commission vs. Hands On Original, Inc.*

48.   Campbell, in communication with the author, October 2014.

49.   Sexton, in communication with the author, October 2014.

50.   Ibid.

51.   Campbell, in communication with the author, October 2014.

52.   "SF Bay Area School Permits Queer Straight Alliance to Bully Students," Pacific Justice Institute, February 5, 2015, accessed December 19, 2016, http://www.pacificjustice.org/press-releases/sf-bay-area-school-permits-queer-straight-alliance-to-bully-students.

53.   Ibid.
54.   Ibid.
55.   Ibid.
56.   In communication with the author, February 2015, name withheld.
57.   "SF Bay Area School Permits Queer Straight Alliance to Bully Students," Pacific Justice Institute.
58.   Todd Starnes, "Students Opposed to LGBT Agenda Shamed in Classroom," FoxNews.com, February 9, 2015, accessed December 19, 2016, http://www.foxnews.com/opinion/2015/02/09/students-opposed-to-lgbt-agenda-shamed-in-classroom.html.
59.   "SF Bay Area School Permits Queer Straight Alliance to Bully Students," Pacific Justice Institute.
60.   In communication with the author, February 2015, name withheld.
61.   Ibid.
62.   John Nickerson, in communication with the author, February 2015.
63.   Ibid.
64.   "SF Bay Area School Permits Queer Straight Alliance to Bully Students," Pacific Justice Institute.
65.   In communication with the author, February 2015, name withheld.
66.   Pacific Justice Institute, in communication with the author, February 2015.
67.   Nicole Hensley, "Mississippi Clerk Resigns Over Supreme Court Ruling on Gay Marriage: 'I Choose to Obey God Rather Than Man,'" NYDailyNews.com, July 1, 2015, accessed December 19, 2016, http://www.nydailynews.com/news/national/clerk-resigns-scotus-ruling-marriage-equality-article-1.2277815.
68.   "Grenada County Clerk Quits Early Over Same Sex Marriage Ruling," Raycom Media, June 27, 2016, accessed December 19, 2016, http://www.nbc12.com/story/29443287/grenada-co-circuit-clerk-resigns-over-same-sex-marriage-ruling.
69.   Linda Barnette, in communication with the author, July 2015.
70.   Franklin Graham's Facebook page, July 6, 2015, accessed December 19, 2016, https://www.facebook.com/FranklinGraham/posts/959422130780635.
71.   Richard L. Mast Jr., Liberty Counsel, letter sent to City of Lake Worth via e-mail on February 23, 2014, accessed December 19, 2016, https://www.liberty.edu/media/9980/attachments/022515_Ltr_Lake_Worth_about_Common_Ground.pdf.
72.   Ibid.
73.   Mat Staver, in communication with the author, March 2013.
74.   Mast Jr., Liberty Counsel, letter sent to City of Lake Worth.
75.   Ibid.
76.   Mike Olive, in communication with the author, March 2013.
77.   Ibid.
78.   Ibid.
79.   Mast Jr., Liberty Counsel, letter sent to City of Lake Worth.
80.   Ibid.
81.   Ibid.
82.   Olive, in communication with the author, March 2013.

83.   Ibid.

84.   William Waters, in communication with the author, March 2013.

85.   Ibid.

86.   Ibid.

87.   The *Lake Worth Tribune* Facebook page, accessed December 19, 2016, https://www.facebook.com/permalink.php?story_fbid=1413843555577342&id =1376829215945443&substory_index=0.

88.   Ibid.

89.   Waters, in communication with the author, March 2013.

90.   The *Lake Worth Tribune* Facebook page.

91.   Mast Jr., Liberty Counsel, letter sent to City of Lake Worth.

92.   Waters, in communication with the author, March 2013.

93.   Olive, in communication with the author, March 2013.

94.   Fr. Jonathan Morris's Twitter account, June 28, 2015, accessed December 19, 2016, https://twitter.com/fatherjonathan/status/615286358169534464.

95.   Fr. Jonathan Morris's Twitter account, June 28, 2015, accessed December 19, 2016, https://twitter.com/fatherjonathan/status/615288009831882753.

96.   Fr. Jonathan Morris's Twitter account, June 28, 2015, accessed December 19, 2016, https://twitter.com/fatherjonathan/status/615286358169534464.

97.   John Zmirak, "Gay Totalitarianism and the Coming Persecution of Christians," The Stream, April 1, 2015, accessed December 19, 2016, https:// stream.org/gay-totalitarianism-coming-persecution-christians/.

98.   "Transcript: Obama's Remarks on Supreme Court Ruling on Same-Sex Marriage," *Washington Post*, June 26, 2015, accessed December 19, 2016, https:// www.washingtonpost.com/news/post-nation/wp/2015/06/26/transcript-obamas -remarks-on-supreme-court-ruling-on-same-sex-marriage/?utm_term= .2d1885553492.

99.   John Nolte, "Obama on Gay Marriage: 'If You Like Your Religion, You Can Keep Your Religion,'" Breitbart, June 27, 2015, accessed December 19, 2016, http://www.breitbart.com/big-government/2015/06/27/obama-on-gay-marriage-if -you-like-your-religion-you-can-keep-your-religion/.

100.   Charles S. Colson, *My Final Word: Holding Tight to the Issues That Matter Most* (Grand Rapids, MI: Zondervan, 2015).

101.   Adelle M. Banks, "Southern Baptist President: God, Not Supreme Court, Has 'Final Authority,'" *Washington Post*, accessed December 19, 2016, https://www.washingtonpost.com/national/southern-baptist-president-god-not -supreme-court-has-final-authority/2015/06/16/e026314a-146e-11e5-8457 -4b431bf7ed4c_story.html?utm_term=.eeb93dcdc344.

102.   Ibid.

103.   Ibid.

104.   Travis Loller, "Baptist President Pastor Ronnie Floyd Vows He Will Never Marry a Same-Sex Couple," MaineToday Media, June 17, 2015, accessed December 19, 2016, http://www.pressherald.com/2015/06/17/baptist-president -pastor-ronnie-floyd-vows-he-will-never-marry-a-same-sex-couple/.

105.   Ibid.

106.   Nigel Boys, "Leading Pastor Promises Civil Disobedience Over Issue of Gay Marriage," All Christian News, June 23, 2015, accessed December 19, 2016, http://allchristiannews.com/leading-pastor-promises-civil-disobedience-over-issue-of-gay-marriage/.

Chapter 11: Boys and Girls and Zi and Zir

1.   Russell Goldman, "Here's a List of 58 Gender Options for Facebook Users," ABC News, February 13, 2014, accessed December 19, 2016, http://abcnews.go.com/blogs/headlines/2014/02/heres-a-list-of-58-gender-options-for-facebook-users/.

2.   Jesse Scardina, "Kittery School Put on Defensive About Transgender Lesson," GateHouse Media, April 17, 2015, accessed December 19, 2016, http://www.seacoastonline.com/article/20150417/NEWS/150419165.

3.   "Attorney General Loretta E. Lynch Delivers Remarks at Press Conference Announcing Complaint Against the State of North Carolina to Stop Discrimination Against Transgender Individuals," US Department of Justice, May 9, 2016, accessed December 19, 2016, https://www.justice.gov/opa/speech/attorney-general-loretta-e-lynch-delivers-remarks-press-conference-announcing-complaint.

4.   "Dear Colleague Letter on Transgender Students," U.S. Department of Justice, May 13, 2016, accessed December 19, 2016, http://www2.ed.gov/about/offices/list/ocr/letters/colleague-201605-title-ix-transgender.pdf; "U.S. Departments of Education and Justice Release Joint Guidance to Help Schools Ensure the Civil Rights of Transgender Students," U.S. Department of Education, May 13, 2016, accessed December 19, 2016, http://www.ed.gov/news/press-releases/us-departments-education-and-justice-release-joint-guidance-help-schools-ensure-civil-rights-transgender-students.

5.   "U.S. Departments of Education and Justice Release Joint Guidance to Help Schools Ensure the Civil Rights of Transgender Students," U.S. Department of Education.

6.   Ronnie Floyd, in communication with the author, May 2016.

7.   Fox & Friends, May 13, 2016.

8.   Noelle Walker, "Texas Lt. Gov. Dan Patrick Speaks Out on President's Transgender Bathroom Directive," NBCUniversal Media, LLC, May 12, 2016, accessed December 19, 2016, http://www.nbcdfw.com/news/politics/Gov-Greg-Abbott-Lt-Gov-Dan-Patrick-to-Speak-at-GOP-Convention-in-Dallas-379193041.html.

9.   Ibid.

10.   Ibid.

11.   "Rep. Black Blasts Obama Administration Directive on School Bathrooms," Black.House.gov, May 13, 2016, accessed December 19, 2016, https://black.house.gov/press-release/rep-black-blasts-obama-administration-directive-school-bathrooms.

12.   Tony Perkins, in communication with author, May 2016.

13.   Ibid.

14.   Janae Stracke, "Supreme Court Stays Ruling Forcing Schools to Allow Transgender Students to Use the Bathroom of Their Choice," CWALAC, August

3, 2016, accessed December 19, 2016, http://concernedwomen.org/supreme-court
-stays-ruling-forcing-schools-to-allow-transgender-students-to-use-the-bathroom
-of-their-choice/.

15.   Donna Braquet, "Inclusive Practice: Pronoun Usage," University of Tennessee, August 26, 2015, accessed December 19, 2016, https://web.archive.org
/web/20150830174500/http://linkis.com/diversity.utk.edu/20/Aib3Y.

16.   Ibid.

17.   Ibid.

18.   Ibid.

19.   Ibid.

20.   Ibid.

21.   Ibid.

22.   Mae Beavers, in communication with author, August 2015.

23.   Ibid.

24.   Julie West, in communication with author, August 2015.

25.   "University of Tennessee Backing Away From Gender-Neutral Pronoun
Suggestion," Media General Communications Holdings, LLC, September 5, 2015,
accessed December 19, 2016, http://wric.com/2015/09/05/university-of-tennessee
-backing-away-from-gender-neutral-pronoun-suggestion/.

26.   Fenit Nirappil, "Careless Email Brings the Nation's Bathroom Wars to
Ocean City, Md.," *Washington Post*, June 15, 2016, accessed December 19, 2016,
https://www.washingtonpost.com/local/md-politics/careless-email-brings-the
-nations-bathroom-wars-to-ocean-city-md/2016/06/14/47caceb8-3260-11e6-8ff7
-7b6c1998b7a0_story.html?utm_term=.14b8ce7f7ec9.

27.   Ibid.

28.   Ibid.

29.   Ibid.

30.   Ibid.

31.   Ibid.

32.   Jessica Anderson, "Ocean City Beach Patrol Captain Draws Fire With
Email on Locker Room Use," *Baltimore Sun*, June 14, 2016, accessed December 19,
2016, http://www.baltimoresun.com/news/maryland/bs-md-oc-locker-rooms
-20160614-story.html.

33.   "Updated: Ocean City Beach Patrol Head Faces Sanctions Over Locker
Room Email," WBOC, June 16, 2016, accessed December 19, 2016, http://www
.wboc.com/story/32226926/ocean-city-beach-patrol-head-faces-sanctions-over
-locker-room-email.

34.   Nirappil, "Careless Email Brings the Nation's Bathroom Wars to Ocean
City, Md."

35.   Ibid.

36.   OC *Today*, "Insensitivity and Loss of Perspective," June 17, 2016,
accessed December 19, 2016, http://www.oceancitytoday.net/p/insensitivity-and
-loss-of-perspective/1538246.

37.   Ibid.

38.   "51 Families Sue Feds, Chicago-Area School District for Violating Student Privacy," Alliance Defending Freedom, May 4, 2016, accessed December 19,

2016, https://www.adflegal.org/detailspages/press-release-details/51-families-sue
-feds-chicago-area-school-district-for-violating-student-privacy.

39. Jeremy Tedesco, in communication with the author, May 2016.

40. *Students and Parents for Privacy v. United States Department of Educa-tion*, case 1:16-cv-04945, accessed December 19, 2016, https://www
.thomasmoresociety.org/wp-content/uploads/2016/05/160504-Palatine-Trans
-Verified-Complaint-dkt-1_Redacted.pdf.

41. Duaa Eldeib and Dawn Rhodes, "Lawsuit Filed After Transgender
Student Gets Locker Room Access in Palatine," *Chicago Tribune*, May 5, 2016,
accessed December 19, 2016, http://www.chicagotribune.com/news/local
/breaking/ct-transgender-palatine-high-school-lawsuit-met-20160504-story.html.

42. *Students and Parents for Privacy v. United States Department of Educa-tion*, case 1:16-cv-04945.

43. Tedesco, in conversation with the author, May 2016.

44. Kellie Fiedorek, "Obama Administration: 'Give Up Privacy or Give Up
Funding,' NC Families, Students Sue," Alliance Defending Freedom, May 11,
2016, accessed December 19, 2016, http://www.adfmedia.org/News/PRDetail
/9955.

45. "Title IX, Education Amendments of 1972," United States Department
of Labor, accessed December 19, 2016, https://www.dol.gov/oasam/regs/statutes
/titleix.htm.

46. Tedesco, in conversation with the author, May 2016.

47. Ibid.

48. *Students and Parents for Privacy v. United States Department of Educa-tion*, case 1:16-cv-04945.

49. Ibid.

50. Ibid.

51. Eldeib and Rhodes, "Lawsuit Filed After Transgender Student Gets
Locker Room Access in Palatine."

52. Ibid.

53. "Trish Regan: 'What About the Civil Rights of Women Who Don't
Want Men in Their Bathrooms?,'" FoxNews.com, accessed December 19, 2016,
http://nation.foxnews.com/2016/05/06/trish-regan-what-about-civil-rights
-women-who-dont-want-men-their-bathrooms.

54. *Privacy Matters and Parent A v. United States Department of Education,
United States Department of Justice, and Independent School District 706, State of
MN*, Case :16-cv-03015, accessed December 19, 2016, http://www.adfmedia.org
/files/PrivacyMattersComplaint.pdf.

55. Ibid.

56. Ibid.

57. Ibid.

58. Ibid.

59. Ibid.

60. Ibid.

61. Ibid.

62. Matt Sharp, in communication with the author, September 2016.

63.   Richard Sandomir, "Curt Schilling, ESPN Analyst, Is Fired Over Offensive Social Media Post," The New York Times Company, April 20, 2016, accessed December 19, 2016, http://www.nytimes.com/2016/04/21/sports/baseball/curt-schilling-is-fired-by-espn.html?_r=0.

64.   Ibid.

65.   Ibid.

66.   Jeff Katz, in communication with the author, April 2016.

67.   Clay Travis, "ESPN Loses 4 Million Subscribers in Past Year," Fox Sports Interactive Media, LLC, August 4, 2016, accessed December 19, 2016, http://www.outkickthecoverage.com/espn-loses-4-million-subscribers-in-past-year-080416.

68.   Winston Churchill, "Never Give In," The International Churchill Society, accessed December 19, 2016, http://www.winstonchurchill.org/resources/speeches/1941-1945-war-leader/103-never-give-in.

Chapter 12: I Wanna Deck Somebody's Halls

1.   Sarah Palin, in conversation with the author, December 2014.

2.   "Nativity Outrage: Alabama Town Threatened With Lawsuit Over Religious Scene," ABC Inc., KTRK-TV Houston, December 21, 2014, accessed December 19, 2016, http://abc13.com/news/alabama-town-threatened-with-lawsuit-over-nativity-scene/445483/.

3.   Ibid.

4.   "Utica Fire Chief Refuses to Remove 'Happy Birthday Jesus' Christmas Sign," CBS Local Media, December 16, 2014, accessed December 19, 2016,http://connecticut.cbslocal.com/2014/12/16/utica-fire-chief-refuses-to-remove-happy-birthday-jesus-christmas-sign/.

5.   "Utica Fire Chief Says 'Happy Birthday Jesus, We Love You' Sign Is Here to Stay," STATter911, December 17, 2014, accessed December 19, 2016, https://www.statter911.com/2014/12/17/utica-fire-chief-says-happy-birthday-jesus-love-sign-stay/.

6.   Ibid.

7.   Robert Richardson, "Piedmont Parade Unofficially 'Keeps Christ in Christmas,'" Sinclair Broadcast Group, December 4, 2014, accessed December 19, 2016, http://abc3340.com/archive/piedmont-parade-unofficially-keeps-christ-in-christmas.

8.   "Editorial on Diversity," *University of Tennessee Daily Beacon*.

9.   Ibid.

10.   University of Tennessee Media Relations Department, in communication with the author, December 2015.

11.   Ibid.

12.   Ibid.

13.   "Editorial on Diversity," *University of Tennessee Daily Beacon*.

14.   Ibid.

15.   John Duncan, in communication with the author, December 2015.

16.   Ron Ramsey, in communication with the author, December 2015.

17.   Paul Walsh, "St. Paul School Kisses Valentine's Day, Other 'Dominant Holidays,' Goodbye," January 28, 2016, accessed December 19, 2016, http://www.startribune.com/st-paul-school-pulls-plug-on-celebrating-dominant-holidays/366834081/.

18.   Ibid.

19.   Ibid.

20.   Scott Masini, in communication with the author, January 2016.

21.   Walsh, "St. Paul School Kisses Valentine's Day, Other 'Dominant Holidays,' Goodbye."

22.   St. Paul Public Schools spokesperson, in communication with the author, January 2016.

23.   Cambridge Public Schools, accessed December 19, 2016, http://peabody.cpsd.us/.

24.   Katie Brace, "Cambridge School Removes Santa Claus From Winter Concert," CBS Local Media, December 12, 2014, accessed December 19, 2016, http://boston.cbslocal.com/2014/12/12/cambridge-school-removes-santa-claus-from-winter-concert/.

25.   Robert Thompson, as seen on *Fox & Friends*, December 15, 2014.

26.   Ibid.

27.   Peter Schworm, "Santa Claus Disinvited From Cambridge School Concert," Boston Globe Media Partners, LLC, December 12, 2014, accessed December 19, 2016, https://www.bostonglobe.com/metro/2014/12/12/santa-disinvited-cambridge-school-holiday-concert/SwmET7k5Y9GeZ8PRvxvzWL/story.html.

28.   Ibid.

29.   Amy Derjue, "Don't Ever Change, Cambridge," Metro Corp., November 14, 2007, accessed December 19, 2016, http://www.bostonmagazine.com/news/blog/2007/11/14/dont-ever-change-cambridge/.

30.   Brock Parker, "Cambridge Mulling Soda Ban Similar to New York City Proposal," Boston Globe Media Partners, LLC, June 18, 2012, accessed December 19, 2016, http://archive.boston.com/yourtown/news/cambridge/2012/06/cambridge_mulling_soda_ban_sim.html.

31.   Laura A. Moore, "Pledge of Allegiance Controversy Grows in Cambridge Public Schools as Committee Member Criticizes Law," The Harvard Crimson, Inc., February 23, 2006, accessed December 19, 2016, http://www.thecrimson.com/article/2006/2/23/pledge-of-allegiance-controversy-grows-in/.

32.   Ibid.

33.   "Salem VA Medical Center Bans Christmas Trees as Holiday Decorations," LIN Television Corporation, November 20, 2015, accessed December 19, 2016, http://wtnh.com/2015/11/20/salem-va-medical-center-bans-christmas-trees-as-holiday-decorations/.

34.   Ibid.

35.   Ibid.

36.   Ibid.

37.   John Sines Jr., in communication with the author, November 2015.

38.   Ibid.

39.   Ibid.

40.   Ibid.

41.   Ibid.

42.   Danner Evans, "Salem VA Hospital Decides to Decorate With Christmas Tree After Meeting," November 20, 2015, accessed December 19, 2016, http://wset.com/news/local/salem-va-hospital-not-putting-up-christmas-tree-some-staff-upset.

43.   Ibid.

44.   Ibid.

45.   "Inclusive Holidays at Cornell," December 23, 2015, accessed December 19, 2016, http://www.wsj.com/articles/notable-quotable-inclusive-holidays-at-cornell-1450914140.

46.   Ibid.

47.   Ibid.

48.   Ibid.

49.   Ibid.

50.   Ashley Rae Goldenberg, "EXCLUSIVE: University of Missouri Student Health Center Staff Banned From Decorating for Holidays," Media Research Center, December 15, 2015, accessed December 19, 2016, http://www.mrctv.org/blog/university-missouri-student-health-center-staff-banned-decorating-holidays.

51.   Ibid.

CHAPTER 13: THE GENERATION THAT MIGHT SAVE FREEDOM

1.   Reagan, "Inaugural Address: January 5, 1967," Ronald Reagan Presidential Library and Museum.

2.   Phil Sanchez, "Teen Makes Soldiers a Part of the Flag They Fight For," LIN Television Corporation, February 19, 2016, accessed December 19, 2016, http://wishtv.com/2016/02/19/teen-makes-soldiers-a-part-of-the-flag-they-fight-for/.

3.   "Maconaquah High School Student's Art Goes Viral," *Kokomo Tribune*, February 19, 2016, accessed December 19, 2016, http://www.kokomotribune.com/news/maconaquah-high-school-student-s-art-goes-viral/article_8f50bd0c-d747-11e5-a123-9f5d3abb36b7.html.

4.   Ibid.

5.   Ibid.

6.   Daniel Craig, "Pa. School Investigating Photo of Student Stepping on American Flag," WWB Holdings, LLC, February 16, 2015, accessed December 19, 2016, http://www.phillyvoice.com/pa-school-investigating-photo-students-stepping-american-flag/.

7.   Ibid.

8.   Todd Starnes, "Teen's Flag-Stomp Stunt at HS Spurs Investigation," FoxNews.com, February 16, 2016, accessed December 19, 2016, http://www.foxnews.com/opinion/2016/02/16/teens-flag-stomp-stunt-at-hs-spurs-investigation.html.

9.   Ibid.

10.   Ibid.

11.   David Hurst, "Photo of Teen Standing on American Flag Prompts School, Police Inquiry," *North Jefferson News*, February 15, 2016, accessed

December 19, 2016, http://www.njeffersonnews.com/cnhi_network/photo-of-teen
-standing-on-american-flag-prompts-school-police/article_564d5b3e-c606-5851
-9482-9dd12ce9c1ca.html.

12.   "School District in Johnstown Promises 'Thorough Review' of Unpatriotic Photo," Cox Media Group, February 14, 2016, accessed December 19, 2016,
http://www.wpxi.com/news/local/school-district-johnstown-promises-thorough
-review/165770075.

13.   Jillian Hartmann, "Family Reacts to Picture of Boy Standing on Flag,"
Sinclair Broadcast Group, February 15, 2016, accessed December 19, 2016, http://
wjactv.com/news/local/family-reacts-to-picture-of-boy-standing-on-flag.

14.   Hurst, "Photo of Teen Standing on American Flag Prompts School,
Police Inquiry."

15.   Ibid.

16.   Ibid.

17.   "Millikin to Look at Anthem Policy," Herald and Review, October 18,
2016, accessed December 19, 2016, http://herald-review.com/news/local/millikin
-to-look-at-anthem-policy/article_250e1ab6-c5e1-5517-ad02-629a49f83b73.html.

18.   "Millikin University President's Email to Campus," Herald and Review,
October 14, 2016, accessed December 19, 2016, http://herald-review.com/full-text
-millikin-university-president-s-email-to-campus/article_26bffc64-0dd6-5573-a7d8
-8eadf870db7b.html.

19.   Ibid.

20.   Ibid.

21.   Ibid.

22.   Debi Daniels, in communication with the author, October 2016.

23.   Ibid.

24.   Ibid.

25.   Ibid.

26.   Ibid.

27.   Anonymous, in communication with the author, October 2016. Some
editorial changes were made to correct grammar and spelling.

28.   Todd Starnes, "School Rejects Teen's Gun-Toting, Flag-Waving Photo,"
FoxNews.com, June 11, 2016, accessed December 19, 2016, http://www.foxnews
.com/opinion/2016/06/11/school-rejects-teens-gun-toting-flag-waving-photo.html.

29.   Darcy Meys, in communication with the author, June 2016.

30.   Starnes, "School Rejects Teen's Gun-Toting, Flag-Waving Photo."

31.   Ibid.

32.   Meys, in communication with the author, June 2016.

33.   Ibid.

34.   Ibid.

35.   Ibid.

36.   Ibid.

37.   Ibid.

38.   Grant Strobl, in communication with the author, September 2016.

39.   Martha E. Pollack and E. Royster Harper, "New Process for Desig-
nating Pronouns for Class Rosters," The Regents of the University of Michigan,

September 27, 2016, accessed December 19, 2016, http://www.provost.umich.edu
/provost%20messages/pronoun_msg.html.

40.   Ibid.

41.   Strobl, in communication with the author, September 2016.

42.   Ibid.

43.   Ibid.

44.   Ibid.

45.   Ibid.

46.   Ibid.

47.   Ibid.

48.   Alex Dunn, in communication with the author, September 2016.

49.   Ibid.

50.   Nancy McCleary and Alicia Banks, "Fayetteville Teacher Placed on
Leave in Flag Controversy," *Fayetteville Observer*, September 20, 2016, accessed
December 19, 2016, http://www.fayobserver.com/news/local/fayetteville-teacher
-placed-on-leave-in-flag-controversy/article_05143376-3259-59d6-aadd
-62ea4df1b6b5.html.

51.   Dunn, in communication with the author, September 2016.

52.   Ibid.

53.   Todd Starnes, "Meet the North Carolina Teen Who Saved the American
Flag," FoxNews.com, September 22, 2016, accessed December 19, 2016, http://
www.foxnews.com/opinion/2016/09/22/meet-north-carolina-teen-who-saved
-american-flag.html.

54.   Mrs. Dunn, in communication with the author, September 2016.

55.   Lee Francis, in communication with the author, September 2016.

56.   "North Carolina Teacher Lee Francis' 10-Day Suspension Without Pay
Upheld," Interactive One, LLC, December 5, 2016, accessed December 19, 2016,
https://newsone.com/3606021/north-carolina-teacher-lee-francis-10-day-suspension
-without-pay-upheld/.

57.   Mrs. Dunn, in communication with the author, September 2016.

58.   Dunn, in communication with the author, September 2016.

59.   Mrs. Dunn, in communication with the author, September 2016.

60.   Jim Langham, "Grandma's Love Is Heartbeat for Parkway Senior Prom
Date," Times Bulletin Media, May 1, 2014, accessed December 19, 2016, http://
www.timesbulletin.com/Content/News/News/Article/Grandma-s-love-is
-heartbeat-for-Parkway-senior-prom-date/2/4/187271.

61.   Austin Dennison, in communication with the author, May 2014.

62.   Delores Dennison, in communication with the author, May 2014.

63.   Langham, "Grandma's Love Is Heartbeat for Parkway Senior Prom Date."

64.   Delores Dennison, in communication with the author, May 2014.

65.   Austin Dennison, in communication with the author, May 2014.

66.   Delores Dennison, in communication with the author, May 2014.

67.   Ibid.

68.   Ibid.

69.   Langham, "Grandma's Love Is Heartbeat for Parkway Senior Prom Date."

70.   Ibid.

71.   Austin Dennison, in communication with the author, May 2014.
72.   Delores Dennison, in communication with the author, May 2014.
73.   Austin Dennison, in communication with the author, May 2014.
74.   Langham, "Grandma's Love Is Heartbeat for Parkway Senior Prom Date."
75.   Delores Dennison, in communication with the author, May 2014.
76.   Austin Dennison, in communication with the author, May 2014.
77.   Delores Dennison, in communication with the author, May 2014.
78.   Austin Dennison, in communication with the author, May 2014.
79.   Ibid.

CHAPTER 14: PROFILES IN COURAGE

1.   Kelvin Cochran, in communication with the author, January 2015.
2.   Ibid.
3.   Kelvin J. Cochran's LinkedIn page, accessed December 19, 2016, https://www.linkedin.com/in/kelvin-j-cochran-280a2754.
4.   *Kelvin J. Cochran v. City of Atlanta, Georgia; and Mayor Kasim Reed*, United States District Court Northern District of Georgia Atlanta Division, accessed December 19, 2016, https://adflegal.blob.core.windows.net/web-content-dev/documents/cochran-v-city-of-atlanta-district-court-complaint.pdf?sfvrsn=4.
5.   Cochran, in communication with the author, January 2015.
6.   *Cochran v. City of Atlanta, Georgia; and Mayor Kasim Reed*, United States District Court Northern District Of Georgia Atlanta Division.
7.   Todd Starnes, "Atlanta Fire Chief: I Was Fired Because of My Christian Faith," FoxNews.com, January 7, 2015, accessed December 19, 2016, http://www.foxnews.com/opinion/2015/01/07/atlanta-fire-chief-was-fired-because-my-christian-faith.html.
8.   Kasim Reed's Facebook page, November 24, 2014, accessed December 19, 2016, https://www.facebook.com/kasimreed/posts/10152925936289669.
9.   Ibid.
10.   Ibid.
11.   Dyana Bagby, "Atlanta Fire Chief Goes on Anti-Gay Crusade in Self-Published Book," Georgia Voice, November 24, 2014, accessed December 19, 2016, https://thegavoice.com/atlanta-fire-chief-goes-anti-gay-crusade-self-published-book/.
12.   Cochran, in communication with the author, January 2015.
13.   Ibid.
14.   Todd Duncan, "Reaction to Atlanta Fire Chief's Firing," Cox Media Group, January 7, 2015, accessed December 19, 2016, http://www.ajc.com/news/reaction-atlanta-fire-chief-firing/rDPNvsQ7FYpe3CgCS20BfJ/.
15.   Cochran, in communication with the author, January 2015.
16.   Dyana Bagby and Patrick Saunders, "Atlanta Mayor Kasim Reed Ousts Anti-Gay Fire Chief," Georgia Voice, January 6, 2015, accessed December 19, 2016, https://webcache.googleusercontent.com/search?q=cache:5LPrMpTSt90J:h ttps://thegavoice.com/anti-gay-atlanta-fire-chief-terminated-mayor/+&cd=4&hl =en&ct=clnk&gl=us.
17.   Ibid.

18.   *Cochran v. City of Atlanta, Georgia; and Mayor Kasim Reed*, United States District Court Northern District Of Georgia Atlanta Division.

19.   Ibid.

20.   Ibid.

21.   Ibid.

22.   Cochran, in communication with the author, January 2015.

23.   Ibid.

24.   Robert White, in communication with the author, January 2015.

25.   Ibid.

26.   Ibid.

27.   Cochran, in communication with the author, January 2015.

28.   W. J. Modder, "First Endorsement on NAVNUPWRTRACOM ltr 1611 Ser Legal/047 of 17 Feb 15," accessed December 19, 2016, https://www .libertyinstitute.org/file/DETACHMENT-FOR-CAUSE-REQ--Redacted.pdf.

29.   Ibid.

30.   Michael Berry, First Liberty Institute (formerly Liberty Institute), letter sent to Captain Jon R. Fahs, USN, Commanding Officer, Navy Nuclear Power Training Command, March 9, 2015, via certified mail RRR, accessed December 19, 2016, https://www.libertyinstitute.org/file/Modder---Response-to-Det-for -Cause-FINAL.pdf.

31.   Ibid.

32.   Ibid.

33.   Michael Berry, in communication with the author, March 2015.

34.   Ibid.

35.   Wes Modder, in communication with the author, March 2015.

36.   Ibid.

37.   Ibid.

38.   Ibid.

39.   Zollie Smith, in communication with the author, March 2015.

40.   Berry, in communication with the author, March 2015.

41.   Ibid.

42.   Modder, in communication with the author, March 2015.

43.   Ibid.

44.   Ibid.

45.   Ibid.

46.   Ibid.

47.   Ibid.

48.   Andrew Tilghman, "Navy Spares Controversial Chaplain Accused of Misconduct," Sightline Media Group, September 14, 2015, accessed December 19, 2016, http://www.militarytimes.com/story/military/2015/09/04/modder-chaplain -navy-fired-intolerant-nnptc-controversy/71695820/.

49.   Megan M. Reid, "Football Coach Fired for Postgame Prayer Takes Action Against School," August 9, 2016, accessed December 19, 2016, http://www .cbsnews.com/news/washington-football-coach-fired-for-post-game-prayer-takes -action-against-school/.

50.   Heather Graf, "Garfield High School Football Team Takes Knee During National Anthem," September 18, 2016, accessed December 19, 2016, http://www.king5.com/sports/high-school/football/garfield-high-school-football-team-takes-knee-during-national-anthem/319577573.

51.   Ibid.

52.   Ibid.

53.   Ibid.

54.   "Entire Seattle High School Football Team Kneels During National Anthem Before Game," KCPQ, September 16, 2016, accessed December 19, 2016, http://q13fox.com/2016/09/16/entire-seattle-high-school-team-kneels-during-national-anthem-before-game/.

55.   Joseph A. Kennedy Equal Employment Opportunity Commission Intake Questionnaire, accessed December 19, 2016, http://firstliberty.org/wp-content/uploads/2016/01/Kennedy-EEOC-Intake-Questionnaire-and-Supporting-Materials_Redacted.pdf.

56.   Ibid.

57.   *Joseph A. Kennedy v. Bremerton School District*, case no. 3:16-cv-05694, accessed December 19, 2016, http://firstliberty.org/wp-content/uploads/2016/08/Filed-Complaint.pdf.

58.   Ibid.

59.   Michael Berry, in communication with the author, August 2016.

60.   Joseph A. Kennedy Equal Employment Opportunity Commission Intake Questionnaire.

61.   *Joseph A. Kennedy v. Bremerton School District*.

62.   Ibid.

63.   Ibid; Joseph A. Kennedy Equal Employment Opportunity Commission Intake Questionnaire.

64.   *Joseph A. Kennedy v. Bremerton School District*.

65.   Ibid.

66.   *Joseph A. Kennedy v. Bremerton School District*, "Complaint Appendix," United States District Court Western District of Washington at Tacoma, accessed December 19, 2016, http://firstliberty.org/wp-content/uploads/2015/12/Kennedy-Complaint-Appendix.pdf.

67.   *Joseph A. Kennedy v. Bremerton School District*.

68.   Ibid.

69.   Joe Kennedy, in communication with the author, August 2016.

70.   Berry, in communication with the author, August 2016.

71.   Kim Davis, in communication with the author, 2015.

72.   Alan Blinder and Tamar Lewin, "Clerk in Kentucky Chooses Jail Over Deal on Same-Sex Marriage," The New York Times Company, September 3, 2015, accessed December 19, 2016, http://www.nytimes.com/2015/09/04/us/kim-davis-same-sex-marriage.html.

73.   Polly Mosendz, "Following Kim Davis Battle Over Same Sex Marriage Licenses, Kentucky Governor Strips Clerk Names From Form," Newsweek LLC, December 22, 2015, accessed December 19, 2016, http://www.newsweek.com/following-kim-davis-battle-new-kentucky-governor-strips-clerk-names-same

-sex-408343; Blinder and Lewin, "Clerk in Kentucky Chooses Jail Over Deal on Same-Sex Marriage."

74.   Davis, in communication with the author, 2015.

75.   Eugene Volokh, "Kim Davis Released From Jail, Plus More on Her Requested Accommodation," *Washington Post*, September 8, 2015, accessed December 19, 2016, https://www.washingtonpost.com/news/volokh-conspiracy /wp/2015/09/08/kim-davis-released-from-jail-plus-more-on-her-requested -accommodation/?utm_term=.2a0fd7dc01fa.

76.   Adam Beam, "ACLU Says Kentucky Clerk Should Have to Reissue Licenses," The Associated Press, November 20, 2015, accessed December 19, 2016, https://web-beta.archive.org/web/20151121181400/https://www.washingtonpost .com/national/aclu-says-kentucky-clerk-should-have-to-reissue-licenses/2015/11/20 /b6202d46-8fd0-11e5-934c-a369c80822c2_story.html.

77.   Adam Beam, "Kim Davis' Lawyers Say Altered Marriage Licenses Are Valid." The Associated Press, October 13, 2015, accessed December 19, 2016, https://web-beta.archive.org/web/20151017053615/https://www.washingtonpost .com/national/kim-davis-lawyers-say-altered-marriage-licenses-are-valid/2015 /10/13/9970a63e-71e5-11e5-ba14-318f8e87a2fc_story.html.

78.   Mat Staver, in communication with the author, September 2015.

79.   Davis, in communication with the author, 2015.

80.   Ibid.

81.   Elizabeth Chuck, "Kim Davis, Kentucky Clerk Blocking Gay Marriages, Has Had Her Own Marital Strife," NBCNews.com, September 3, 2015, accessed December 19, 2016, http://www.nbcnews.com/news/us-news/clerk-who-denied -gay-marriage-licenses-has-been-divorced-multiple-n420216.

82.   Davis, in communication with the author, 2015.

83.   Ibid.

84.   Ibid.

85.   Todd Starnes, "Judicial Tyranny: Kentucky Judge Does With a Gavel What Bull Connor Did With Dogs and Fire Hoses," FoxNews.com, September 4, 2015, accessed December 19, 2016, http://www.foxnews.com/opinion/2015/09/04 /christian-intimidation-kentucky-judge-does-with-gavel-what-bull-connor-did-with -dogs-and-fire-hoses.html.

86.   Davis, in communication with the author, 2015.

87.   Ibid.

88.   Ibid.

89.   Ibid.

90.   Ibid.

91.   Staver, in communication with the author, September 2015.

92.   Ibid.

93.   Davis, in communication with the author, 2015.

94.   Ibid.

CONCLUSION: THE SHINING CITY ON A HILL

1.   "Reagan's Farewell Speech," PBS, *American Experience*, accessed December 19, 2016, http://www.pbs.org/wgbh/americanexperience/features/primary-resources/reagan-farewell/.

2.   Ibid.

3.   Joseph Hoyt, "Hurst L.D. Bell Player Stands For National Anthem a Day After ACL Surgery," DallasNews.com, September 12, 2016, accessed December 19, 2016, http://sportsday.dallasnews.com/high-school/high-schools/2016/09/12/hurst-ld-bell-player-stands-national-anthem-day-acl-surgery.

4.   Todd Starnes, "This School Loves America!," ToddStarnes.com, August 31, 2016, accessed December 19, 2016, http://www.toddstarnes.com/column/an46b577ddiwvn2zbm19n04trxiou4.

5.   Aubrey McKay, "Police Investigating Flag Burning at High School in Heber City," KSTU, September 2, 2016, accessed December 19, 2016, http://fox13now.com/2016/09/02/police-investigating-flag-burning-at-high-school-in-heber-city/.

6.   Reagan, "Inaugural Address: January 5, 1967," Ronald Reagan Presidential Library and Museum, accessed December 19, 2016, https://reaganlibrary.archives.gov/archives/speeches/govspeech/01051967a.htm.

7.   *We Were Soldiers*, directed by Randall Wallace (Los Angeles: Paramount Pictures, 2002).

8.   "Reagan's Farewell Speech," PBS.

9.   Ibid.

CONNECT WITH US!

CHARISMA HOUSE

(Spiritual Growth)

Facebook.com/CharismaHouse

@CharismaHouse

Instagram.com/CharismaHouse

SILOAM

(Health)

Pinterest.com/CharismaHouse

MEV — MODERN ENGLISH VERSION

(Bible)

www.mevbible.com